1001
INVENTIONS & AWESOME
FACTS
FROM MUSLIM CIVILIZATION

WASHINGTON, D.C.

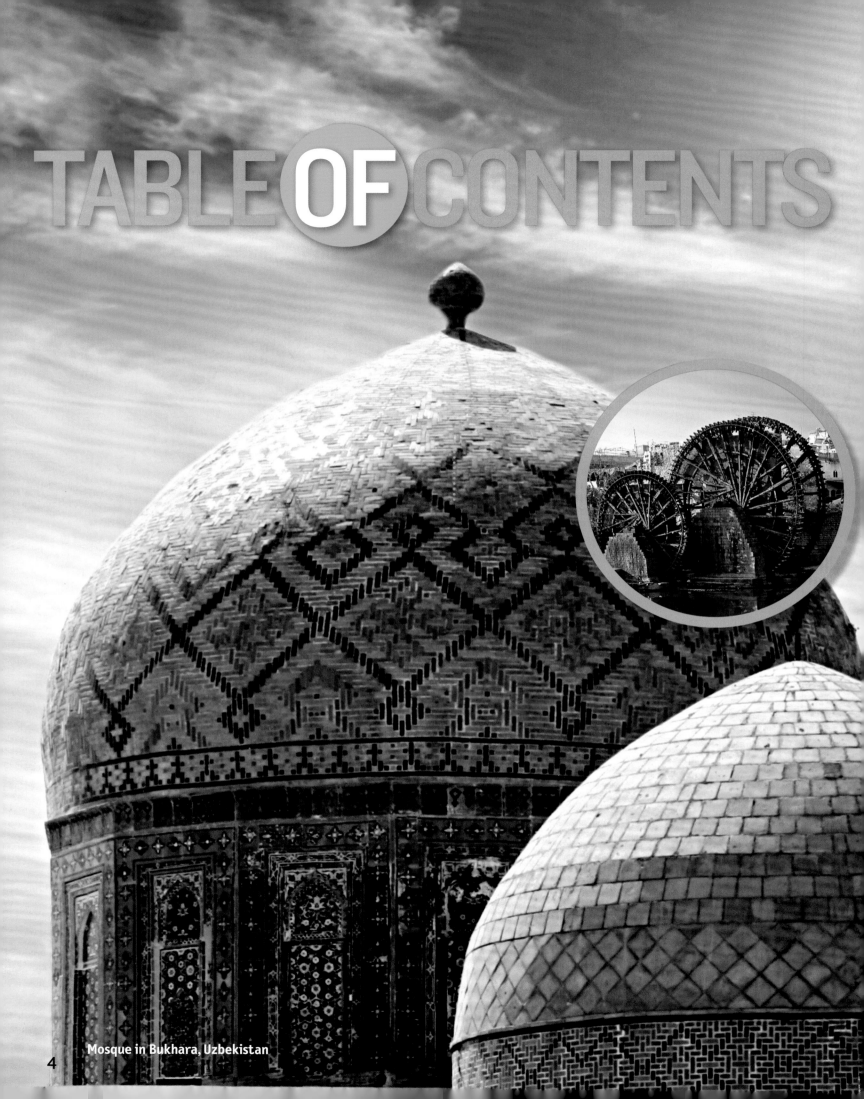

TABLE OF CONTENTS

Mosque in Bukhara, Uzbekistan

Imagine a time and place where people from different countries, cultures, religions, and backgrounds work together to discover new knowledge, understand more about the world, and develop new inventions while sharing them openly and freely. A world in which the common language is science and that language is used for the benefit of everyone. A world in which progress is based on the sharing of ideas and working collaboratively.

Such a time and place existed. It was a long time ago and has almost been forgotten.

1001 Inventions & Awesome Facts from Muslim Civilization takes you to that world and introduces you to some of the men and women who helped form the basis of much of modern science, technology, medicine, and the understanding of our world. These men and women studied science from previous civilizations and other cultures under the umbrella of Muslim culture and civilization. They built upon this knowledge and in turn passed the achievements on to the modern world. These important advancements took place during medieval times, or what some call "the Middle Ages." It was a time when it seemed there was little to no innovation happening. But in Muslim civilization, which stretched from Spain to China, the period was known as "the Golden Age."

More than 300 years ago, the great Sir Isaac Newton remarked that if he had seen farther than others, it was because he was standing on the shoulders of giants. This expression of humility, and of appreciation for our predecessors, has been repeated by hundreds of scientists, scholars, engineers, and inventors ever since. In this book you will meet some of those "giants": scholars, scientists, inventors, engineers, architects, explorers, medical specialists, astronomers, and teachers. Their developments and achievements still touch our modern lives.

The initiative *1001 Inventions* brings this underappreciated time and place to life. *1001 Inventions* has a powerful and fascinating story to tell, since the influence of Muslim heritage can be found today in our homes, schools, hospitals, farms, supermarkets, airports, parks, and gardens in countless ways.

Millions of people around the world have experienced *1001 Inventions*, through interactive exhibitions, best-selling books, and the award-winning movie *Library of Secrets*, starring Oscar winner Sir Ben Kingsley, which has been downloaded more than 20 million times.

This new book, published by National Geographic in partnership with the Foundation for Science, Technology and Civilisation, introduces more than 1,001 amazing facts about inventions from the Golden Age. I sincerely hope it will amaze and inspire you to stand on the shoulders of giants yourselves to see farther than anyone has ever done before.

Professor Salim Al-Hassani
Chief Editor and Chairman, FSTC

10 FAST FACTS
YOU NEED TO KNOW ABOUT

1

We often think that people from a thousand years ago were living in the "Dark Ages." But in **MUSLIM CIVILIZATION** from the 7th century onward there were amazing advances and inventions **THAT STILL INFLUENCE OUR EVERYDAY LIVES.**

2

PEOPLE LIVING IN THE MUSLIM WORLD SAW WHAT THE **EGYPTIANS, CHINESE, INDIANS, GREEKS, AND ROMANS** HAD DISCOVERED AND SPENT THE NEXT **ONE THOUSAND YEARS** ADDING NEW DEVELOPMENTS AND IDEAS.

3

EXPLORERS DREW DETAILED **MAPS,** INCLUDING THE EARLIEST MAP SHOWING AMERICA, SAILED THE HIGH SEAS, AND TOOK THE FIRST **GIRAFFE** TO CHINA.

4

ENGINEERS IN THE MUSLIM WORLD DESIGNED INTRIGUING MACHINES, INCLUDING A MECHANICAL **ELEPHANT CLOCK** THAT WAS POWERED BY FALLING METAL BALLS AND CONTROLLED BY A HIDDEN WATER SYSTEM.

5

NEW FOODS LIKE **APRICOTS, ORANGES, AND RICE** SPREAD FAR AND WIDE, AND FARMERS USED PUMPS TO WATER CROPS AND WINDMILLS TO GRIND PRODUCE.

6

ARABIC BOOKS WERE TRANSLATED INTO LATIN. THE SHARED KNOWLEDGE HELPED BRING ABOUT A NEW RUSH OF DEVELOPMENT IN EUROPE.

MUSLIM CIVILIZATION

7 A WOMAN NAMED **FATIMA AL-FIHRI** founded the world's first university, where you can still study today. People also made breakthroughs in chemistry, physics, and mathematics.

8 Doctors could treat all kinds of diseases, fix your broken leg, give you an eye operation, and stitch you up after surgery using **CATGUT.**

9 **ARCHITECTS** BUILT DOMES LARGER THAN EVER BEFORE AND DESIGNED DISTINCTIVE **ARCHES** AND **TILE** PATTERNS.

10 **ASTRONOMERS** MAPPED THE STARS AND GAVE SOME OF THEM NAMES WE STILL USE. ONE EVEN MENTIONED THE GALAXY WE NOW CALL ANDROMEDA. OTHERS WORKED OUT HOW TO PREDICT THE MOON'S PHASES AND LUNAR AND SOLAR ECLIPSES.

Decorative Arabic reliefs and tiles in Nasrid Palace, in present-day Grenada, Spain

THE GOLDEN AGE OF

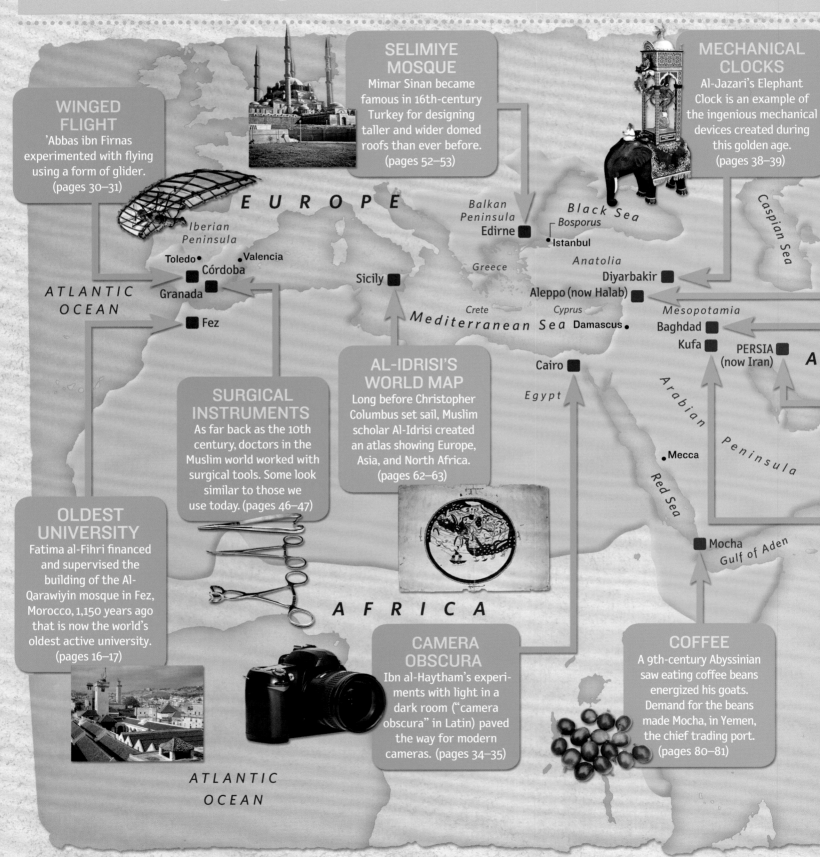

WINGED FLIGHT
'Abbas ibn Firnas experimented with flying using a form of glider. (pages 30–31)

SELIMIYE MOSQUE
Mimar Sinan became famous in 16th-century Turkey for designing taller and wider domed roofs than ever before. (pages 52–53)

MECHANICAL CLOCKS
Al-Jazari's Elephant Clock is an example of the ingenious mechanical devices created during this golden age. (pages 38–39)

EUROPE

Iberian Peninsula

Toledo • ■ Córdoba • Valencia

ATLANTIC OCEAN

Granada

■ Fez

Balkan Peninsula — *Bosporus* — *Black Sea*
Edirne ■ • Istanbul

Greece — *Anatolia*
Diyarbakir ■
Aleppo (now Halab) ■
Crete — *Cyprus* — *Mesopotamia*
Sicily ■ *Mediterranean Sea* Damascus • Baghdad ■
Kufa ■ PERSIA (now Iran) ■
Caspian Sea

SURGICAL INSTRUMENTS
As far back as the 10th century, doctors in the Muslim world worked with surgical tools. Some look similar to those we use today. (pages 46–47)

AL-IDRISI'S WORLD MAP
Long before Christopher Columbus set sail, Muslim scholar Al-Idrisi created an atlas showing Europe, Asia, and North Africa. (pages 62–63)

Cairo ■
Egypt

Arabian Peninsula
• Mecca
Red Sea

OLDEST UNIVERSITY
Fatima al-Fihri financed and supervised the building of the Al-Qarawiyin mosque in Fez, Morocco, 1,150 years ago that is now the world's oldest active university. (pages 16–17)

AFRICA

CAMERA OBSCURA
Ibn al-Haytham's experiments with light in a dark room ("camera obscura" in Latin) paved the way for modern cameras. (pages 34–35)

■ Mocha
Gulf of Aden

COFFEE
A 9th-century Abyssinian saw eating coffee beans energized his goats. Demand for the beans made Mocha, in Yemen, the chief trading port. (pages 80–81)

ATLANTIC OCEAN

MUSLIM CIVILIZATION 7TH TO 17TH CENTURIES

ASTROLABES
"Merriam" al-Astrulabiya was skilled at making very accurate astrolabes, complex gadgets for finding directions, telling time, and observing the sun and stars. (pages 24–25)

Welcome to the Golden Age of Muslim civilization, during which men and women of different faiths and cultures worked together to create thousands of inventions and discoveries that changed the world. Stretching over three continents, from Spain and northern Africa through the Middle East to Indonesia and China, Muslim civilization contributed to advances in science, mathematics, medicine, technology, architecture, and more. Check out the map for highlights of things invented or discovered in this period.

MAP KEY

Lands under Muslim control at various times from the 7th century onward

■ Point of interest

• Other city

HOUSE OF WISDOM
In the early 9th century the top scientists and scholars from many regions of the Muslim world gathered at the House of Wisdom to study, debate, and make new discoveries. (pages 32–33)

ZHENG HE'S WOODEN SHIPS
Zheng He became admiral of the Chinese fleet, sailing in the early 1400s the biggest wooden ships the world had ever seen. (pages 64–65)

WINDMILLS
Five hundred years before windmills appeared in Europe, they were a common sight in parts of the Muslim world. (pages 84–85)

DISTILLATION
Jabir ibn Hayyan perfected the distillation process, which is still used in the creation of perfume, gasoline, plastics, and more. (pages 20–21)

S   I   A

Arabian Sea

India

PACIFIC OCEAN

South China Sea

Mindanao

Sumatra

Borneo

Java

INDIAN OCEAN

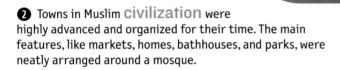

1 You might be surprised to learn that many of the **conveniences** and **comforts** that you enjoy today were part of the everyday lives of people living in Muslim civilization a thousand years ago.

2 Towns in Muslim **civilization** were highly advanced and organized for their time. The main features, like markets, homes, bathhouses, and parks, were neatly arranged around a mosque.

3 Most **homes** in Muslim civilization had built-in air-conditioning, inner courtyards, gardens, and terraces. By contrast, most people in medieval cities elsewhere lived in far less comfortable **dwellings**.

4 Walls around houses had to be **taller** than the height of a **camel rider** to protect the privacy of the people inside.

5 To provide **relief** from the hot, desert climate, town planners created **shade** by designing narrow, covered streets, indoor and outdoor fountains, and court-yards with elaborate gardens.

6 People of different **faiths and ethnic backgrounds** lived near each other and worked together in towns under Muslim rule.

7 Shopping for food, spices, books, and other goods was done at an open-air market called a *souk*.

8 People still shop at *souks* in **Morocco, Turkey,** and other **Muslim countries**.

ABOUT TOWNS

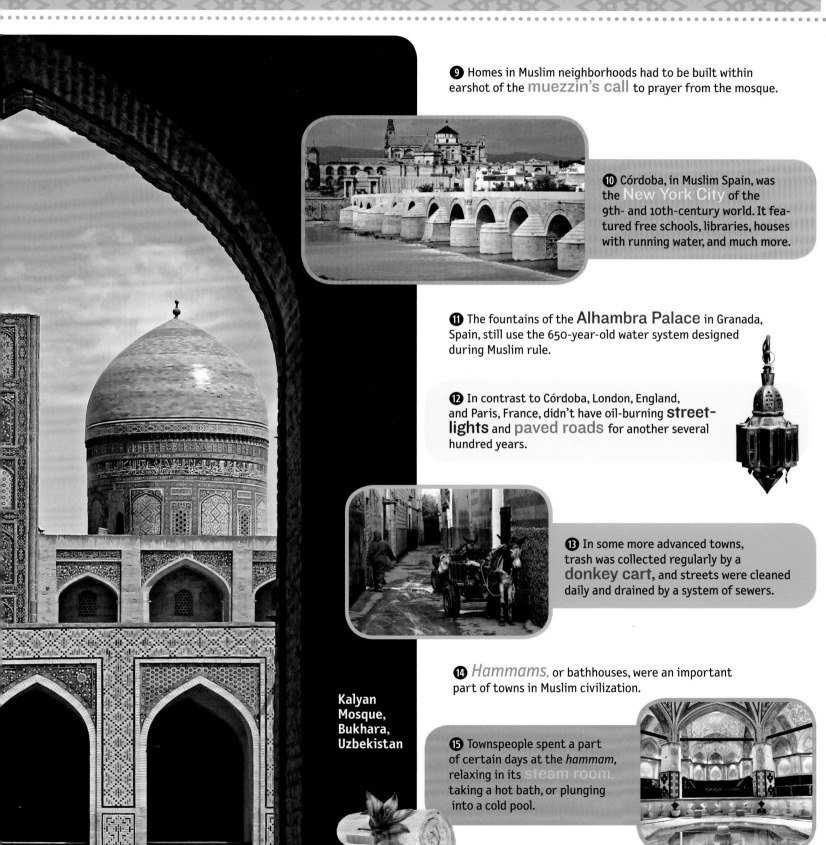

9 Homes in Muslim neighborhoods had to be built within earshot of the **muezzin's call** to prayer from the mosque.

10 Córdoba, in Muslim Spain, was the New York City of the 9th- and 10th-century world. It featured free schools, libraries, houses with running water, and much more.

11 The fountains of the **Alhambra Palace** in Granada, Spain, still use the 650-year-old water system designed during Muslim rule.

12 In contrast to Córdoba, London, England, and Paris, France, didn't have oil-burning **streetlights** and **paved roads** for another several hundred years.

13 In some more advanced towns, trash was collected regularly by a **donkey cart,** and streets were cleaned daily and drained by a system of sewers.

14 *Hammams,* or bathhouses, were an important part of towns in Muslim civilization.

Kalyan Mosque, Bukhara, Uzbekistan

15 Townspeople spent a part of certain days at the *hammam,* relaxing in its steam room, taking a hot bath, or plunging into a cold pool.

15 FACTS ABOUT GARDENS

1 In Muslim civilization gardens were a symbol of an **earthly Paradise** and a perfect place to **sit and think.**

2 Beginning in the 8th century the **designing** and **planting of gardens** spread across the Muslim world from Spain to India.

3 Numerous references in the Quran to Paradise gardens, like **Eden,** influenced designers.

4 In the 10th century gardens began to include **shallow canals** and **fountains** and flower beds arranged in **geometric patterns.**

5 You can still see such **gardens at the Taj Mahal in India,** at the Alhambra in Spain, and elsewhere in Europe, where formal gardens designed with similar features were created centuries later.

6 **Water was scarce** in much of the Muslim world, so garden fountains and canals were the **ultimate display of wealth.**

7 Muslim engineers invented **ingenious ways** to control the display and flow of water in garden fountains so the fountains would be both **beautiful** to look at and **soothing** to listen to.

Longwood Gardens, Pennsylvania, U.S.A.

8 The **12 lions** around a garden fountain at the **Alhambra** in Spain formed a water clock when they were created 650 years ago. Back then, water spouted from the mouth of a different lion each hour.

9 Flowers such as **tulips, irises**, and **carnations** all made their way from Muslim civilization to Europe and beyond.

10 Gardens also were used for **botanical experiments,** providing shade, and growing food.

11 **Glass rooms** called "conservatories" evolved from Turkish kiosks, or *koshks*, and later were added to homes in Europe and elsewhere.

12 A *koshk* was a domed hall with open, arched sides. **Bandstands and pavilions** in city parks today trace back to them.

13 In Muslim civilization *koshks* were usually **attached to a mosque** and often **overlooked gardens.**

14 Gardens even inspired their own kind of Arabic poetry called *rawdhiya.*

15 One of the most famous kiosks, **Cinili Koshk,** was built in 1473 at Topkapi Palace in Istanbul, Turkey. **It is two stories tall and topped with a dome.**

1 EVERYONE in the Muslim world wanted to LEARN NEW THINGS and share their discoveries.

2 A THIRST for KNOWLEDGE LED TO THE FIRST SCHOOL, ESTABLISHED IN A MOSQUE IN MEDINA IN WHAT IS NOW SAUDI ARABIA IN 622.

3 Traveling teachers, known as *AHL AL-'ILM* ("THE PEOPLE WITH KNOWLEDGE"), helped spread learning to other Muslim towns and cities.

4 By the LATE 9TH CENTURY almost every mosque had an ELEMENTARY SCHOOL for boys and girls.

5 ACCORDING TO IBN HAWQAL, A TRAVELING GEOGRAPHER, THE CITY OF PALERMO, IN MUSLIM SICILY, IN THE LATE 10TH CENTURY HAD 300 MOSQUES THAT TAUGHT VARIOUS SUBJECTS.

25 SMART FACTS

6

Kids began school at the AGE OF SIX, much as they do now.

7 Among the early skills schoolchildren learned were how to write verses from the Quran and the 99 NAMES OF ALLAH (God).

8

Each Muslim school had arched hallways leading to a courtyard for LESSONS OUTSIDE, a prayer hall, living rooms for students, and a room for washing before praying.

9 Students learned mostly through REPETITION and MEMORIZATION. Today many Muslim students still memorize all 6,239 verses of the Quran.

10 Wealthy people HIRED TUTORS to teach their children in their HOMES.

11 IN 1066 THE FIRST *MADRASA*, A SCHOOL SEPARATE FROM A MOSQUE, WAS BUILT IN BAGHDAD.

12 Classroom time was SUPER SERIOUS —no talking, laughing, or joking!

13 There were FOUR DIFFERENT KINDS OF MUSLIM SCHOOLS: regular (primary) schools, houses of readers (high schools), houses of *hadiths* (religious schools), and medical schools.

14 Most schools had LIBRARIES filled with books written in Arabic on ADVANCED TOPICS like chemistry, physics, and astronomy.

15

EDUCATION IN MUSLIM CIVILIZATION WAS FREE,

and some students were provided with books, pocket money, and a place to live.

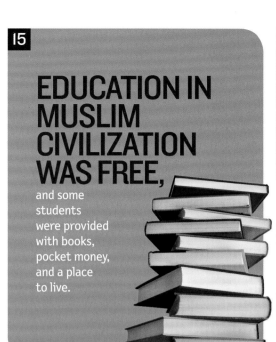

16

FUNDS CALLED *AWQAF* were set up to build schools and to pay for things like teachers' salaries and meals for students.

18

A quest for **ADVANCED EDUCATION** among scholars of the Muslim world led to the spread of universities—ultimately sparking **A REVIVAL OF LEARNING** throughout Europe.

17

By the 15th century, **THE OTTOMANS REVOLUTIONIZED SCHOOLS** by setting up a kind of learning center called a *KULLIYE.* Each complex had a mosque, school, hospital, and dining area.

ABOUT SCHOOLS

19

"UNIVERSITY" IN ARABIC IS *JAMI'AH,* AND THE WORD FOR "MOSQUE" IS *JAMI'.* In early Muslim civilization, many scholars saw a clear connection between learning and faith.

20

The MOST SOUTHERLY of the big universities was in TIMBUKTU IN MALI, WEST AFRICA. By the 12th century it had about **25,000 STUDENTS.**

21

FATIMA AL-FIHRI used her fortune and talent to build a mosque with a school called Al-Qarawiyin in Fez, Morocco. It is now the **WORLD'S OLDEST ACTIVE UNIVERSITY.** You can still study there today.

22

SOME SCHOOLS ATTACHED TO MOSQUES IN THE MEDIEVAL MUSLIM WORLD ARE CONSIDERED TO BE THE WORLD'S OLDEST UNIVERSITIES.

23

AL-QARAWIYIN was equipped with high-tech gear for the time, such as astronomy instruments, astrolabes, sundials, and sand and water clocks. Students calculated time in a "timers room," supervised by *Al-Muwaqqit* ("the timekeeper").

24

Much LIKE COLLEGE KIDS TODAY, students at universities in the Muslim world took **ENTRANCE EXAMS, JOINED STUDY GROUPS,** and **HAD TO PASS FINAL EXAMS TO GRADUATE.**

25

EUROPEAN STUDENTS TRAVELED TO AND FROM MUSLIM CITIES TO STUDY AT COLLEGES AND TO LEARN ARABIC, CONTRIBUTING TO THE SPREAD OF **ISLAMIC KNOWLEDGE, IDEAS, AND STYLES.**

15 HEAD-TURNING

1 Baghdad was the **Paris** of the 9th century.

2 Popular fashions like **high-heeled shoes** and lightweight pants for summer first came on to the scene in Muslim Spain more than a thousand years ago.

3 Ziryab, a famous 8th- to 9th-century musician and stylist from Baghdad, sparked a fashion movement in the Muslim world when he moved to Córdoba, in **Muslim Spain.**

4 Ziryab was a major trendsetter of his time, influencing everything from **hairstyles** to **clothing styles.**

5 As students left Córdoba, they took with them the **trends** pioneered by Ziryab, eventually spreading them throughout Europe and North Africa.

6 People in Muslim Spain began to follow a fashion calendar, changing their **styles** based on the season like we do now.

Traditional leather slippers at a *souk* in Morocco

7 They'd wear brightly colored clothes made of cotton, silk, and flax in the hot season, then change to warm, dark wools and cottons for **winter.**

FASHION FACTS

8 Women in Muslim Spain went from wearing their hair in a single braid down the back to a bolder, shorter cut with bangs.

9 Men began shaving their beards—a nod to Ziryab's clean-cut look.

10 Ziryab opened a salon and cosmetology school close to Alcazar, the emir's palace in Córdoba, Spain.

11 Today there is a street, a hotel, a club, or a cafe named after Ziryab in every country in the Muslim world.

12 Leather and cork-soled sandals became all the rage in Muslim Spain and a staple of the export trade.

13 Two medieval Muslim writers even penned a book detailing how to make these sandals, down to the specific stitching.

14 Some shoemakers put sand below the heel to make it higher and to act as a shock absorber, creating one of the earliest forms of high heels.

15 Today's global Muslim fashion industry is estimated to be worth around $96 billion.

1
Medieval times are often imagined as SMELLY, dark, and unclean, but in 10th-century Muslim civilization people were very concerned about hygiene.

2
The COSMETIC PRODUCTS used in Muslim civilization a thousand years ago could almost compete with those we have today.

3
Cleanliness is vital in Islam, and WUDHU'—washing parts of the body—is always done before prayers.

4
According to the Quran, a Muslim MUST WASH face, hands, head, and feet BEFORE PRAYING.

5
A 13th-century ROBOTIC wudhu' machine that looked like a PEACOCK shot eight spurts of water from its head—just enough to wash with.

6
Other machines even HANDED YOU A TOWEL to dry off!

7
To make SOAP, a mixture of oil, al-qali (a salt-like substance), and sweet- or spicy-smelling ingredients was BOILED and left to harden in a mold.

8
Lye (sodium hydroxide), perfumed and colored soaps, and liquid and solid soaps also were made by CHEMISTS in the Muslim world.

9
MEDIEVAL MUSLIMS went to great lengths to keep up their appearance.

10
AL-ZAHRAWI, a physician and surgeon from Muslim Spain, wrote about hair and skin care, TEETH WHITENING, and gum strengthening.

11
He considered cosmetics to be a branch of medicine that he called "MEDICINE OF BEAUTY."

12
Al-Zahrawi also wrote about NASAL SPRAYS, mouthwashes, and hand creams.

13
Recipes for BREATH FRESHENERS date back to ancient times and include ingredients such as charcoal, fruit, and dried flowers.

14
Al-Zahrawi's concept of molded perfumed sticks may be the earliest versions of LIPSTICK and roll-on deodorant.

15
The benefits of SUNSCREEN were also discussed by Al-Zahrawi.

16
Al-Zahrawi suggested HAIR-REMOVING STICKS, hair dyes that turned blond hair to black, and lotions for straightening curly hair.

17
AL-KINDI, a scholar from Iraq, wrote a book on perfumes. It was PACKED WITH RECIPES for fragrant oils, creams, and scented waters.

18
Al-Kindi's book also described 107 METHODS and recipes for perfume making and perfume-making equipment.

19
At first only WEALTHY PEOPLE used perfumes, but later they became more available to all.

20
The ALEMBIC, a glass container used in distillation, still bears its Arabic name.

21
Chemists made PERFUMES by distilling plants and flowers. Some of these ingredients, like jasmine and citrus fruits, are still used in perfumes.

22
Muslims also used HERBS AND SPICES to make perfume.

23
The knowledge about perfumes made its way from the Muslim world to southern FRANCE, which had the perfect climate and soil for perfume making.

24
Southern France's perfume industry continues to thrive, 700 YEARS LATER.

25
Every single day 170,000 BOTTLES of perfume are sold in France alone.

26
In 2006 a HALF-OUNCE BOTTLE of a particular perfume was sold to a wealthy client for $234,450.

27
According to tradition, the Prophet Muhammad scrubbed his teeth with a twig of *miswak* before each prayer time. Its use is still popular.

28
More than 1,000 YEARS ago, the Muslim musician and fashion icon ZIRYAB, "THE BLACKBIRD," introduced toothpaste to Andalus.

29
The EXACT INGREDIENTS of Ziryab's toothpaste are unknown, but it was said to have been both "functional and pleasant to taste."

30
Today more than ONE BILLION TUBES of toothpaste are purchased each year just in the United States.

31
Ziryab also introduced the USE OF SALT to clean clothes.

32
Muslim methods and ideas about hygiene FILTERED INTO EUROPE BY WAY OF MERCHANTS, travelers, and Crusaders.

50 Fresh Facts ABOUT KEEPING CLEAN

33 In keeping with the Islamic tradition of cleanliness, the *HAMMAM*, or bathhouse, became an institution in every Muslim town.

36 It's still customary in many parts of the Muslim world for a BRIDE-TO-BE to be groomed at a *hammam* before her wedding.

39 PUBLIC BATHS made a comeback in Europe in the 17th century after tourists raved about Turkish baths.

42 There was a TURKISH BATH on the doomed R.M.S. *Titanic.*

45 At Mahomed's INDIAN VAPOR BATHS, clients sat in flannel tents and were given a massage by a person reaching in through slits in the flannel.

46 HENNA, the reddish-brown herbal paste commonly used to create elegant designs on women's hands, has been used as a hair dye for 6,000 years.

47 Men used henna to DYE THEIR BEARDS, following the tradition of the Prophet Muhammad.

48 Henna, which is ANTIBACTERIAL and antifungal, is used to treat rashes.

34 The *hammam* brought friends, neighbors, relatives, and workers together regularly to RELAX and CATCH UP.

40 The first TURKISH BATH in Europe, called a *BAGNIO*, opened as early as 1679 in London, England. Others were built in Scotland.

49 Henna is also a natural HAIR CONDITIONER.

35 Bathhouses were used by men and women but at SEPARATE TIMES. Women usually bathed during the day and men at night or very early in the morning.

37 The *hammam* is believed to be the origin of most MODERN HEALTH and fitness clubs around the world.

41 Picking up on Muslim style, Turkish baths were DOMED BUILDINGS with horseshoe arches and geometrical lattice windows.

43 Some *hammams* from THE MEDIEVAL MUSLIM ERA are still in use in places like Morocco and Turkey.

50 In 2011 a woman in India set a world record by DECORATING 170 HANDS with henna in just over 24 hours!

38 *Hammams* had STRICT RULES. Men had to keep their lower half covered, and women were forbidden to enter the *hammam* if men were present.

44 In the late 1700s the Indian Sake Dean Mahomed opened a bathhouse in England and became known as the "SHAMPOOING SURGEON."

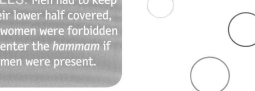

15 PLAYFUL FACTS

1 Chess **developed** more than a thousand years ago—so long ago that we don't know if it began in India or Persia.

2 An Icelandic story tells of the Danish king **Knut the Great** playing chess in 1027.

3 Chess may be based on the Indian game *Chaturanga,* which means **"having four limbs"**—a likely reference to India's army, which had four branches: soldiers, horsemen, chariots, and elephants.

4 Persians changed the name to *Chatrang* and used it in **war games.**

5 At the time, the playing pieces were *Shah* (the king); *Firzan* (a general, who became the **queen** in modern games); *Fil* (an **elephant** that is now the bishop); *Faras* (Arabic for "horse"); *Rukh* (a **chariot** that is now the castle, or rook); and *Baidaq* (the **pawn**).

6 A 13th-century manuscript from Spain shows **women playing chess.**

7 The **rules** of chess have not changed in nearly 500 years.

8 There are **I69,5I8,829,I00,544,000,000,000,000,000** ways to play the first ten moves in chess.

ABOUT CHESS

Chessboard

9 Travelers going from Persia to Spain took the game with them and **introduced chess to Europe.**

10 A Russian chess champion won a match with a move used by the Arab master **Al-Suli** 1,000 years ago.

11 The word **"checkmate"** comes from the Persian word *Shahmat,* meaning "the king is dead."

12 In the 18th and 19th centuries people traveled miles to watch the **"Iron Muslim,"** a chess-playing robot whose moves were actually made by a chess master hiding below the board.

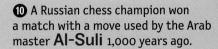

13 Fifteen different chess masters operated the "Iron Muslim" during its **85-year reign** over other top players of the day.

14 Today chess is played everywhere. About **three million chess sets** are sold every year in the United States alone.

15 Two German men set a record in 2010 for the **longest** chess game to date: 40 hours and 20 minutes.

1 The study of astronomy in the Muslim world included scholars from many countries and cultures.

2 Keeping a close watch on the sky helped Muslims find the direction of Mecca.

3 The Quran encourages the exploration of the universe.

4 Muslim civilization was the first to use observatories and large instruments to study the heavens.

5 WORKING IN TEAMS LET ASTRONOMERS STUDY PLANETS AND STARS IN MORE DETAIL THAN EVER BEFORE.

6 The Toledan Tables are astronomical charts that predict the movements of the moon, sun, and planets and take their name from Toledo, a city in Muslim Spain.

7 The tables were written in the 9th century by Al-Zarqali, known in Europe as Arzachel.

8 For 300 years Muslim-ruled Toledo was the world's center for astronomy and science.

9 Caliph Al-Ma'mum set up a government-funded observatory in Baghdad so astronomers could work together in one place.

10 Scientists at Al-Ma'mum's observatory discovered that the solar apogee, the point at which the sun is farthest from the Earth, changes over time.

Ahmad al-Mizzi's quadrant; foreground: armillary sphere

11 We now know the solar apogee changes because the whole solar system moves within our galaxy.

12 The Maragha Observatory, built in northern Persia (now Iran) in 1263, had a library with more than 40,000 books.

13 The astronomer Jamal al-Din introduced instruments from the observatory to China in 1267.

14 The foundations of the Maragha Observatory still stand in Iran.

15 The 15th-century astronomer-mathematician Ulugh Beg created an observatory in Samarkand (now in Uzbekistan) while he was Sultan.

16 Ulugh Beg calculated the length of a year at 365 days, 6 hours, 10 minutes, and 8 seconds—just 62 seconds longer than the figure used today!

17 In the 9th century 'Abbas ibn Firnas built a glass planetarium in his house that showed images of stars and planets.

18 HIS PLANETARIUM EVEN FEATURED ARTIFICIAL THUNDER AND LIGHTNING.

19 Many astronomical instruments created in the early Muslim world greatly influenced the development of modern astronomy.

20 These new kinds of astrolabes, sextants, and quadrants measured the height of stars more accurately than ever before.

21 SEXTANTS WERE THE GPS OF THE MEDIEVAL WORLD.

quadrants helped make possible the European age of exploration.

23 An amazing observatory built by Taqi al-Din in Istanbul, Turkey, had an impressive array of extremely large instruments.

24 Large instruments made more accurate measurements possible.

25 THE OBSERVATORY IN DAMASCUS, SYRIA, HAD A 20-FOOT (6-M) QUADRANT AND A 56-FOOT (17-M) SEXTANT.

26 Today some of the largest optical telescopes are in the Canary Islands.

27 The need to know prayer times and the direction of Mecca led to substantial improvements in the astrolabe, an ancient instrument.

28 An astrolabe shows how the 3-D sky would look if it were flat.

29 People used astrolabes to tell time day or night, navigate on land, and calculate sunrise and sunset.

30 Astrolabes are sometimes called the pocket watches of the medieval world.

31 Observations made with astrolabes helped lead to the birth of modern astronomy.

32 The astrolabe is considered the most important astronomical observational device before the invention of the telescope.

to build an astrolabe because the makers had to do extensive calculations, engrave all the parts, and then assemble them all by hand.

34 THE OLDEST KNOWN ASTROLABE MADE IN THE MUSLIM WORLD IS FROM 10TH-CENTURY BAGHDAD.

35 Using a huge astrolabe, astronomer Ibn Yunus recorded more than 10,000 observations of the sun's position during a 30-year period.

36 The astrolabe was based on the ancient Greek model of the universe described by Ptolemy that showed the Earth at the center.

37 In 1387 Geoffrey Chaucer, author of *The Canterbury Tales,* gave his young son an astrolabe made to work for Oxford, England.

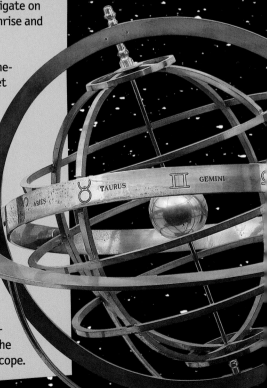

75 OUT OF THIS WORLD FACTS ABOUT

developed in Toledo, Spain, in the 11th century by Al-Zarqali, changed star mapping forever.

39 The universal astrolabe could be used at any location.

40 Jabir ibn Aflah, who lived in the 1100s, designed the first portable celestial globe to measure coordinates of planets and stars.

41 Since ancient times astronomers have used 3-D models of the heavens called armillary spheres.

42 These spheres have rings set at different angles to show the paths of planets and stars.

43 By the 10th century the Muslim world was producing two kinds of complex armillary spheres: demonstrational and observational.

44 DEMONSTRATIONAL ARMILLARY SPHERES PUT THE EARTH AT THE CENTER WITH THE SUN, TROPICS, EQUATOR, AND POLAR CIRCLES MOVING AROUND IT.

45 Observational armillary spheres had sighting devices on the rings but did not have the Earth at the center.

46 Using armillary spheres, astronomers produced flat charts of the heavens, which were then used to make astrolabes.

47 THE ALMAGEST, BY 2ND-CENTURY B.C.E. GREEK SCHOLAR PTOLEMY, HAD AN IMPORTANT INFLUENCE ON ASTRONOMERS OF THE MUSLIM WORLD.

48 Ninth-century astronomer Al-Farghani, inspired by Ptolemy's work, wrote several important books on astronomy.

49 The medieval Italian poet Dante probably gained his astronomical knowledge by studying the writings of Al-Farghani in Latin.

50 One of Al-Farghani's most important inventions was the Nilometer. Created in 861, it measured the water level of the Nile at Cairo and predicted when the river would flood each year.

51 Scientist Al-Battani combined elements of the celestial globe and the armillary sphere to create a new instrument called *al-baydha*, meaning "the egg."

52 The creation of the egg allowed astronomers to assign stars exact coordinates.

53 Al-Battani is also credited with timing new moons, calculating the length of solar years, and predicting eclipses.

54 Star maps created in the Muslim world were used in Europe and the Far East for centuries.

55 Today the names of more than 165 stars reflect their Arabic origins.

56 THE ASTRONOMER 'ABD AL-RAHMAN AL-SUFI WAS THE FIRST TO MENTION A STAR SYSTEM BEYOND OUR MILKY WAY GALAXY.

57 In 964 Al-Sufi named his find "little cloud." Today we call it the Andromeda galaxy.

58 The Andromeda galaxy is about 2.6 million light-years from Earth.

59 Our Milky Way galaxy contains between 200 and 400 billion stars.

60 The Milky Way is about 1,000 light-years thick, 100,000 light-years wide, and 300,000 light-years around.

61 The terms "zenith" and "azimuth" are of Arabic origin.

62 The astronomer Qutb al-Din al-Shirazi and his student Kamal al-Din al-Farisi explained that rainbows are caused by the refraction of the sun's rays in raindrops.

63 According to Copernicus, Ibn Rushd, a philosopher and astronomer, may have observed sunspots.

64 The 17th-century astronomer Galileo Galilei built on Latin translations of works written by astronomers of the Muslim world.

65 Six hundred years before Galileo, Muslim astronomer Al-Biruni explored the idea that the Earth rotated on its own axis.

66 Al-Biruni is sometimes referred to as the Leonardo da Vinci of his day.

67 Astronomer-scientist Thabit ibn Qurra lived in Baghdad, where he revised many Arabic versions of ancient Greek and Syriac science texts before his death in 901.

68 IT WAS EASIER FOR EARLY CIVILIZATIONS TO OBSERVE PLANETS AND STARS WITH THE NAKED EYE BECAUSE THERE WERE NO BRIGHT CITY LIGHTS.

69 Human eyes can take up to an hour to adjust to the night sky. This "night vision" makes it easier to see things that are farther away and less bright in the sky.

70 There are five planets that can be easily seen with the naked eye: Mercury, Venus, Jupiter, Mars, and Saturn.

71 Unlike some earlier thinkers, the scholars of Muslim civilization did not believe that the stars and planets were living beings.

72 The Quran talks about orbits and other astronomical phenomena.

73 The groundbreaking observations and discoveries made by astronomers during Muslim civilization had a huge impact on astronomy in the Western world.

74 Among those influenced by these medieval astronomers was Nicolaus Copernicus, a Renaissance scholar from Poland who is often considered the founder of modern astronomy.

75 Copernicus relied heavily on work done by Al-Battani, Ibn al-Shatir, Nasir al-Din al-Tusi, and other astronomers of the Muslim world.

ASTRONOMY

1 In Muslim civilization **astronomers** were fascinated by the phases of the Moon.

2 Astronomers in early Muslim civilization **calculated precisely** when the **crescent moon** would appear—important information for followers of Islam.

3 The crescent moon marks the beginning of Ramadan and other months in the Islamic calendar.

4 Al-Kindi, a 9th-century Iraqi, developed a type of **trigonometry** that dealt with **spheres** rather than flat surfaces.

5 People needed **spherical trigonometry** to find the direction of Mecca, the holiest place of Islam, from any point on Earth.

6 Astronomer Muhammad Abu al-Wafa' al-Buzjani discovered that the **moon** travels at **different speeds** during different phases.

7 The Danish astronomer Tycho Brahe is often credited with discovering this lunar phenomenon, but his discovery came 600 years after Al-Buzjani's.

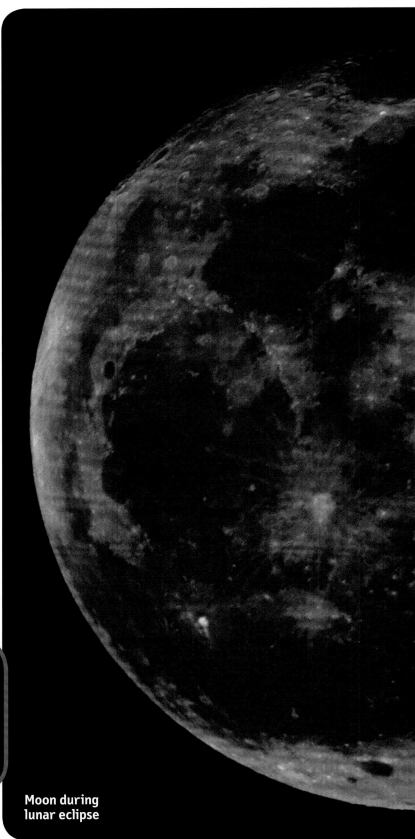

Moon during lunar eclipse

THE MOON

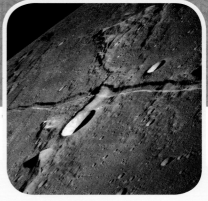

8 A **crater on the moon** is named after Abu al-Wafa' al-Buzjani.

9 The Islamic calendar has **12 months** that begin and end according to the lunar cycle.

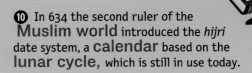

10 In 634 the second ruler of the **Muslim world** introduced the *hijri* date system, a **calendar** based on the **lunar cycle,** which is still in use today.

11 The *hijri,* or Islamic calendar, is only **354** or **355 days** long, 11 days shorter than calendars based on the Earth's revolution around the sun.

12 Ibn al-Haytham studied the moon at different positions in the sky and discovered that its **larger appearance** near the horizon is an **optical illusion.** The moon's real size never changes.

13 The moon's surface has more than 650 **dark and light patches,** caused by craters and other formations. Thirteen of these are named for Muslim astronomers.

14 **Lunar formations** are part of what creates the "man in the moon" phenomenon we can see from the Earth.

15 The moon has been known by many names: "Luna" by the Romans, "Selene" by the Greeks, and *Al-Qamar* by Arabs.

1 Humans have been **fascinated** by the stars since the beginning of time. The world's oldest star map— **carved into a mammoth's tusk**—is believed to be about **35,000 YEARS OLD!**

2 The wonder of the **STARRY SKIES** impressed the scholars of Muslim civilization. In line with earlier thinkers, they looked for **ORDER AND LOGIC** in what they saw.

3 Today we still know many constellations by names from **ANCIENT GREEK** legends, including **HERCULES the HERO** and **PEGASUS the WINGED HORSE.**

4 Ninth-century scholars at the **HOUSE OF WISDOM** in Baghdad translated and studied texts about astronomy from **GREEK, ROMAN,** and other early civilizations.

5 **MUSLIM ASTRONOMERS BUILT OBSERVATORIES TO STUDY THE STARS, MOON, AND PLANETS.** THESE OBSERVATORIES WERE THE HIGH-TECH LABORATORIES OF THEIR DAY.

25 Stellar FACTS ABOUT

6 The **FIRST WRITTEN RECORD** of a star system outside our own galaxy came from **ABD AL-RAHMAN AL-SUFI** in **964.**

7 Al-Sufi's *BOOK OF FIXED STARS,* an update to Greek astronomer Ptolemy's star catalog, became the standard constellation handbook for **SEVERAL CENTURIES.**

8 "FIXED STARS" referred to **CELESTIAL OBJECTS** THAT DID NOT SEEM TO MOVE IN RELATION TO OTHER STARS.

9 TODAY WE KNOW THAT STARS IN CONSTELLATIONS DO CHANGE POSITION—THEY'RE JUST SO FAR AWAY, WE CAN'T SEE THEM MOVE.

10 Al-Sufi's book identified and illustrated **48** CONSTELLATIONS.

11 Astronomers in the Muslim world made better and better **CELESTIAL GLOBES** to mark the positions of the stars and constellations in the sky.

12 **AL-SUFI** gave the **POSITION, SIZE,** and **COLOR** of each constellation.

13 Stars can be **RED, BLUE,** or **YELLOW.**

14 Cold stars are **RED;** hot stars are **BLUE.**

15 STAR MAPS AND ASTRONOMICAL TABLES from the Muslim world were used in Europe and the Far East for centuries.

16 ANCIENT GREEK STARGAZERS named many constellations after mythical figures, like ORION THE HUNTER.

18 To astronomers of the Muslim world CASSIOPEIA resembled a hand stained with henna.

17

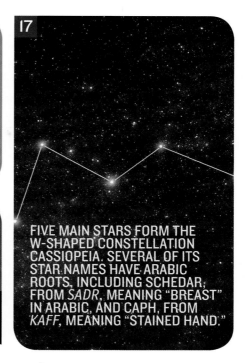

FIVE MAIN STARS FORM THE W-SHAPED CONSTELLATION CASSIOPEIA. SEVERAL OF ITS STAR NAMES HAVE ARABIC ROOTS, INCLUDING SCHEDAR, FROM *SADR*, MEANING "BREAST" IN ARABIC, AND CAPH, FROM *KAFF*, MEANING "STAINED HAND."

CONSTELLATIONS

19 ORION, one of the MOST RECOGNIZABLE constellations, is joined by his hunting dogs, CANIS MAJOR and CANIS MINOR.

20 ASTRONOMERS of Muslim civilization added ARABIC NAMES and their own sightings of STARS.

21 Muslim astronomers recorded and named more than 1,000 STARS.

22 ONE HUNDRED AND SIXTY STARS are known worldwide by their Arabic names, including Aldebaran ("Follower" of the Pleiades) and Altair ("The Flying Eagle").

23 TODAY 88 CONSTELLATIONS ARE RECOGNIZED BY THE INTERNATIONAL ASTRONOMICAL UNION.

24 The "modern family" of CONSTELLATIONS includes 19 land animals, 13 humans, 10 water creatures, 9 birds, 2 centaurs, a dragon, a unicorn, AND A HEAD OF HAIR!

25

You can still see parts of a star map on the dome of a bathhouse in an 8th-century palace in a desert in Jordan.

29

15 SOARING FACTS

1 Since the beginning of time every civilization has seen **birds flying** and **dreamed of taking flight themselves.**

2 The Muslim civilization's **fascination with flight** was reinforced by the belief that when the human soul reaches the highest level of goodness it **rises above the Earth.**

3 In his *Book of Kings*, Persian poet Al-Firdawsi recounted the tale of King Kai Kawus, who was tempted by evil spirits to invade heaven on a flying throne. **The eagles carrying him grew tired, and he crashed.**

4 In 852 a Spanish Muslim named 'Abbas ibn Firnas made an early **parachute jump when he leaped** off the Great Mosque of Córdoba (Spain) **wearing a reinforced cloak.**

5 **Twenty-three years later,** 65-year-old Ibn Firnas made the first controlled flight using what **we would call a hang glider.**

6 Ibn Firnas's hang glider resembled **a bird costume made of silk and covered with eagle feathers.**

7 The story goes that Ibn Firnas **hung in the air for more than ten minutes** using his glider before crashing to the ground.

8 The **rough landing** made the flight pioneer realize the important role a bird's tail plays in a safe landing. **Today all planes touch down with rear wheels first.**

Chinese red dragon kite

ON FLIGHT

A model of Ibn Firnas's hang glider

9 Leonardo da Vinci made his **famous drawings of birdlike flying machines** almost seven centuries after 'Abbas ibn Firnas's experiments with flight.

10 In the 17th century, a Turk named Hazarfen Ahmed Celebi **used an eagle-feathered glider** to fly across **the Bosporus**, a strait that flows through **Istanbul, Turkey.**

11 In 1971 a Turkish **postage stamp** was created to honor Hazarfen Ahmed Celebi's **famous flight**.

12 **Great snipes** hold the record for the fastest long-distance, nonstop flight of **any living bird.**

13 The **first manned rocket** was said to have been invented by Lagari Hasan Celebi in 1633.

14 Lagari Hasan Celebi's **gunpowder-fueled rocket** carried him **high into the sky,** where he spread out wings and glided down before plunging into the water. For his risky flight Celebi was **rewarded with a pouch of gold** from the Sultan.

15 **Birds also influenced the thinking of the Wright brothers,** whose successful flight in 1903 paved the way for **modern aviation.**

1

A THOUSAND YEARS AGO, **BAGHDAD** BOASTED THE TOP INTELLECTUAL ESTABLISHMENT OF THE DAY: THE *BAYT AL-HIKMA*, OR **HOUSE OF WISDOM.**

2

Drawing on Persian, Indian, and Greek texts, the **HOUSE OF WISDOM SCHOLARS** accumulated one of the greatest **COLLECTIONS OF KNOWLEDGE** in the known world, then built on it through their own discoveries.

3

THIS **LEARNING CENTER** WAS THE 9TH-CENTURY BRAIN-CHILD OF FOUR GENERATIONS OF RULERS, OR **CALIPHS**, WHO BROUGHT THE **TOP SCHOLARS** FROM ALL OVER THE MUSLIM WORLD UNDER ONE ROOF.

4

RESEARCH AND DISCOVERIES AT THE HOUSE OF WISDOM PROVIDED A FOUNDATION FOR MUCH OF WHAT WE KNOW TODAY.

5

The House of Wisdom featured a massive library, with books on every subject written in many languages.

25 BRAINY

6

This intellectual powerhouse turned BAGHDAD into the headquarters for the arts, sciences, and writing and played a major part in the spread and development of **KNOWLEDGE** in these fields.

7

THE HOUSE OF WISDOM WAS OPEN TO TO MEN AND WOMEN OF ALL FAITHS.

8

CALIPH AL-MA'MUN USED **CAMELS** TO CARRY HUNDREDS OF BOOKS AND MANUSCRIPTS FROM OTHER PARTS OF THE MUSLIM WORLD TO THE HOUSE OF WISDOM.

9

THE LIBRARY **GREW** SO LARGE THAT AL-MA'MUM BUILT EXTENSIONS TO HOUSE DIFFERENT BRANCHES OF **KNOWLEDGE.**

10

SO MANY **SCHOLARS** WANTED TO COME THAT AL-MA'MUN KEPT HAVING TO EXPAND THE STUDY CENTERS.

11

CALIPH AL-MA'MUN IS SAID TO HAVE encouraged translators and scholars to add to the House of Wisdom library by paying them the weight of each **COMPLETED BOOK IN GOLD.**

12

AL-MA'MUN BUILT AN ASTRONOMY CENTER IN BAGHDAD AND SET UP DOZENS OF LEARNING CENTERS ALL OVER THE MUSLIM WORLD.

13

SCHOLARS MET EACH DAY FOR READING, WRITING, AND DISCUSSION, USING SEVERAL LANGUAGES, INCLUDING ARABIC, PERSIAN, GREEK, AND SYRIAC.

14

EXPERTS WORKED TO TRANSLATE WRITINGS FROM OTHER CIVILIZATIONS INTO ARABIC SO SCHOLARS COULD READ, DEBATE, AND BUILD ON THEM.

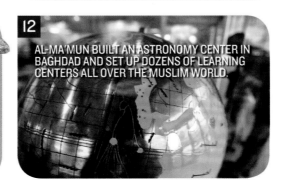

15

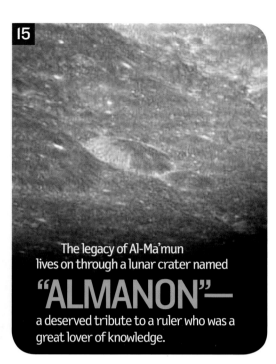

The legacy of Al-Ma'mun lives on through a lunar crater named **"ALMANON"**— a deserved tribute to a ruler who was a great lover of knowledge.

16

OTHER CITIES IN THE ISLAMIC WORLD **FOLLOWED BAGHDAD'S LEAD AND** ESTABLISHED THEIR OWN VERSIONS OF THE HOUSE OF WISDOM IN THE **9TH AND 10TH CENTURIES.**

17

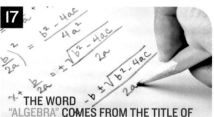

THE WORD "ALGEBRA" COMES FROM THE TITLE OF THE BOOK *AL-JABR WA-'L-MUQABALAH,* BY AL-KHWARIZMI, A SCHOLAR AT THE HOUSE OF WISDOM DURING THE EARLY 9TH CENTURY.

18

The three Banu Musa brothers, mathematicians and inventors of machines and trick devices, Al-Khwarizmi, the "father of algebra," and Al-Kindi, philosopher, mathematician, and inventor of decryption, are among the House of Wisdom's most famous **SCHOLARS.**

FACTS ABOUT THE HOUSE OF WISDOM

19

SOME LIBRARIES WERE SUPER-LAVISH: TOPPED WITH DOMES, WITH NUMEROUS ROOMS FILLED WITH BOOKS AND SURROUNDED BY GARDENS WITH LAKES.

20

AT ONE POINT BAGHDAD HAD **36** LIBRARIES AND MORE THAN A **HUNDRED** BOOK DEALERS.

21

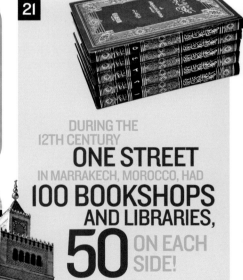

DURING THE 12TH CENTURY **ONE STREET** IN MARRAKECH, MOROCCO, HAD **100 BOOKSHOPS** AND LIBRARIES, **50** ON EACH SIDE!

23

MANY MUSLIM TOWNS ALSO HAD BOOKSHOPS, WHERE PEOPLE WOULD COME TO BUY BOOKS, EAT AND DRINK, AND SHARE IDEAS.

22

DURING MUSLIM CIVILIZATION, **HUNDREDS OF LIBRARIES OPENED,** MAKING MANY THOUSANDS OF BOOKS AVAILABLE TO READERS.

24

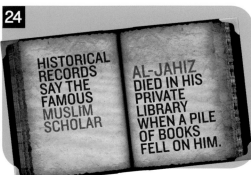

HISTORICAL RECORDS SAY THE FAMOUS MUSLIM SCHOLAR AL-JAHIZ DIED IN HIS PRIVATE LIBRARY WHEN A PILE OF BOOKS FELL ON HIM.

25

THE LIBRARY OF THE ZAYTUNA MOSQUE IN TUNISIA HAD MORE THAN **100,000 BOOKS.**

33

❶ Much of what we know about the **eye and vision** was influenced by scientists in Muslim civilization, beginning in the 9th century.

❷ The scholars of Islam inherited **two theories about vision** from the Greeks. One said we see because our eyes send out invisible, laser-like rays that make objects visible. The other said we see because something representing an object **enters our eyes.**

❸ Figuring out how the eye works is one of the most outstanding **scientific legacies** of Muslim civilization.

❹ Ninth-century philosopher and scientist Al-Kindi was the first to lay down the foundations of **modern-day optics** by questioning earlier theories of vision.

❺ Al-Kindi has been called "one of the 12 giant minds of history."

❻ One century later **Ibn al-Haytham**, a mathematician, astronomer, and physicist, used experiments to build on Al-Kindi's work and provide a more detailed theory of vision.

❼ Al-Kindi's **meticulous experiments** helped Ibn al-Haytham prove that we see because of **light rays** coming from the objects, not from the eye.

❽ **Scientific theories** were often accepted without proof. Ibn al-Haytham was among the first to use experiments to check theories. His *Book of Optics* is still a **brilliant example** of writing on the scientific method.

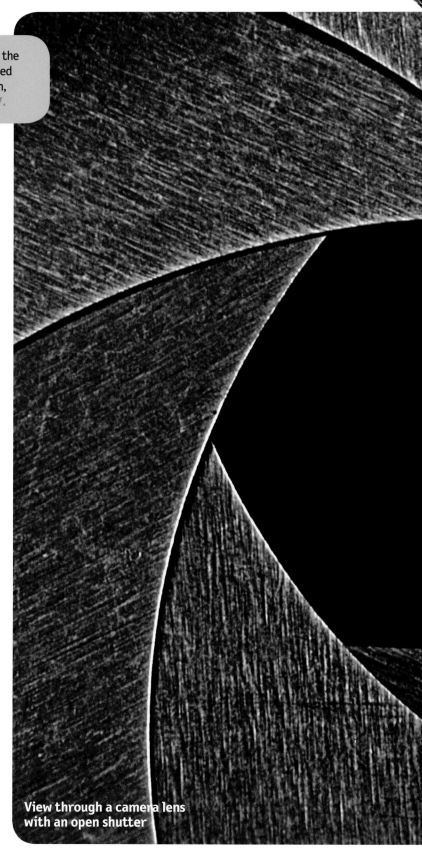

View through a camera lens with an open shutter

VISION FACTS

9 Leonardo da Vinci may have learned from Ibn al-Haytham's book after it was translated from Arabic into Latin.

10 Ibn al-Haytham experimented with the **pinhole camera** while under house arrest in Cairo, Egypt.

11 One day Ibn al-Haytham noticed that light coming through a **tiny hole** in the shutters projected an image of the outside world onto the opposite wall of his dark room.

12 After discovering that the smaller the hole, the more focused the light and the sharper the image, Ibn al-Haytham confirmed light travels in a straight line. This led to the **camera obscura,** a forerunner to the modern camera.

13 The camera obscura had a large, dark chamber the size of a small room with a pinhole opening for light to shine through. The image projected by the light was traced onto a drawing surface to produce a picture.

14 The **earliest** known surviving photograph was shot in France in 1827, using a camera obscura.

15 "Camera obscura" is the Latin translation of "dark room," as originally used by Ibn al-Haytham, which in modern Arabic is *qamara*.

1 A THOUSAND YEARS BEFORE EUROPEANS MADE SIGNIFICANT ADVANCES IN THE FIELD, SCHOLARS IN MUSLIM CIVILIZATION WERE **CREATING NEW MATHEMATICAL KNOWLEDGE** AND BROADENING THE SCOPE OF **MATH.**

2 NEXT TIME YOU DO YOUR **ALGEBRA HOMEWORK,** YOU HAVE MUSLIM MATHEMATICIAN AL-KHWARIZMI TO THANK. THE "FATHER OF ALGEBRA" INTRODUCED NEW CONCEPTS IN MATH IN BAGHDAD AROUND 830.

3 MATHEMATICAL INVENTIONS FROM MUSLIM CIVILIZATION INCLUDE **THE CREATION OF ALGEBRA,** ADDITIONS TO GEOMETRY, THE DECIMAL NUMBERING SYSTEM, THE SINE AND COSINE, AND MANY OTHERS OF **LASTING INFLUENCE.**

4 AL-KHWARIZMI IS KNOWN IN **LATIN** AS **ALGORITMI,** THE SOURCE OF THE MATH AND COMPUTER TERM "ALGORITHM."

5 ALGEBRA REVOLUTIONIZED THE WAY PEOPLE LOOKED AT **NUMBERS** AND BROKE AWAY FROM GEOMETRY, WHICH WAS THE ROOT OF THE GREEK CONCEPT OF MATH.

25 NIFTY

6 AL-KHWARIZMI'S book, *Al-Jabr wa-'l-Muqabala,* introduced the basics of the algebra we study today.

7 **AL-KARAJI,** another mathematician, BUILT ON THE RULES OF ALGEBRA and started an algebra school that THRIVED FOR SEVERAL hundred years.

8 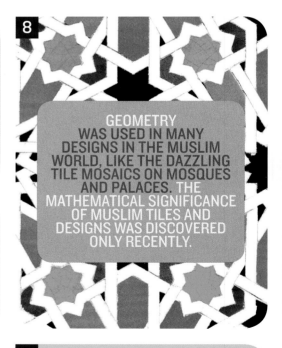 GEOMETRY WAS USED IN MANY DESIGNS IN THE MUSLIM WORLD, LIKE THE DAZZLING TILE MOSAICS ON MOSQUES AND PALACES. THE MATHEMATICAL SIGNIFICANCE OF MUSLIM TILES AND DESIGNS WAS DISCOVERED ONLY RECENTLY.

9 MUSLIMS WERE THE FIRST TO GIVE **ZERO** A MATHEMATICAL PROPERTY. Without this contribution, there would be no way to tell the difference between numbers like **23 and 203.**

10 EVEN POETS LOVED MATH IN MUSLIM CIVILIZATION. THE POET WE KNOW TODAY AS UMAR AL-KHAYYAM CONTRIBUTED TO ALGEBRA WITH HIS IDEAS ABOUT SOLVING COMPLEX EQUATIONS.

11 **ALGEBRA** MADE ITS WAY TO EUROPE BY THE **12TH** CENTURY.

12 THE NUMBERS WE USE TODAY **(0, 1, 2,...9)** COME FROM THE ARABIC SYMBOLS USED MORE THAN **1,000** YEARS AGO.

13 MUSLIMS HAD TWO COUNTING, OR NUMERICAL, SYSTEMS: ONE in which numbers were written as letters of the alphabet; AND ANOTHER in which numbers were written using ancient Babylonian symbols.

14 THE TWO TRADITIONAL MUSLIM COUNTING SYSTEMS WERE EVENTUALLY REPLACED BY NEW NUMBERS KNOWN AS **ARABIC NUMERALS,** DEVELOPED FROM AN ANCIENT INDIAN SYSTEM.

15 ARABIC NUMERALS WERE ALSO KNOWN AS *GHUBARI NUMBERS* BECAUSE MUSLIMS INITIALLY USED DUST (*GHUBAR*) BOARDS TO MAKE CALCULATIONS.

16 ARABIC NUMERALS MADE CALCULATIONS MUCH EASIER THAN THE ROMAN SYSTEM, WHICH USED LETTERS LIKE **X, V, I, L, C, AND M** FOR NUMBERS, OR OTHER SYSTEMS BASED ON DOTS, PICTOGRAPHS, OR FINGER COUNTING.

17 Arabic numerals also led to the introduction of **SIMPLE FRACTIONS** and decimal fractions (a fraction in which the bottom number is a power of ten).

3/4

18 BEGINNING IN THE 11TH CENTURY, STUDENTS STUDYING IN MUSLIM LEARNING CENTERS IN NORTH AFRICA AND SOUTHERN EUROPE INTRODUCED ARABIC NUMERALS TO THE REST OF EUROPE.

NUMBER FACTS

23 WITH A BETTER UNDERSTANDING FOR MATH, PEOPLE WERE ABLE TO USE IT AS A PRACTICAL TOOL IN BUSINESS AND EVERYDAY LIFE.

19 Al-Biruni, one of the greatest Muslim scholars, used **TRIGONOMETRY** to come up with a figure for the **EARTH'S CIRCUMFERENCE** that is very close to the accepted value today.

20 IN THE EARLY **9TH CENTURY** AL-KHWARIZMI CONSTRUCTED TABLES THAT COULD HELP CALCULATE MISSING VALUES IN **ASTRONOMICAL TABLES** THAT DEFINE THE LOCATIONS OF **STARS.**

21 TODAY TRIGONOMETRY IS USED TO **CALCULATE** DISTANCES TO THE STARS, MEASURE THE HEIGHTS OF BUILDINGS AND TREES, AND MUCH MORE.

22 THE SCHOLARS AT THE HOUSE OF WISDOM IN BAGHDAD AND AT UNIVERSITIES IN CAIRO, EGYPT, PICKED UP WHERE THE GREEKS LEFT OFF, THEN ADDED THEIR OWN CONTRIBUTIONS TO **GEOMETRY.**

24 IN THE 10TH CENTURY, IBN AL-HAYTHAM WAS THE FIRST MATHEMATICIAN TO FIGURE OUT HOW TO FIND ALL EVEN PERFECT NUMBERS— A SET OF UNIQUE NUMBERS THAT HAS FASCINATED THINKERS SINCE ANCIENT TIMES.

25

COMPLEX GEOMETRIC PATTERNS WERE USED IN MUSLIM ARCHITECTURE TO COVER WALLS, CEILINGS, FLOORS, AND ARCHES.

15 TIMELY FACTS

❶ Seven hundred years ago, people in Muslim civilization designed clever clocks that were powered by **water.**

❷ Ancient Egyptians introduced **water clocks,** also known as *clepsydras,* around 1500 B.C.E. that measured time by the flow of water in a small bowl. They could be used 24/7 in any weather.

❸ One of the oldest water clocks was found in the tomb of the Egyptian pharaoh Amenhotep I, who died around 1500 B.C.E.

❹ Water clocks were used in ancient Greece to time the length of speeches. Scholars in the Muslim world improved upon early Greek and Indian clocks and **pioneered** many ideas in mechanical design.

❺ In Greek *clepsydra* means "water thief."

❻ The study of **timekeeping** is known as **horology.**

❼ Timekeeping was very important to Muslims, who had to know when to perform each of the five daily prayers.

❽ Clocks also helped keep track of important religious events, such as when to begin and end the daily fast during Ramadan when it was hard to see the dawn or sunset.

Modern clock mechanisms

ABOUT CLOCKS

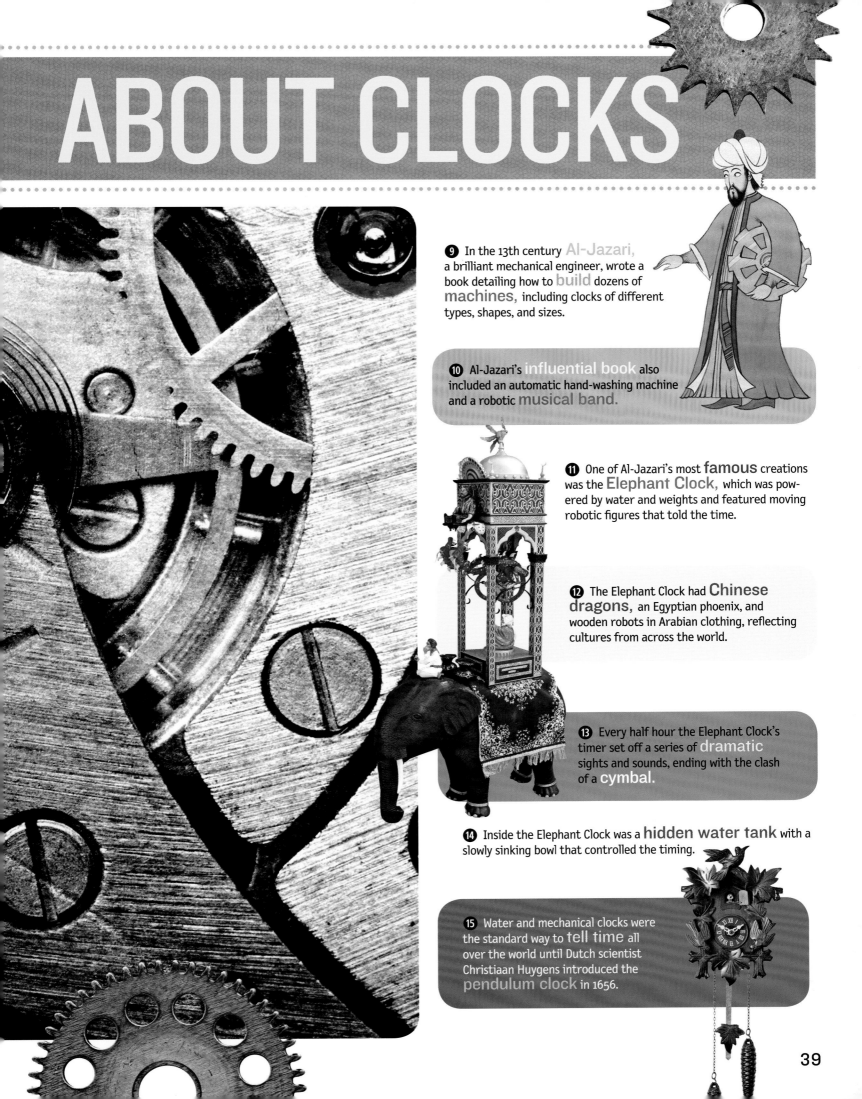

9 In the 13th century Al-Jazari, a brilliant mechanical engineer, wrote a book detailing how to build dozens of machines, including clocks of different types, shapes, and sizes.

10 Al-Jazari's influential book also included an automatic hand-washing machine and a robotic musical band.

11 One of Al-Jazari's most famous creations was the Elephant Clock, which was powered by water and weights and featured moving robotic figures that told the time.

12 The Elephant Clock had Chinese dragons, an Egyptian phoenix, and wooden robots in Arabian clothing, reflecting cultures from across the world.

13 Every half hour the Elephant Clock's timer set off a series of dramatic sights and sounds, ending with the clash of a cymbal.

14 Inside the Elephant Clock was a hidden water tank with a slowly sinking bowl that controlled the timing.

15 Water and mechanical clocks were the standard way to tell time all over the world until Dutch scientist Christiaan Huygens introduced the pendulum clock in 1656.

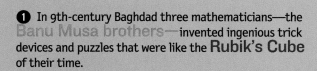

1 In 9th-century Baghdad three mathematicians—the **Banu Musa brothers**—invented ingenious trick devices and puzzles that were like the **Rubik's Cube** of their time.

2 More than **300 million** Rubik's Cubes have been sold worldwide. Stacked end to end, they would **stretch** from the North Pole to the South Pole!

3 The **record** for solving a Rubik's Cube is **6.24 seconds**.

4 The Banu Musa brothers built upon Greek knowledge and helped kick-start the development of **mechanical technology**.

5 **Al-Biruni**, another scholar in the medieval Muslim world, wrote about **number puzzles**.

6 It took a few centuries for **Europe** to catch up with the innovative thinkers of Muslim civilization.

7 Like the Banu Musa brothers, many of the Muslim scholars studied at the **House of Wisdom**, a famous scientific academy in Baghdad founded in the 9th century.

8 Published around 850, the Banu Musa brothers' *Book of Ingenious Devices* illustrated more than **100 trick gadgets and machines**.

Sudoku, a modern version of a mind game

ABOUT GAMES

9 Some of the brothers' **funnier** trick devices involved fake animals and sounds and relied on water and air pressure, siphons, valves, and floats to make them work.

10 The brothers are credited with developing the earliest robotic devices, including birds that could sing and flap their wings.

11 The Banu Musa brothers also are credited with creating the on-off switch and the gas mask.

12 The brothers' "magic flask" had two spouts that could be filled with different-color liquids. The liquids would mysteriously swap places inside the flask so the "wrong" color would come out of each spout.

13 The brothers' automatic flute player, which used steam to produce flute sounds, may be the world's first programmable machine—not that different from a computer you might program today.

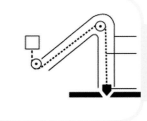

14 These devices provided hours of entertainment and showed an incredible level of skill and craftsmanship.

15 The "Drinking Bull" featured a robotic bull that gave a contented sigh after drinking water.

41

15 MUSIC FACTS

1 Medieval Muslim **musicians** played the *qitara,* an early version of the guitar.

2 The musical scale has its roots in early Muslim civilization. Do, re, mi, fa, sol, la, ti sound close to the names of some letters of the Arabic alphabet, such as *dal, ra, mim,* and *fa.*

3 Roving musicians, merchants, and travelers helped spread Arabic **music** to Europe.

4 A handsome singer called Ziryab was a very **popular musician** in 9th-century Muslim Spain.

5 Al-Farabi, a 10th-century philosopher and musician, developed the *rababah* (an early type of violin) and the *qanun* (similar to a table zither). He wrote *The Great Book of Music,* which was first translated into Hebrew, then Latin.

6 As **entertainer** to the court of the Umayyad Caliph in Córdoba, Ziryab was paid a monthly salary of 200 golden dinars.

7 Today the guitar is considered the most popular instrument in the world.

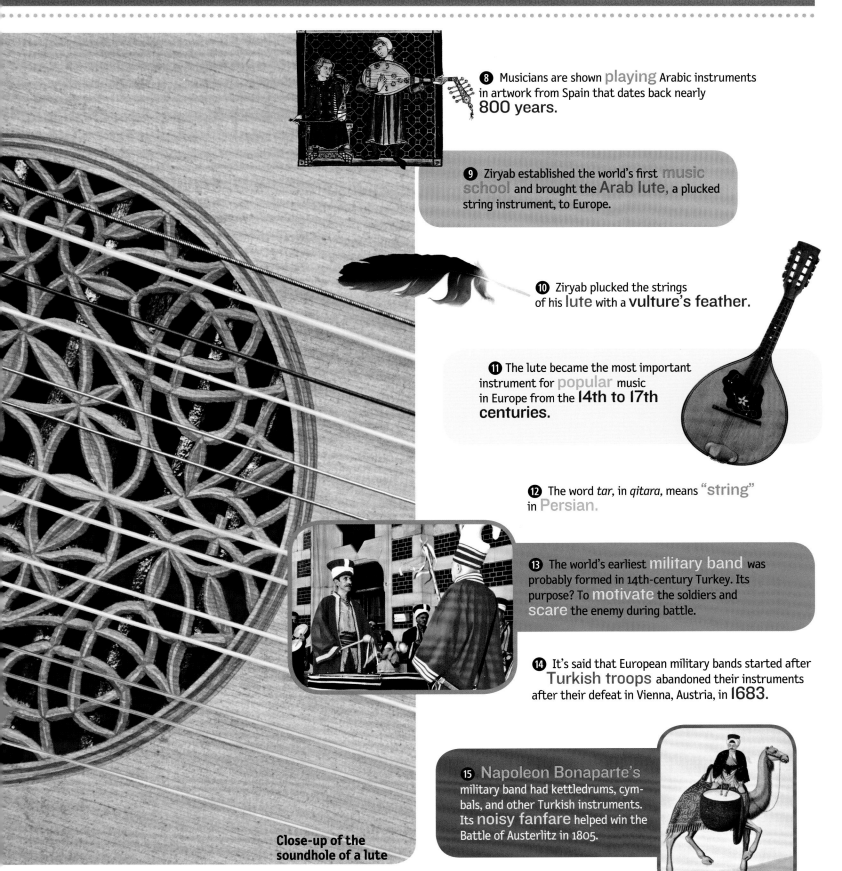

8 Musicians are shown playing Arabic instruments in artwork from Spain that dates back nearly **800 years.**

9 Ziryab established the world's first music school and brought the Arab lute, a plucked string instrument, to Europe.

10 Ziryab plucked the strings of his lute with a vulture's feather.

11 The lute became the most important instrument for popular music in Europe from the **14th to 17th centuries.**

12 The word *tar*, in *qitara*, means "string" in Persian.

13 The world's earliest military band was probably formed in 14th-century Turkey. Its purpose? To motivate the soldiers and scare the enemy during battle.

14 It's said that European military bands started after Turkish troops abandoned their instruments after their defeat in Vienna, Austria, in **1683.**

15 Napoleon Bonaparte's military band had kettledrums, cymbals, and other Turkish instruments. Its noisy fanfare helped win the Battle of Austerlitz in 1805.

Close-up of the soundhole of a lute

1

Pharmacies, hospitals, and medical schools were **common** in the early Muslim world.

2

Unlike healing centers in ancient Greece, the **pioneering** health-care system in Muslim civilization focused on diagnosis and treatment rather than on **miraculous cures.**

3

Hospital patients in the early Muslim world might take **syrups**, pills, and powders; undergo surgery; or have a **cast** put on a broken leg.

4

Muslim rulers competed with each other to create the best hospitals that were **open to all.**

5

The **first** major **hospital** was **built** in Cairo, Egypt, between 872 and 874. It was named for Ahmad ibn Tulun, a Muslim ruler in Egypt.

6

Unlike in the Western world today, **herbal medicine** in the 10th-century Muslim world was not seen as alternative medicine.

7

A thousand years ago in the Muslim world medical care was **free** for everyone and included very advanced treatments—even **music therapy.**

8

Because Muslims are **honor-bound** by the Quran to care for the sick, early hospitals treated people of **all faiths,** rich or poor, man or woman.

9

The earliest hospitals in Muslim civilization began in **Baghdad** in the 8th century.

10

Patients with **leprosy** could get treatment at Al-Qayrawan hospital in 9th-century Tunisia, even though many people thought the disease was a **sign of evil.**

11

Al-Nuri Hospital in Damascus, Syria, had inspectors who made sure the care met the **highest standards.**

12

Damascus's highly advanced hospital was one of the first **teaching hospitals** in the world.

13

Doctors in Muslim civilization were required to have **rigorous medical training** in a teaching hospital, much like doctors are today.

14

Muslim hospitals were built in southern Spain and other areas of Europe that were part of **Muslim civilization.**

15

Muslim hospitals were funded by **charitable gifts** called *awqaf.*

16

Muslim scientist Sinan ibn Thabit ibn Qurra started **mobile** hospital services for rural areas.

17

In the 13th century Ibn al-Nafis accurately described how in the **lungs,** blood coming from the heart mixes with the air.

18

Ibn al-Nafis was **not credited** with this great discovery until **1957!**

19

In the 17th century an English doctor named William Harvey discovered the complete blood **circulatory** system.

20

Eleventh-century doctor and philosopher Ibn Sina developed a method for treating **fractured bones** that is still used today.

21

Ibn Sina was known in the West as the "Prince of Physicians."

22

Ibn Sina wrote a highly **influential** medical textbook: the *Code of Laws in Medicine,* or **the Canon.**

23

The *Canon* was printed in Rome in 1593 and went on to become a **standard text** in European medical schools.

24

The *Canon* influenced the layout of modern medical textbooks, such as *Gray's Anatomy,* first published in 1858 and now the leading Western medical encyclopedia.

25

Medical books written in the 11th-century Muslim world were **translated** from Arabic into Latin to help spread the knowledge in Europe.

26

The first book solely on **pediatrics,** or children's medicine, was written by Tunisian-born Ibn al-Jazzar al-Qayrawani back in the 9th century.

27

The first known alphabetical classification of medical terms was called *Kitab al-Ma'a,* or *The Book of Water.* The odd title comes from the fact that *Al-Ma'a,* which means "the water," is the first entry.

28

The Book of Water was rediscovered by the modern world, and in 1996 it was published by the government of Oman.

29

Medical books from the Muslim world a thousand years ago show that physicians back then were very skilled at treating **eye diseases.**

30

The *Notebook of the Oculist,* written in the 10th century, describes **130 eye diseases.**

31

As early as the year 1000, physicians in the Muslim world were working to find ways to **prevent blindness.**

32

Of the 30 ophthalmology textbooks written during early Muslim civilization, **14 still exist.**

50 Healing Facts About MEDICINE

Al-Qayrawan hospital in Tunisia

33
Al-Kindi, a 9th-century scholar, was the first doctor to systematically determine the dosage for some drugs.

36
Edward Jenner is credited as the pioneer of vaccination. Unlike inoculation, Jenner used cowpox rather than smallpox itself to provide protection.

39
Pharmacies existed in Iraq more than a thousand years ago.

42
In 1967 the Turkish Postal Authority issued a stamp commemorating the 250th anniversary of the first smallpox vaccination.

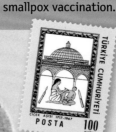

45
Ibn Sina's *Canon* had 142 herbal remedies made from plants, trees, seeds, and spices.

46
Al-Zahrawi had his patients swallow drugs in parcels made of catgut—the forerunner to present-day capsules.

47
Thanks to translations from Arabic to Latin by **Constantine the African**, a Tunisian scholar, medicine from the Muslim world found its way to Europe.

48
The largest encyclopedia of drug usage still in existence—*Dictionary of Simple Remedies and Food*— was written by the Spanish Muslim Ibn al-Baytar in the 13th century.

34
Tribes in the Middle East and Africa were among the ancient peoples who knew of a life-saving process called inoculation.

37
The word "vaccination" is derived from the Latin word *vacca*, meaning "cow."

40
Smallpox was one of the deadliest diseases in the world until 1980, when it was wiped out as the result of a worldwide vaccination campaign.

43
In 1721 Lady Mary Montagu, wife of the English ambassador to **Istanbul**, brought the idea of inoculation to England from Turkey, where it was well-known.

49
Ibn al-Baytar had a system of classifying plants centuries before Swedish scientist Carl Linnaeus set up his.

35
In inoculation, or immunization, patients are given a controlled dose of a disease-causing organism so that their immune system learns to fight off the disease.

38
In 1796 Jenner infected a young boy with cowpox, believing that it would immunize him against the smallpox virus. Lucky for all, the process worked.

41
It is estimated that more than 300 million deaths worldwide in the 20th century can be attributed to smallpox.

44
Spanish doctor Al-Zahrawi wrote the first illustrated book on medicine and surgery.

50
Ahmad ibn Tulun Hospital in Egypt was the first to include a mental health department.

1 If you lived **a thousand years ago** in Muslim Spain, two types of surgery could have been performed on you: **GENERAL AND ORTHOPEDIC (BONES).**

2 Al-Zahrawi, a 10th-century **SPANISH MUSLIM SURGEON,** is considered the **"father of modern surgery."**

3 IF YOU EVER NEED SURGERY, YOU CAN THANK AL-ZAHRAWI FOR CREATING MANY OF THE **medical instruments** used, including a **scalpel for cutting.**

4 **DON'T GET SCARED!** Al-Zahrawi was so concerned about his patients that **he invented A KNIFE with a HIDDEN BLADE.**

5  ALTHOUGH SURGERY WAS STILL DANGEROUS AND PAINFUL, AL-ZAHRAWI'S TOOLS WOULD HAVE HELPED TREAT PATIENTS SUFFERING FROM BONE DISEASES, TUMORS, AND WOUNDS AS WELL AS ASSISTING IN CHILDBIRTH.

25 FACTS ABOUT SURGERY YOU

6 Another tool Al-Zahrawi invented was the **LITHOTRIPTER,** an instrument for **crushing hard deposits in the body, like bladder stones.**

7 A **30-chapter book** written by Al-Zahrawi included illustrations of his **surgical instruments** and explained HOW AND WHAT TO USE THEM FOR, making it an IMPORTANT SURGICAL HANDBOOK for centuries to come.

8 There were sketches of more than **200 DIFFERENT MEDICAL TOOLS** in Al-Zahrawi's book!

9 AL-ZAHRAWI'S MEDICAL BOOK WAS **translated** INTO **Latin** SO THAT EUROPEAN DOCTORS COULD LEARN FROM IT.

10  IN THE 12TH CENTURY, A MUSLIM DOCTOR NAMED IBN ZUHR IMPROVED UPON ONE OF AL-ZAHRAWI'S **surgical drills by adding a diamond on the tip.**

11 AL-ZAHRAWI PIONEERED THE USE OF **catgut** for **MAKING INTERNAL STITCHES IN A PATIENT.** SURGEONS STILL USE A SIMILAR MATERIAL.

12 **CATGUT** is a **THIN, NATURAL FIBER MADE FROM THE INTESTINES OF ANIMALS** that can be absorbed by the body.

13 CATGUT HAS BEEN USED THROUGHOUT HISTORY TO MAKE STRINGED MUSICAL INSTRUMENTS AND SNARE DRUMS.

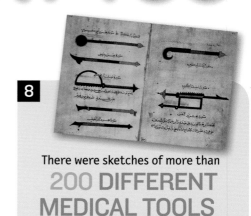

14 DOCTORS IN MUSLIM CIVILIZATION TACKLED SERIOUS EYE DISEASES AND EVEN PERFORMED **eye surgery.**

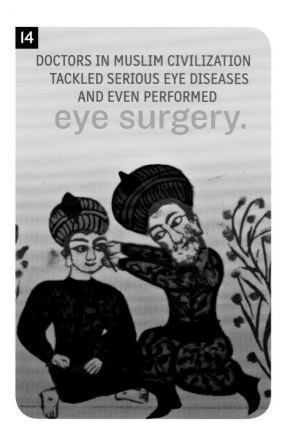

15 Al-Mawsili, a 10th-century Iraqi, **INVENTED A HOLLOW NEEDLE** for **sucking cataracts out of patients' eyes so they could see again.**

16 Muslim scholars produced some of the **first accurate diagrams** of the structure of the **HUMAN EYE.**

17 PIONEERING OPHTHALMOLOGISTS OF MUSLIM CIVILIZATION USED MODERN TERMS TO DESCRIBE THE ANATOMY OF THE EYE IN ARABIC, SUCH AS **retina, uvea, and cornea.**

CAN OPERATE ON

18 A 15TH-CENTURY **ILLUSTRATED MANUSCRIPT** by Turkish physician Serefeddin Sabuncuoglu showed very advanced surgery techniques.

19 SABUNCUOGLU'S BOOK WAS ALSO THE FIRST TO SHOW **FEMALE SURGEONS** at work.

20 THREE ORIGINAL, **HANDWRITTEN COPIES** OF SABUNCUOGLU'S NEARLY 600-YEAR-OLD BOOK **STILL EXIST!**

25 IBN ZUHR AND AL-RAZI WERE AMONG THE **FIRST DOCTORS TO TEST TREATMENTS ON ANIMALS BEFORE USING THEM ON HUMANS.**

21 Followers of Islam are **FORBIDDEN TO DRINK ALCOHOL,** SO PHYSICIANS IN THE EARLY MUSLIM WORLD HAD TO FIND HERBAL MEDICINES TO **calm their patients.**

22 Surgeons in the early Muslim world described a method for **inhaling drugs** THAT PUT A PATIENT TO SLEEP.

23 SOPORIFIC, OR SLEEP, **sponges** WERE USED IN EUROPE UNTIL THE 1840S.

24 ABU MARWAN ABD AL-MALIK IBN ZUHR, A 12TH-CENTURY MUSLIM DOCTOR, WAS THE FIRST SURGEON TO PROVE A TRACHEOTOMY—A SURGERY IN WHICH A HOLE IS MADE IN THE WINDPIPE TO AID BREATHING—COULD BE DONE SAFELY.

1 From geography to gemstones, scholars developed exciting new ideas about the natural sciences during Muslim civilization.

2 Many areas of science, including geology, meteorology, botany, and zoology, are linked to ideas from a thousand years ago.

3 Scientists in Muslim civilization used observation and experimentation to explore and explain such natural phenomena as earthquakes and the formation of mountains.

4 The boundaries of the Muslim world gave scholars a wide range of geographical regions to study.

5 INFORMATION ABOUT MINERALS, PLANTS, AND ANIMALS WAS GATHERED FROM AS FAR AWAY AS THE MALAY ISLANDS.

6 Al-Hamdani, a 10th-century scholar, wrote three books about ways to look for gold, silver, and other minerals in Arabia.

7 The 11th-century scholar Ibn Sina's *The Book of Cure* presented his observations and theories about how the Earth works.

8 The Latin translation of Ibn Sina's book influenced the study of earth science in Europe for more than 300 years.

9 Al-Biruni, another 11th-century Muslim scholar, took the lead in studies about minerals.

10 Al-Biruni's works included a focus on diamonds, rubies, sapphires, and other gemstones.

11 Like other scientists in the medieval Muslim world, Al-Biruni built upon the work of scholars in earlier civilizations.

12 Al-Biruni classified gemstones by color, shape, and hardness.

13 "Hardness" is the ability of a mineral to scratch the surface of softer minerals.

14 Al-Biruni used crystal shape to help him decide whether a gemstone was a quartz or a diamond.

15 Today scientists and jewelers use similar techniques to identify gemstones.

16 Carnelian, a reddish brown gemstone, is prized by Muslims because the Prophet Muhammad is said to have worn a ring with this stone.

17 Carnelians are often engraved with verses from the Quran.

18 Al-Biruni studied India's Ganges River basin and accounts of other geologic formations from the Baltic Sea to Mozambique.

19 Al-Biruni could speak Greek, Sanskrit, and Syriac and wrote all of his books in Arabic and Persian.

20 BY FINDING FOSSILS OF OCEAN LIFE IN ROCKS HIGH ABOVE SEA LEVEL, AL-BIRUNI PROVED THE OCEAN HAD ONCE COVERED PARTS OF INDIA.

21 Al-Biruni's work became a key reference on precious stones.

22 By observing the moon's effects on the ocean, Al-Biruni figured out that tides changed based on the phases of the moon.

23 Al-Biruni discussed the possibility of the Earth being in motion without rejecting it.

24 Like other scholars of the time he believed the Earth was a sphere and discussed the possibility that it rotates on its axis.

25 Six hundred years later the Italian astronomer Galileo Galilei proved Al-Biruni was correct.

26 Al-Biruni also measured latitudes and longitudes and came up with the concept of antipodes, places that are directly opposite each other on the Earth's surface.

27 ONE OF THE EARLIEST EXPLANATIONS OF WHY THE SKY IS BLUE WAS WRITTEN IN THE 9TH CENTURY BY AL-KINDI.

28 Al-Kindi reasoned that the color midway between darkness and light was blue.

29 Al-Kindi was partly right. The sky is not really blue—that's just the way light acts on the atmosphere.

30 Since ancient times some people have believed that stars and planets had souls and minds.

31 Ibn Hazm, a 10th-century scholar from Córdoba, dared to say that "stars are celestial bodies with no mind or soul."

32 Ibn al-Haytham, another earth science innovator, searched for ways to control flooding along the Nile River. A thousand years later his idea became a reality when the powerful Aswan Dam was completed in present-day Egypt.

33 IBN AL-HAYTHAM'S EXPERIMENTS WITH RAYS OF LIGHT LED TO A DETAILED THEORY OF VISION.

34 His observations paved the way for others to figure out that rainbows are caused by a refraction of sunlight in raindrops.

35 Why does the moon seem to grow in size when it is low in the sky? Ibn al-Haytham said it was a visual trick played by the brain.

36 Later a scholar named Kamal al-Din al-Farisi experimented with glass jars full of water to find out how rainbows are made.

37 Scholars also studied the shape of the Earth, the amount of water versus land, and how rivers, seas, winds, and sea storms formed.

38 Like the ancient Greeks, geographers in Muslim civilization believed the world was round, not flat, and made detailed measurements of the globe.

Sand dunes of Erg Chebbi, in Morocco

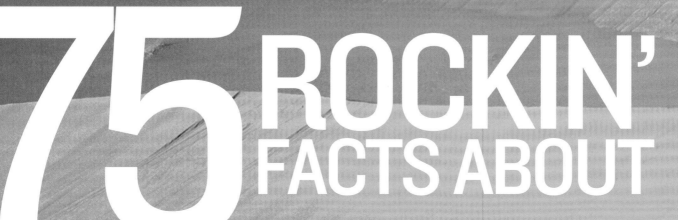

75 ROCKIN' FACTS ABOUT

39 Scientists now know that the Earth is slightly pear-shaped.

40 Beginning in the 9th century, people in Muslim civilization made very accurate measurements of the Earth, building on the ancient Greek astronomer Ptolemy's findings.

41 NINTH-CENTURY CALIPH AL-MA'MUN HIRED A GROUP OF MUSLIM ASTRONOMERS TO MEASURE THE DISTANCE AROUND THE EARTH.

42 They measured the distance around the Earth to be 25,012 miles (40,253 km). The current measurement is 24,897 miles (40,068 km) at the Equator.

43 Two centuries later Al-Biruni used an equation to calculate the Earth's circumference that "didn't require walking in deserts."

44 In the early 9th century, mathematician, scientist, and astronomer Al-Battani improved existing values for the length of the year and of the seasons that are very close to today's.

45 Observing the seasons led Muslim scholars to study and calculate the tilt of the Earth on its axis.

46 In the late 10th century, mathematician and astronomer Al-Khujandi built a huge observatory to observe the sun.

47 Al-Khujandi calculated the tilt of the Earth's axis relative to the sun and made a list of latitudes and longitudes of major cities.

48 MUSLIM SCIENTISTS STUDIED WEATHER PATTERNS ON LAND AND AT SEA AND WROTE BOOKS ON METEOROLOGY THAT WERE MUST-READS FOR SAILORS.

49 Ahmed ibn Majid, a great Muslim navigator, learned about currents and the monsoons that helped carry vessels to India.

50 Ninth-century Muslim inventor 'Abbas ibn Firnas invented a weather simulation room in which hidden mechanisms created thunder and lightning.

51 Farmers in Muslim lands followed the *Calendar of Córdoba*, an almanac of weather, planting, and harvesting times.

52 MUSLIM SCHOLARS ALSO EXPANDED THE STUDY OF ANIMALS, CALLED ZOOLOGY, DURING THE 9TH AND 10TH CENTURIES.

53 The most famous Muslim writer on animals was the Iraqi Al-Jahiz, who recognized the influence of environment on animals.

54 Al-Jahiz sometimes rented the contents of entire bookshops so he could read all of the books.

55 Though he wrote poetry and fiction, he mixed in scientific observations about things like camouflage and mimicry.

56 Al-Jahiz also investigated animal behavior and communication, especially among insects.

57 Al-Asmai, an Iraqi scholar, was likely the first Muslim scientist to contribute to zoology, botany, and animal husbandry.

58 Al-Asmai's expertise was in breeding horses and camels.

59 Merino wool, most likely from Morocco, resulted from centuries of careful sheep breeding.

60 Today Merino wool is popular among cyclists, hikers, runners, and other outdoor lovers.

61 The concept of pedigree—tracing the ancestry of an animal, especially the horse—originated in Muslim Spain and is used throughout the world today for all kinds of animals.

62 Arabians, which were originally bred as war horses and for their endurance in the desert, are now one of the world's most popular breeds of riding horses.

63 THE MUSLIM WORLD ALSO MADE SIGNIFICANT ADVANCES IN BIOLOGY, ESPECIALLY IN BOTANY—THE STUDY OF PLANTS.

64 A thousand years ago gardens in Muslim civilization were like scientific field laboratories tended by scholars who took detailed notes about the plants they grew.

65 Migrants to the Muslim world, homesick for their native lands, brought fruit trees, like date and pomegranate, then learned how to grow them in the new climate.

66 Some of the greatest botanists of medieval times came from Muslim civilization.

67 Ibn Bassal, a botanist in Toledo, Spain, came up with a way of classifying ten types of soil and explained which ones were best for raising which crops.

68 Al-Ghafiqi, a physician and botanist from Córdoba, Spain, made herbal medicines from plants he collected in Spain and Africa.

69 Ibn al-Baytar, another botanist of the Muslim world, collected plants and herbs from Spain to Syria.

70 He wrote a book outlining the medical uses for 3,000 plants.

71 Ibn Al-Awwam, a 12th-century scholar from Seville, in Muslim Spain, described in great detail how to grow 585 plants and 50 fruit trees.

72 His book also listed ways to fertilize plants and keep them safe from diseases.

73 The knowledge of plants that botanists in Muslim civilization collected and developed led to the cultivation of many useful, beautiful, and nutritious plants.

74 These plants improved the lives of people in other parts of the world, and they enriched gardens throughout Europe.

75 When Europeans colonized the New World, they brought with them many of the plants discovered, studied, and grown in the Muslim world.

EARTH SCIENCE

15 CRYSTAL CLEAR FACTS

1 Beginning in the 8th century, Egypt, Iraq, Syria, and Muslim Spain produced vast amounts of glassware either by **blowing liquid glass** into molds or by cutting it from crystal.

2 Muslims inherited the Roman glass industry in Syria and Egypt and improved it by developing their own glassmaking techniques.

3 **Glassmakers** in the Muslim world were skilled in using both blown and **wheel-turned** techniques.

4 They also made many kinds of glass objects, including **bottles**, **vases**, and **cups**.

5 Many amazing examples of ancient glass have been uncovered in excavations of *Al-Fustat*, or "Old Cairo," in Egypt.

6 Samarra, near Baghdad, in Iraq, was well celebrated for its glass, especially mosaic glass called millefiori.

7 Samarra's glassmakers were also famed for the small, heavy but graceful blue or **green bottles** often used for **perfume**.

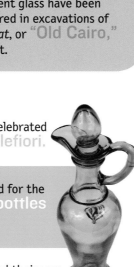

8 Many Andalusian **crystal pieces** found their way to churches and monasteries throughout Europe.

Window in the Sultan's room in the Topkapi Palace in Istanbul, Turkey

ABOUT GLASS

9 Finds from *Al-Fustat* include glass weights in **many colors** stamped with the **names of rulers,** some dating from the year 708.

10 Most of what is **known** about Muslim glassware has been learned from **surviving items,** archaeological **digs,** and **writings** of the time.

11 A 9th-century Iraqi nicknamed Ziryab ("The Blackbird") introduced the use of **crystal glasses** to Muslim Spain after his arrival there.

12 Credit for making glasses out of crystal goes to 'Abbas ibn Firnas, a Cordoban scholar who created a **crystal industry** using rocks mined near Badajos, Spain.

13 'Abbas ibn Firnas also experimented with using glass **lenses to magnify** the writing in ancient scripts for translators.

14 Ziryab replaced the heavy **metal goblets** and **gold cups** commonly found on the banquet tables of Andalusia in Muslim Spain with delicate crystal drinking glasses.

15 By the 13th and 14th centuries **glassware** from Syria was in **great demand** around the world.

1 Muslim civilization gave rise to many new architectural IDEAS AND STYLES.

2 ENGINEERS in the Muslim world improved upon many architectural features used by earlier civilizations.

3 The Muslim architecture of North Africa and Muslim-ruled Spain is often CALLED "MOORISH" architecture.

4 Architectural advances spread from Muslim-ruled SPAIN AND SICILY to the rest of Europe a thousand years ago.

5 Islamic features in the GREAT MOSQUE OF CÓRDOBA in Spain made it an inspiration for much of European architecture.

11 Mimar Sinan began as an ORDINARY CARPENTER and ended up designing 477 buildings for three Ottoman Sultans.

12 Sinan's designs emphasized the importance of HARMONY between architecture and landscape.

13 Suleymaniye Mosque, which crowns one of the SEVEN HILLS of Istanbul, Turkey, is one of Sinan's best-known works.

14 Features in Suleymaniye Mosque show that Sinan may have been the FIRST "GREEN" ARCHITECT.

15 Smoke from candles and lamps in the mosque was channeled into a filter room before escaping into the outside air.

21 "Minaret" comes from the Arabic word *manarah*, meaning "lighthouse," a reference to the LIGHT OF ISLAM.

22 Sinan built the Selimiye Mosque in Edirne, Turkey, so well that it has withstood EARTHQUAKES since the 1570s!

23 MATH SKILLS helped Muslims to create many new kinds of arches, including the horseshoe, pointed, and ogee.

24 Architects use arches to SPAN LARGE OPENINGS and carry HEAVY LOADS.

25 The respect Muslims held for the arch is reflected in an Arabic saying that means "THE ARCH NEVER SLEEPS."

35 FACTS TO BUILD ON

Inside of Suleymaniye Mosque in Istanbul, Turkey

6 TRAVELERS, SCHOLARS, and invaders who passed through Muslim lands helped spread Muslim innovations in architecture.

7 Some even took MUSLIM ARCHITECTS AND CRAFTSMEN home with them.

8 Muslim architecture was a symbolic expression of the power of God and the BEAUTY OF LIFE IN PARADISE.

9 Domes, towers, and archways gave buildings A FEELING OF SPACE AND MAJESTY.

10 ROSE WINDOWS in European churches may have been inspired by a circular window in an 8th-century Muslim palace.

16 The soot was then used to make ink that also repelled BOOKWORMS AND BUGS.

17 Sinan figured out a way to MAKE DOMES BIGGER AND HIGHER.

18 Under the Ottomans, domes grew large enough to COVER ENTIRE SANCTUARIES.

19 For Muslims the DOME SYMBOLIZED THE VAULT OF HEAVEN.

20 THE MINARET, a tower used by muezzins to call people to prayer, is an essential feature of a mosque.

26 The HORSESHOE ARCH, which gave a greater feeling of openness, was created by expanding the top of a basic arch.

27 This arch, known in Britain as the "MOORISH ARCH," was popular during Queen Victoria's reign (1837–1901).

28 By tapering the top of an arch, Muslim architects created the POINTED ARCH, which reached Europe by way of Sicily in the early 11th century.

29 The ogee arch, which originated in Muslim India, resembles TWO S-SHAPED CURVES facing each other.

30 The ogee arch, which became known as the "GOTHIC ARCH" in Europe, can be seen in many churches in the West.

31 Muslim architects figured out a way to make VAULTS—arched ceilings—bigger, higher, and fancier.

32 A STALACTITE VAULT, or *muqarnas*, has a dome that looks like a honeycomb.

33 Muslim architects imitated the graceful curve of PALM TREE branches in their designs.

34 THE TAJ MAHAL, in India, is one of the world's most famous and widely visited examples of Islamic architecture.

35 To see all of these architectural innovations under one roof, VISIT THE GREAT MOSQUE in Córdoba, Spain.

WHAT YOU KNOW ABOUT
ARCHITECTURE

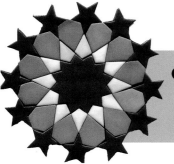

❶ **New colors, techniques, and decorations** made the pottery of Muslim civilization among the world's finest.

❷ Pottery was used for everyday activities, such as **cooking and washing,** as well as for trade and decoration.

❸ Everyday pottery was **used and then thrown away,** much the way we do with paper cups and plates today.

❹ One 14th-century historian estimated the value of pottery that ended up daily on trash heaps to be about a **thousand dinars**—about 10 pounds (4.5 kg) of gold!

❺ By **adding more lead to their glazes,** Muslims made pots that were **leakproof and able to hold liquid.**

❻ Potters in the Muslim world discovered that adding tin oxide to lead glaze produced a **pure white porcelain** similar to that being made in China.

❼ **Blue-on-white** decoration became a **signature of the Abbasid potters.**

IDEAS ON POTTERY

8 **Baghdad and Samarra, Iraq,** were among the **chief pottery** centers in Muslim civilization.

9 Three types of pots were most often made: white pots decorated with cobalt blue, pots decorated with two-tone stripes, and pots that had a **special metallic luster.**

10 Eighth-century potters in Iraq revolutionized pottery by developing a process called **"luster"** that made clay objects look as though they were made of precious **metals.**

11 Islamic law **prohibits the use of gold or silver** containers, so the luster technique became a way of making luxury items without breaking the law.

12 The luster technique was also used to make decorative tiles that made the outsides of mosques and castles appear to **shimmer.**

13 **Unglazed pots** for everyday use, such as carrying water and eating and drinking, **were called** *qâdûs.*

14 Iznik, Turkey, was a **thriving pottery** center widely known for its blue-and-white tiles even to this day.

15 **Iznik pottery** typically featured **floral designs** painted on with **glazes** of cobalt blue, turquoise, and green and then outlined in black with tomato-red highlights.

Handcrafts for sale in a market in Morocco

1 **Advances in geometry** CREATED A WHOLE NEW KIND OF ART IN MUSLIM CIVILIZATION.

2 **Geometric art** BROUGHT TOGETHER MATH, SPACE, SHAPE, AND PATTERN.

3 **Interlacing, flowing lines create complex** PATTERNS THAT SEEM TO CHANGE SHAPE RIGHT BEFORE YOUR EYES.

4 This type of geometric art is called "arabesque."

5 EACH UNIT OF AN ARABESQUE PATTERN CAN STAND ALONE BUT ALSO HELPS TO **COMPLETE THE OVERALL DESIGN.**

25 CREATIVE FACTS ABOUT

6 THE COMPLEXITY OF ARABESQUE encouraged **deep thought,** which made it **ideal for decorating** MOSQUES, TOMBS, AND SHRINES.

7 Arabesque is most often used to **decorate walls,** ceilings, carpets, furniture, tiles, and textiles.

8 MUSLIMS FELT THAT ARABESQUE'S INFINITE DESIGN MOVED BEYOND THE MATERIAL WORLD AND EXTENDED INTO ANOTHER **spiritual level.**

9 THE TOPKAPI SCROLL IS A COLLECTION OF **114 geometric patterns** drawn by master builders from Persia in the 15th or 16th century.

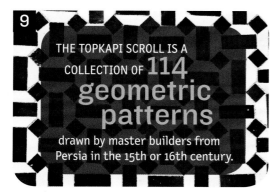

10 UNLIKE RELIGIOUS ART IN THE WEST, ART IN MUSLIM CIVILIZATION DOES NOT FEATURE HUMANS OR ANIMALS. THE PROPHET MUHAMMAD SPOKE OUT AGAINST PORTRAYING HUMAN OR ANIMAL FORMS IN ART BECAUSE IT IS TOO MUCH LIKE THE WORSHIP OF IDOLS, RATHER THAN OF ALLAH (GOD).

11 ARABESQUE OFTEN USED DESIGNS INSPIRED BY NATURE, ALONG WITH **geometric shapes.**

12 THIS INSPIRATION INCLUDED THE GOLDEN RATIO, a **measurement that appears in nature and is pleasing to the eye.**

13 The golden ratio OCCURS WHEN THE WIDTH OF SOMETHING IS ROUGHLY TWO-THIRDS OF ITS HEIGHT.

14 The nautilus shell is an example of a natural occurrence of a simple and beautiful golden ratio.

15 THE *IKHWAN AL-SAFA* (BROTHERS OF PURITY), A GROUP OF 10TH-CENTURY SCHOLARS, DISCOVERED THAT IF YOU LIE DOWN AND SPREAD YOUR HANDS OUT, YOUR toes and the tips of your fingers WILL TOUCH THE EDGE OF AN imaginary circle.

16 Divine proportion and the geometric patterns OF MUSLIM CIVILIZATION HAD AN ENORMOUS IMPACT ON WESTERN ART.

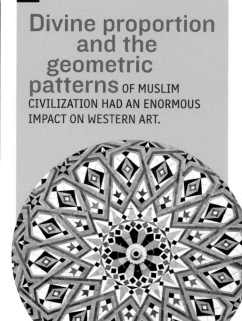

17 The ideal **human body** is eight heads long, the **foot** and the **face** are each an eighth of the body's length, **the forehead** is a third of the face, and the **face** is four noses or four ears. **Check yours out!**

18 LEONARDO DA VINCI'S "VITRUVIAN MAN" SHOWS THE PROPORTIONS OF THE HUMAN BODY DESCRIBED BY THE **Brothers of Purity.**

ART AND DESIGN

19 ARABESQUE DESIGNS were often paired with the use of ARABIC CALLIGRAPHY to write verses from the Quran.

20 Calligraphy IS ONE OF THE MOST RECOGNIZABLE FORMS OF ISLAMIC ART.

21 The Alhambra, a 14th-century palace and fortress in Granada, Spain, CONTAINS SOME OF THE FINEST EXAMPLES OF ARABESQUE ART.

22 ARTISTS IN MUSLIM CIVILIZATION USED linseed oil TO IMPROVE THEIR PAINTS, GLAZES, AND INKS.

23 BEGINNING IN THE 14TH CENTURY, EUROPEAN ARTISTS STARTED USING imported linseed-oil paint INSTEAD OF TEMPERA PAINTS TO ACHIEVE RICHER COLORS.

24 TEMPERA PAINT IS MADE FROM egg, water, honey, and dye.

25 M.C. ESCHER, A 20TH-CENTURY ARTIST BEST KNOWN FOR USING GEOMETRIC SHAPES TO TRICK THE EYE, WAS INSPIRED BY ALHAMBRA TILE PATTERNS.

1 The carpets, cushions, and cloths of Muslim civilization are **world-famous** for their quality materials and **jewel-like** colors.

2 By the mid-9th century the textiles of Muslim Spain had an international reputation, with everyone from queens to commoners seeking out the region's rich, colorful fabrics.

3 Different cities were known for different fabrics. **Córdoba, in Muslim Spain,** housed one manufacturing center with **13,000 active looms,** producing silk for making curtains, shawls, robes, and more.

4 **Camel, goat, and sheep hair** were used to make fabric for clothes, much like camel-hair coats and mohair sweaters worn today.

5 **Muslim silk** was so valued in Europe that Pope Sylvester II was buried in Persian silk cloth when he died in 1003.

6 Queen Beatrice of Portugal used silks with golden borders imported from Muslim Spain at her wedding in 1383.

7 The **popularity** of Muslim silk in Britain exploded to the point that by 1700 it threatened the local textile industry, forcing the government to limit its import.

Carpets made in Iran (formerly Persia)

ABOUT FABRIC

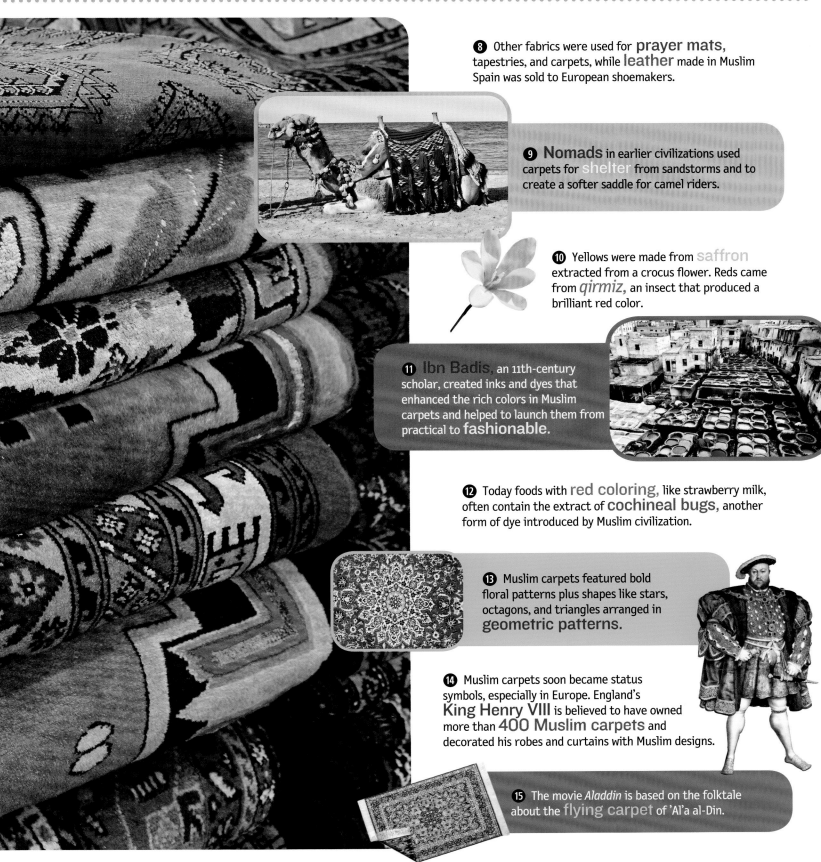

8 Other fabrics were used for **prayer mats,** tapestries, and carpets, while **leather** made in Muslim Spain was sold to European shoemakers.

9 **Nomads** in earlier civilizations used carpets for shelter from sandstorms and to create a softer saddle for camel riders.

10 Yellows were made from saffron extracted from a crocus flower. Reds came from *qirmiz,* an insect that produced a brilliant red color.

11 Ibn Badis, an 11th-century scholar, created inks and dyes that enhanced the rich colors in Muslim carpets and helped to launch them from practical to **fashionable.**

12 Today foods with red coloring, like strawberry milk, often contain the extract of **cochineal bugs,** another form of dye introduced by Muslim civilization.

13 Muslim carpets featured bold floral patterns plus shapes like stars, octagons, and triangles arranged in **geometric patterns.**

14 Muslim carpets soon became status symbols, especially in Europe. England's **King Henry VIII** is believed to have owned more than **400 Muslim carpets** and decorated his robes and curtains with Muslim designs.

15 The movie *Aladdin* is based on the folktale about the **flying carpet** of 'Al'a al-Din.

1 Muslim civilization learned about paper in 751 from captured Chinese soldiers, who passed along the secrets of papermaking.

2 It was a lot cheaper to make books with paper than with more expensive materials like parchment or papyrus.

3 Artists used reed pens called *qalams* and different colors of ink to write on paper in a decorative script known as Arabic calligraphy.

4 The town of Jativa in Muslim Spain was famous for the thick, glossy paper produced in its mills.

5 Muslim papermakers pioneered the use of the trip hammer, a tool for beating linen rags or tree roots into the pulp used to make paper.

6 A large number of early Arabic manuscripts dating from the 10th to the 12th centuries are written on paper.

7 The boom in paper production meant that thousands of copies of a book could be made, and more books meant more people had the chance to learn.

8 Hemp, a crop grown in Syria, turned out to be a great source of low-cost, high-quality paper.

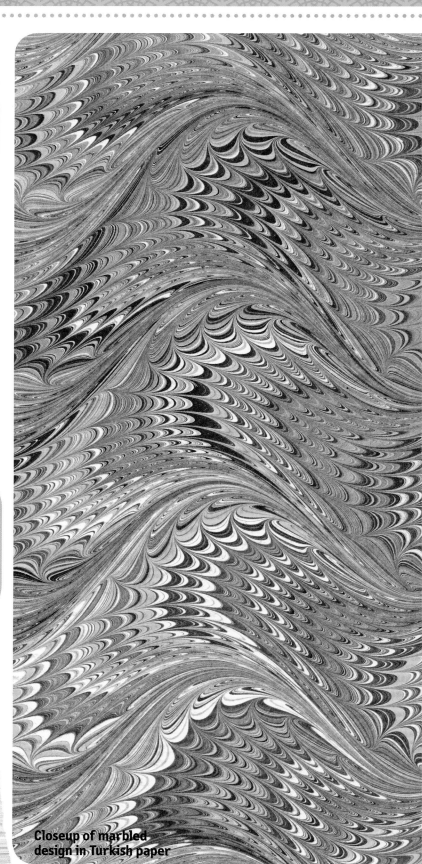

Closeup of marbled design in Turkish paper

ABOUT PENS AND PAPER

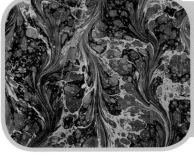

9 Today more than one million books are published worldwide each year.

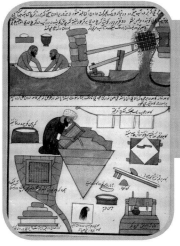

10 All the hand mixing and mashing that went into making paper in China was done by mills in Muslim civilization. Mills started in Baghdad and spread to other cities to meet the demand.

11 Gold and silver inks were used on blue paper to create impressive front pages for books.

12 In 953 the Sultan of Egypt, tired of having ink stain his hands and clothes, asked for a leakproof pen that held its own ink. What he got was much like today's fountain pen.

13 Papermaking was started in Europe by Muslims living in Spain and Sicily in the 10th century.

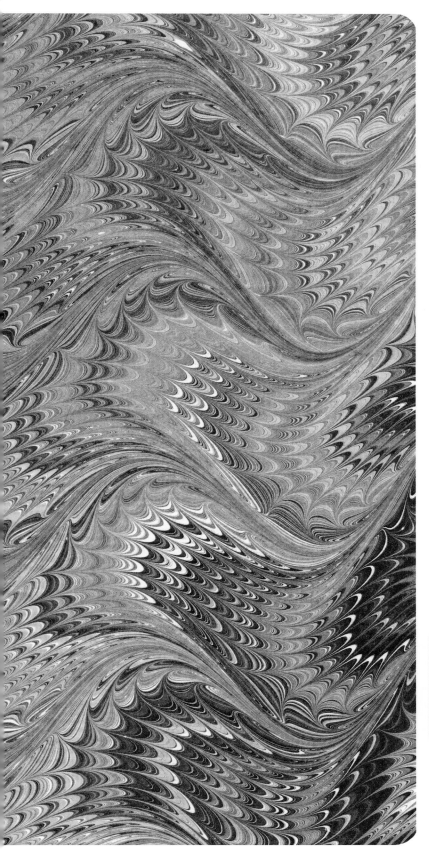

14 Muslim artists used inks and dyes to create patterns on paper called marbling. By the 1550s marbled paper became prized by Europeans, who referred to it as "Turkish paper."

15 The Muslim world was using block printing as early as the 10th century, some 500 years before Johannes Gutenberg started printing with moveable letters.

1 Maps made during Muslim civilization usually showed **south at the top** and **north at the bottom—** **UPSIDE DOWN TO A WESTERN VIEW TODAY.**

2 THE CHINESE INTRODUCED **paper** to Baghdad in the 8th century, which MADE IT POSSIBLE FOR THE MUSLIM WORLD TO CREATE MAPS FOR EVERYONE TO USE.

3 In the 9th century, astronomers in the Muslim world were **SO ACCURATE IN THEIR CALCULATIONS** OF **THE EARTH'S CIRCUMFERENCE** THAT THEY WERE ONLY 125 MILES (201 KM) OFF THE 24,897 MILES (40,068 KM) ACCEPTED TODAY.

4 In 1073 Turkish geographer Mahmud al-Kashghari created **A CIRCULAR WORLD MAP** showing where various languages were spoken.

5 In 1154 the Muslim geographer Al-Idrisi finished **the first atlas,** which showed most of North Africa, Asia, and Europe. This was about a hundred years before Marco Polo wrote about his travels to China and back.

25 GLOBAL FACTS

6 AL-IDRISI SPENT **15 years** CREATING **70 maps** for the atlas of Roger II, King of Sicily.

7 Chistopher Columbus studied maps created by Muslim geographers to make the voyages that helped him to reach the Americas.

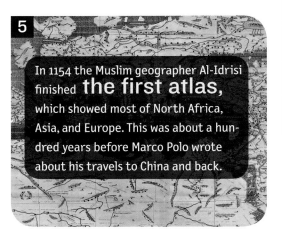

8 Ibn Majid, **A MASTER NAVIGATOR FROM ARABIA,** guided the Portuguese explorer **Vasco da Gama** around Africa's Cape Horn to India in the 15th century.

9 The **earliest known** description of a **magnetic compass** is in a collection of stories written by the Persian Muhammed al-Awfi in 1233.

10 One of the most important navigators of the 16th century, Turkish admiral **PIRI REIS,** wrote a manual of sailing directions called *THE BOOK OF SEA LORE.*

11 *The Book of Sea Lore,* which included more than **200 charts and maps,** was a guide to the coasts, islands, ports, and waterways of the Mediterranean.

12 Originally printed in 1521, *The Book of Sea Lore* **was a must-read for navigators** for more than a century.

13 Piri Reis is best known for the incredibly accurate "MAP OF AMERICA" HE CREATED IN 1513.

14 The "MAP OF AMERICA" was compiled using numerous other maps, including Arab and Portuguese ones and one made by Columbus on his third voyage to the THE AMERICAS.

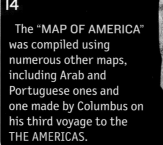

15 The Columbus map that Piri Reis used was lost after Columbus sent it to Spain in 1498, so the Piri Reis version is the only record we have of it.

16 THE "MAP OF AMERICA" SHOWS MOUNTAINS (NOW CALLED THE ANDES) IN SOUTH AMERICA THAT SPANISH EXPLORERS CLAIMED TO HAVE FOUND FIRST IN 1527—14 YEARS *AFTER* PIRI REIS MADE HIS MAP.

17 PIRI REIS DREW HIS "MAP OF AMERICA" ON THE HIDE OF A GAZELLE, A KIND OF African antelope.

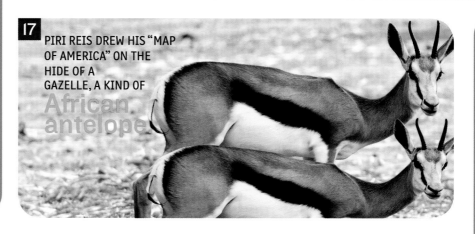

Want to know how people saw the world 1,000 YEARS AGO? Take a look online at *The Book of Curiosities*, written in Egypt in the 11th century (see page 92).

ABOUT GEOGRAPHY

18 Piri Reis drew a second map covering the northwestern part of the Atlantic Ocean, including NEWFOUNDLAND, on Canada's east coast.

19

The earliest known maps were inscribed on clay tablets MORE THAN 3,500 YEARS AGO IN BABYLON.

20 Building on the work of the Romans, scholars in Muslim Spain created triangulation, A METHOD STILL USED TO SURVEY LAND AND CREATE MAPS.

21 Muslim sailors weren't lost at sea BECAUSE THEY DEVELOPED COURSE-PLOTTING INSTRUMENTS AND BECAME MASTER NAVIGATORS.

22 TO CHART THE EARTH'S FEATURES, GEOGRAPHERS IN THE EARLY MUSLIM WORLD USED ASTROLABES, INSTRUMENTS THAT CALCULATE HEIGHT AND DISTANCE.

25

23 Trouble finding your way? THE NAVIGATION TECHNIQUES OF THE PAST HAVE ALL CONTRIBUTED TO MODERN DIRECTIONAL DEVICES LIKE GLOBAL POSITIONING SYSTEMS (GPS).

24 Today's GPS is extremely accurate. A 2011 STUDY SHOWED THAT GPS IS OFTEN ACCURATE TO WITHIN 3 FEET (1 M).

63

1

People in Muslim civilization **loved to travel and learn**. "Seek knowledge even from as far as China," the Prophet Muhammad commanded his followers.

2

The Palestinian geographer Al-Muqaddasi **explored almost every corner** of the 10th-century Muslim world, making observations and taking notes.

3

Thanks to journals kept by Muslim travelers and geographers, we know what life was like in the **medieval world**.

4

Al-Dimashqi, a 14th-century geographer, told about life on the Malay Islands, where towns and cities were surrounded by **dense forests**.

5

The **giraffe** was introduced to China from Africa, thanks to Zheng He's voyages.

6

Al-Dimashqi's accounts said a giant bird called *al-Rukh* and **white elephants** lived on the Malay Islands.

7

Imagine having to find your way to Mecca on foot or by camel **without a map!** That's why early Muslims needed a strong knowledge of geography and astronomy.

8

According to Islam, it is the duty of all able-bodied Muslims to give every effort to make at least one *hajj*, or pilgrimage, to Mecca.

9

Hajj is an Arabic word meaning "to set out for a place."

10

Many Muslims expanded **geographic knowledge** by writing about the people and places they saw while on their *hajj*.

11

Since the 7th century people have traveled thousands of miles on **horseback**, camel, or by foot to make the *hajj*.

12

Traders and travelers wrote some of the first detailed Arabic descriptions of **China**.

13

Many famous **European explorers** used maps and information from the Muslim world.

14

In addition to travel by land, Muslim traders **sailed the seas** to foreign lands, gaining new knowledge of sea routes.

15

In the late 800s, Al-Ya'qubi described in his *Book of the Countries* the color, breezes, and fish in the **seven seas** he'd have to cross to reach China.

16

Before the 15th and 16th centuries **Vikings** were the only Europeans who are positively known to have traveled great distances by sea.

17

Ibn Khurradadhbih wrote a book about the main Muslim **trade routes**, which included China, Japan, Korea, and Java.

18

He mentioned "Waqwaq" islands (probably present-day Japan), lying "East of China."

19

The Arab Ibn Fadlan traveled to northern Europe in 921, where he met European merchants he described as "tall as date palms" camped along the **Volga River**.

20

Travelers' tales of **sea monsters** and giant land animals led to the creation of elaborate Arabic folk tales, such as *The Thousand and One Nights* and *The Seven Voyages of Sinbad the Sailor*.

21

Ibn al-Jazzar, a 10th-century doctor, wrote *Traveler's Provision*, a guide to **medical problems**—useful at home and on the road.

22

Reconstruction of Baghdad's **medieval canals** in 1895 wouldn't have been possible without the detailed descriptions of a 10th-century geographer named Suhrab.

23

Scholars in Muslim civilization believed, as did the ancient Greeks, that the **Earth was round**.

24

Using his own notes, travel accounts, and the work of earlier scholars, Al-Idrisi created a comprehensive **atlas** of the 12th-century world.

25

In 1325 a 21-year-old Moroccan named Ibn Battuta set out for Mecca on a journey that would last **29 years** and take him to the four corners of the known world.

26

Ibn Battuta traveled more than **75,000 miles** (120,000 km) and met thousands of people, including many rulers and leaders.

27

Of the **44 countries** that Ibn Battuta visited he called China "the safest and best country" for travelers.

28

Ibn Battuta's account of life in medieval Mali, West Africa, is the **only record** we have today of the area at that time.

29

Ibn Battuta is often called the **Muslim Marco Polo**.

30

The world's largest themed shopping mall, which is in **Dubai**, United Arab Emirates, is named after Ibn Battuta.

31

In 1271 Marco Polo was only **17 years old** when he left his home in Venice, Italy, to travel to China and back—a 24-year-long journey.

32

One of history's record-breaking naval explorers was a 15th-century Mongolian Muslim from China known as **Zheng He**.

33
Zheng He was named **Admiral of the Chinese fleet** and traveled to 37 countries between 1405 and 1433.

36
Each of Zheng He's ships could have a crew of up to **500**.

39
When Zheng He's navy was on the move, it **resembled a small city**.

43
Zheng He's ships were often called "swimming dragons" because they were decorated with **dragon eyes** to help them "see."

46
Zheng He's fleet included tankers that carried **fresh water** for drinking.

40
His first fleet included **27,870 men on 317 ships**.

47
The seven voyages that Zheng He made in the name of trade and diplomacy were called the **"Treasure Ship"** voyages.

48
In 1962 a rudder post of a **treasure ship** was found in an old boatyard in China. It was 36 feet (11 m) long—suitable for a boat 500 feet (152 m) in length.

50 Facts About EXPLORATION

34
Zheng He was not only a powerful man but also a striking figure. Some accounts say he weighed more than **220 pounds** (100 kg) and was more than **6.5 feet** (2 m) tall, with a stride like a tiger's.

37
Some ships in Zheng He's fleet were more than **400 feet** (122 m) long and 180 feet (55 m) wide.

41
Flags, lanterns, and even carrier pigeons were used to **communicate** between ships and coordinate the fleet's movements.

44
Zheng He's ships carried all kinds of live animals, including celestial horses (zebras), celestial stags (oryx), and camel-like birds (ostriches).

49
Zheng He's journeys were a great success—not only in the search for **new minerals, medicines, and species**, but also in drawing tribute from many of the nations with whom he traded and made diplomatic links.

42
Modern shipbuilders don't know how these floating cities were **made without metal**.

45
Working in pairs, **otters** were used to herd fish into nets to help feed the large crews.

50
Ironically, less than **a hundred years** after Zheng He's death in 1433, China banned seagoing trade and multimast sailing ships.

35
Zheng He built the **largest navy** the world had seen until then, helping to present China as a superpower.

38
By comparison, Columbus's ship *Niña* was only 75 feet (23 m) long.

Camel caravan crossing the Sahara near Morocco

65

15 TANTALIZING TIDBITS

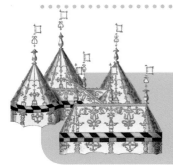

1 From the time they were used by nomadic Arab desert dwellers, tents have **served as shelters and meeting places.**

2 Tents of the Ottoman Turks were **elaborately decorated** royal structures used for practical and social occasions, such as grand parties and ceremonies.

3 Whether traveling for war or hunting trips or to any kind of ceremony, the Sultan **always had his tent with him.**

4 During travel or a military campaign large tent cities were formed. There were **royal tents for the rulers** and **lesser tents for ordinary people and soldiers.**

5 Military tents sometimes had different colors, which may have been a way to tell regiments apart.

6 The Wawel tent collection in Krakow, Poland, has an **oval tent** with a diameter of 79 feet (24 m) and a height of 12 feet (3.7 m).

7 Inspired by Turkish royal tents, French King Louis XIV had many ceremonial tents. This helped to **create a tent craze** across Europe in the late 17th century.

Bedouin camp in the Sahara

ABOUT TENTS

Ottoman tent-pole banner holders, 8th century

8 One account about a Sultan's travels says that it took **600 camels just to carry the tents!**

9 **The round, domed tents** used by Ottoman Turks may have been **inspired by yurts,** felt tents **still used by nomads** in Mongolia and Central Asia.

10 The Ottomans were also inspired by **Persian and Byzantine** tent creations and created their own tent design style and furniture.

11 Turkish royal tents had brightly colored **silk crowns,** richly patterned **carpets** and **cushions,** and raised sections to add majesty.

12 Today visitors can experience the **beauty and grandeur** of these kinds of tents at the Royal Castle of Wawel in Krakow, Poland.

13 **Two tents** always accompanied a Sultan on his travels: one to live in **during a stop** and another for tent pitchers to **march ahead** and set up in the next location.

14 Royal tents were called "walled palaces."

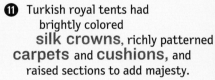

15 **Tents were often very large.** One tent built in 1744 in Vauxhall Gardens, London, England, had a dining area with 14 tables!

15 RICH FACTS ABOUT

1 Trade was a major part of life in early Muslim civilization, and goods were bought and **sold across three continents.**

2 Trade was so important that Muslim rulers created laws, contracts, loans, and more, which still influence trade today.

3 Buyers and sellers in Muslim civilization used checks! The word "check" comes from the Arabic *şakk*, which is a written vow to honor payment for merchandise upon delivery.

4 Ever wonder where the idea for a rest stop came from? In the Muslim world important trade routes had rest stops called "caravansaries" about every 19 miles (30 km).

5 Caravansaries provided free food, shelter, and entertainment **to travelers** for up to three days.

6 Land trade was mainly along the Silk Route, a 7,000-mile (11,265-km)-long trade route linking China to markets in the Muslim world and Europe.

7 Lots of items traded in the Muslim world were **highly prized,** such as textiles, metal, tooled leatherwork, carpets, illustrated manuscripts, enameled glass, and soaps.

Silk scarves in a bazaar

TRADE AND MONEY

8 Many cities **gave their names to the famous goods they produced:** muslin from Mosul, Iraq; gauze from Gaza; and damask cloth from Damascus, Syria.

9 **Giant camel caravans** traveled enormous distances **to trade** with foreign lands.

10 **What's that smell you say?** Don't get too close to the campfires because while on caravan, travelers used dried animal dung as fuel!

11 Traders in the Muslim world used **gold and silver coins,** called "dinars" and "dirhams," as international currency.

12 **The first Caliph to create his own coins** was Caliph Abd al-Malik ibn Marwan, who ruled from 685 to 705. His were also the **first gold coins** to carry an **Arabic inscription.**

13 Trade with Maldive Islanders, who paid for goods with **cowrie shells,** spread the use of this form of currency to distant areas of the Muslim world.

14 It is believed that **two giant gold Islamic coins** existed in the early 1600s. One of these coins was 8 inches (20 cm) in diameter and weighed in at 26.5 pounds (12 kg) of **pure gold!**

15 **Coins from the medieval Muslim world** have been found in modern-day Germany, Finland, and Scandinavia, showing how widespread trade was during this time.

1 Muslim civilization gave rise to a thriving industry of mining rubies, emeralds, sapphires, and other precious stones.

2 About a thousand workers mined cinnabar to make mercury in Almadén, in Muslim Spain.

3 Egypt was a great source of emeralds, while carnelian and onyx were mined in Yemen and Muslim Spain.

4 The largest and most famous sapphire in the world is the Star of India. It is 563 carats!

5 Beginning in the 14th century divers harvested precious pearls in the Persian Gulf and the Arabian Sea.

6 Pearl divers would tie a rope around their waist and swim to the bottom of the sea to collect oysters containing pearls. When they ran out of breath, they would tug on the rope to be pulled up to the boat again.

7 Big or small? Pearls can be found in lots of different sizes and colors.

8 Coral was collected from reefs off the coast of North Africa near Sicily and Sardinia.

An aigrette, or ornament, with pearls, diamonds, and emeralds from a late 17th-century Ottoman headdress

ON JEWELS

9 Today **coral mining is banned** in many countries around the world.

10 People loved to use pearls and coral to make prayer beads, jewelry, and to adorn their weapons.

11 **Precious stones** were **polished with emery** found in Nubia and Ceylon (now Sri Lanka).

12 One of the **precious items mined was salt**, which was referred to as "white gold" in the Muslim world.

13 **Huge camel caravans carried salt** from mines in Yemen, Persia, Armenia, and North Africa to markets far and wide.

14 Pictures of natural things, such as **leaves or flowers**, were often used as inspiration for jewelry designs.

15 Today because **coral is so scarce**, beads made with it are **very expensive**. A single, 2-inch (50-mm) bead can cost as much as $50,000.

1 THE CHINESE DISCOVERED HOW TO MAKE **SALTPETER** (POTASSIUM NITRATE), A KEY INGREDIENT IN **GUNPOWDER**, IN THE 1ST CENTURY.

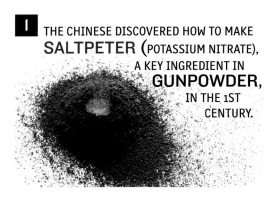

2 Although the Chinese used gunpowder to put on **great fireworks shows,** they could not figure out the correct proportions to make powerful explosions.

3 CHEMISTS IN MUSLIM CIVILIZATION IMPROVED UPON THE WORK OF THE CHINESE AND FOUND A WAY TO USE GUNPOWDER TO CREATE STRONG EXPLOSIONS FOR FIREARMS.

5 Muslim civilization improved on the **design of cannons** that could be held in your hand.

4 THE USE OF GUNPOWDER BY ISLAMIC ARMIES WAS A MAJOR ADVANTAGE IN THEIR BATTLES AGAINST THE CRUSADERS, CHRISTIAN ARMIES TRYING TO OVERTHROW MUSLIM CONTROL OF JERUSALEM FROM THE 11TH TO 14TH CENTURIES.

25 FACTS ABOUT WAR AND WEAPONS

6 Muslim civilization was the first to make huge **SPLIT-BARREL GUNS.**

7 Fifteenth-century Ottomans had **LARGER AND MORE POWERFUL CANNONS** THAN ANY BEING USED IN EUROPE AT THE TIME.

8 The **largest** of these cannons was ordered by Ottoman Sultan Mehmed II in 1453 during the **siege of Constantinople.**

10 A DECORATIVE INSCRIPTION in Arabic was made on the **muzzle** of Sultan Mehmed's cannon.

9 MADE OF BRONZE, THE CANNON WEIGHED **18 tons** and was so long it had to be cast in two pieces and screwed together.

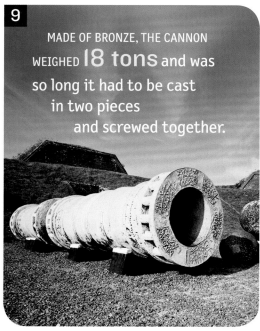

11 OVERALL, THE CANNON WAS MORE THAN 17 FEET (5 M) LONG AND 2 FEET (.6 M) IN DIAMETER WITH A BARREL THAT WAS ALMOST 10 FEET (3 M) LONG.

13 In 1867 **Queen Victoria** requested Sultan Mehmed's cannon to show in England. At the time it was known as **"the most important cannon in Europe."**

12 Able to **FIRE A CANNONBALL UP TO A MILE,** no cannon as impressive had ever been built before.

14 SULTAN ABDUL AZIZ gave Queen Victoria Mehmed's cannon as a gift, and it is now on display in the Fort Nelson Museum, in Portsmouth, England.

15

SULTAN MEHMED'S CANNON IS NOW PART OF THE COLLECTION OF THE ROYAL ARMOURIES, ALONG WITH **70,000** other examples of weapons from ancient times to the present.

16 A 13TH-CENTURY SYRIAN SCHOLAR NAMED HASAN AL-RAMMAH WROTE ONE OF **THE MOST IMPORTANT BOOKS** ON MILITARY TECHNOLOGY, *THE BOOK OF HORSEMANSHIP AND INGENIOUS WAR DEVICES.*

17 Al-Rammah's book was packed full of **DIAGRAMS OF WEAPONS,** including the first description of a military rocket.

18 Another diagram in Al-Rammah's book was of the first torpedo, a kind of rocket made to skim along the surface of the water.

TO BATTLE WITH

19 THE **pear-shaped torpedo** WAS MADE OF IRON AND GUIDED BY **two rudders.**

20 The torpedo carried a **MIXTURE OF EXPLOSIVES** and IRON FILINGS, sealed with a layer of felt.

21 WITH A SPEAR AT THE FRONT, THE TORPEDO WOULD LODGE IN THE WOODEN HULL OF AN ENEMY SHIP BEFORE THE EXPLOSIVES DETONATED.

22 IN MUSLIM CIVILIZATION THIS TORPEDO WAS CALLED **"the egg,** which moves itself and burns when it hits the target."

23 Al-Rammah's book **FEATURED A TREBUCHET,** a weapon used for **flinging missiles.**

24 The book by Al-Rammah described **DOZENS OF RECIPES FOR MAKING EXPLODING GUNPOWDER.**

25 THE NATIONAL AIR AND SPACE MUSEUM IN WASHINGTON, D.C., U.S.A., HAS A MODEL OF WHAT AL-RAMMAH'S ROCKET MAY HAVE LOOKED LIKE IN ITS COLLECTION.

1
During the 800 years in which the Muslims ruled Spain, THEY BUILT INGENIOUS CASTLES.

2
Following a practice called *SPOLIA*, some early Islamic castles reused older masonry from Roman structures.

3
To WITHSTAND A SIEGE, some cities in Syria and elsewhere in the early Muslim world had castles, high walls, and gates.

4
Governors of towns lived in castles called "CITADELS," usually built on high land at the city's edge.

5
Citadels were often surrounded by walls, and each was LIKE ITS OWN CITY, with a mosque, guards, offices, and living spaces.

11
The military defenses and CASTLES IN JERUSALEM and other Muslim strongholds impressed the Crusaders from Europe.

12
Crusaders took the NEW ARCHITECTURAL IDEAS HOME with them and used them in their own buildings.

13
During peace times CRAFTSMEN FROM EUROPE were sometimes hired by Muslims to help them repair or build castles.

14
Greeks and Romans used arrow slits, but Muslims IMPROVED THE DESIGN and made them standard features in their castles.

15
Arrow slits allowed bowmen to shoot out but PROTECTED THEM from return fire.

21
BATTLEMENTS are a series of cutouts and raised sections on the top walls that provided cover for defenders.

22
Today battlements are used as DECORATIVE FEATURES in certain styles of architecture.

23
European castles built after the Crusades used many of the DEFENSIVE FEATURES of Muslim castles in the Middle East.

24
HEARST CASTLE in California combines several architectural styles, including Mexican, Baroque, and Islamic.

25
Islamic castles often had very LARGE WATER STORAGE CISTERNS.

Citadel in Aleppo (now Halab), Syria

35 FACTS TO FORTIFY

6
Keeps, arrow slits, barbicans, machicolations, parapets, and battlements were KEY FEATURES of Muslim strongholds.

7
The central, fortified tower within a castle is called a KEEP.

8
While Muslim keeps were usually ROUND, keeps in Christian Europe were SQUARE.

9
THE TOWER OF LONDON is probably the most famous example of a European castle with square towers.

10
From a round tower the enemy could be seen from any direction, and there were NO CORNERS for attackers to hide behind.

16
A BARBICAN, a walled entrance passage, helped to confine enemies so defenders could attack them from above.

17
The word "barbican" is taken from the Persian *bab al-khanah*, meaning "GATE HOUSE."

18
The stone walls of castles were REINFORCED WITH WOOD BEAMS as steel is used to reinforce walls today.

19
MACHICOLATIONS are holes or gaps in the overhanging floor of a parapet, the open walkway around the top of a castle.

20
Muslim defenders used machicolations to DROP BOILING OIL, molten lead, and even missiles on their attackers!

26
During the 14th and 15th centuries THE ALHAMBRA was built as a military complex overlooking Granada, in Muslim Spain.

27
The Alhambra takes its name from an Arabic word meaning "THE RED CASTLE," or "the red fort."

28
The fortress section of the Alhambra, dating from the 12th century, is referred to as THE ALCAZABA.

29
The Alcazaba was the MILITARY HEADQUARTERS for the Nasrid, the last Muslim dynasty in Spain.

30
The most significant watchtower at the Alcazaba is the 87-foot (29-m)- high *TORRE DE LA VELA*.

31
"Alcazaba" is taken from the Arabic word *al-qasbah*, meaning "A WALLED FORTIFICATION" in a city.

32
Albarrana towers— detached towers connected to the outer walls by a bridge—were another MUSLIM INNOVATION.

33
ALBARRANA TOWERS first appeared in castles in Muslim Spain in the 12th century.

34
The word "albarrana" is derived from the Arabic *barrani*, which MEANS "EXTERIOR."

35
Albarrana towers WERE RARELY USED outside Muslim Spain.

YOUR KNOWLEDGE ABOUT
CASTLES AND KEEPS

1 **Have you ever cracked a code?** Bet you didn't know you could trace many code-breaking techniques to Muslim civilization.

2 In 9th-century Muslim civilization mail was sent by carrier pigeon, giving new meaning to the term "air mail"!

3 Because of the use of birds for mail in the Muslim world, confidential messages needed a way to be kept private, so encryption, or coding, was used.

4 The citadel in Cairo, Egypt, which was the communication nerve center of the time, had about 1,900 pigeon "mailmen."

5 By studying the Arabic text of the Quran, Al-Kindi, a 9th-century scholar from Baghdad, noticed that certain letters were used more frequently than others.

6 He used this observation to come up with a code-breaking method based on what he called "frequency analysis."

7 In this kind of code, letters are replaced by symbols or other letters. A decoder can figure out what the letters or symbols stand for, substitute other letters for the symbols, and read the message.

8 If a message written in English were encoded using this method, the most common symbol would represent the letter *e* since it appears most frequently.

COMMUNICATION

9 Al-Kindi's book, *Treatise on Deciphering Cryptographic Messages,* laid the foundations for **modern cryptology** by encouraging people in other cultures to figure out new ways to encode messages.

10 Frequency analysis using substitution ciphers became the basic tool for breaking codes that used **a text alphabet**.

11 Before Al-Kindi's work, many thought that **substitution ciphers were unbreakable.**

12 **"Cryptanalysis"** is the 20th-century word for the **study of codes and ciphers** begun by Al-Kindi.

13 **Using cryptanalysis,** the Allies in World War II were able to decipher German military encryptions made by a typewriter-like machine called "Enigma."

14 The **Germans' secret messages sent by Enigma** were decrypted by Polish and British code breakers.

15 Journalist Simon Singh names **Al-Kindi** as the originator of the first method of **code breaking** in *The Code Book,* published in 1999.

1
Farmers in the 9th-century Muslim world launched an AGRICULTURAL REVOLUTION when they began using new methods to grow crops.

2
During Muslim civilization people TRAVELED as far east as China and as far west as Spain, seeking new knowledge about agriculture and botany.

3
This new information was CATALOGED in huge agricultural manuals for all to read.

4
These MANUALS taught farmers how to raise the finest animals, GROW NEW SPECIES of plants, irrigate fields, use fertilizers, and fight PESTS.

5
The agricultural system in the early Muslim world was one of the most COMPLEX AND SCIENTIFIC ever devised.

6
The changes in agriculture IMPROVED the economy, city growth, LIFESTYLES, cooking, clothing, and more.

7
12th-century botanist Ibn al-Awwam BUILT UPON STUDIES of Egyptian, Greek, and Persian scholars to develop his *Book of Agriculture*.

8
Ibn al-Awwam's book was a HOW-TO GUIDE FOR FARMERS on everything from how to grow trees to beekeeping.

9
His book also had tips about how to keep pests away from CROPS and even told people how to COOK the food they grew.

10
Farmers in the Muslim world learned how to GROW different crops in different seasons on the same land. This is called "CROP ROTATION."

11
Crop rotation, the use of giant waterwheels called *NORIAS*, and the development of the water pump made it possible to grow new crops and have four harvests each year.

12
Rice, CITRUS FRUITS, plums, apricots, artichokes, saffron, and SUGARCANE were among the new crops grown in the Muslim world.

13
Rice, sugarcane, and cotton require a lot of WATER TO GROW.

14
It reportedly took 8,000 *NORIAS* to supply water to all the rice plantations in Valencia, in Muslim Spain.

15
Using underground canals called *QANATS* to transport water kept it from evaporating.

16
Canals brought WATER from snowcapped MOUNTAINS to fields in the dry climate of Andalus, in southern Spain.

17
Year-round fresh fruit and veggies meant HEALTHY EATING for more people.

18
Rice mixed with butter, oil, fat, and milk became a FAVORITE FOOD.

19
There were even COOKBOOKS full of rice recipes.

20
Today RICE is eaten by more people than any other kind of grain.

21
U.S. farmers produce more than 20 BILLION POUNDS of rice each year.

22
COTTON from India was imported to Sicily and Spain by Muslims and became a major crop.

23
The spread of cotton, silk, and wool gave people a choice in what kind of clothes TO WEAR.

24
The COTTON PLANT is called *algodon* in Spanish, from the Arabic *al-qutn*.

25
SUGARCANE found its way to Zanzibar, Ethiopia, and Spain thanks to Muslim traders.

26
Today some of the BEST SUGAR comes from Zanzibar, now part of Tanzania in East Africa.

27
The word "CANDY" comes from the Persian *qand*, meaning "sugar" or "sweet."

28
Baskets and floor coverings were made from ESPARTO GRASS, which grows wild in parts of Spain.

29
A fig tree cutting from what is now Jordan planted in Muslim Spain grew so well that more cuttings were made, and soon FIG TREES spread across all of Spain.

30
Oranges, lemons, and limes may not have become so popular in the WESTERN WORLD without the orchards in Muslim lands.

31
The average person will eat 12,888 ORANGES in a lifetime.

32
ORANGE TREES from India were PLANTED in Jordan, Iraq, Syria, Turkey, Palestine, and Egypt.

50 FACTS ABOUT FARMS to Feed On

33
Fresh or dried figs are a good source of sugar, and DRIED FIGS stay fresh for more than a year.

36
A camel can be as tall as a BASKETBALL HOOP is high and weigh as much as three motorcycles.

39
The *Calendar of Córdoba of 961*, written by Ibn Bassal, was like a *FARMER'S ALMANAC*. It told when to plant, water, and harvest.

42
Farmers no longer had to do whatever big LANDOWNERS demanded.

45
Farmers spread PIGEON DROPPINGS on their fields for fertilizer.

46
Pigeons were housed in CUBBYHOLES in huge mud-brick structures called PIGEON TOWERS.

47
RUINS of pigeon towers still stand in the Middle East.

48
Farmers fed MILLIONS OF PEOPLE in Muslim Spain, equal to a large proportion of the population of EUROPE at the time.

34
The oldest known FIG TREE is 2,300 YEARS OLD.

40
The *CALENDAR* told farmers that in March roses would bloom and quails would appear. It was also the TIME to plant cucumbers and eggplants.

49
Sugarcane, cotton, and rice were brought to the AMERICAS from Spain and Portugal after the end of Muslim rule there.

37
Better breeding created more animals, which meant MORE MEAT and wool could be bought AT LESS COST.

43
Contracts spelled out what workers were expected to do and what they would BE PAID.

35
By carefully picking and choosing ANIMALS to breed, farmers created BIGGER AND STRONGER horses and camels.

41
The boom in crops brought new freedoms for farmers. Unlike in the European system, they had the RIGHT TO WORK for themselves and to rent, buy, or sell land.

50
French, British, and Dutch COLONISTS made their fortunes in the Americas by growing these crops.

38
Math, engineering, and astronomy SKILLS came in handy for figuring out water levels for IRRIGATION and charts for planting and harvesting crops.

44
As OUTPUT GREW every city came to have its own MARKET GARDENS, orchards, and fruit and olive plantations.

Sugarcane farmer in Pakistan

15 HOT FACTS

❶ It's believed that an Abyssinian goat herder in what is now Ethiopia discovered coffee **1,200 years ago** when his goats got an energy boost after eating some red berries. People soon began boiling the berries to make coffee.

❷ People in parts of the Muslim world were sipping coffee as early as the **9th century.** The drink didn't catch on in Europe for another **700 years.**

❸ Travel and **trade** spread the **popular drink** to Yemen, Mecca, Damascus, Baghdad, and Istanbul and to Europe and beyond.

❹ Today more than **1.5 billion** cups of coffee are consumed around the world every day—enough to fill 300 Olympic-size swimming pools!

❺ Ripe coffee beans are red and are called coffee cherries.

❻ Coffee was just what some Muslims needed to help them stay awake during **late night prayers.**

❼ Cappuccino coffee gets its name from the color of the robes worn by Christian Capuchin monks.

❽ Coffee shops in England were nicknamed **"penny universities"** because you could listen to and talk with some of the greatest minds of the day for the **price of a cup of coffee.**

Modern cup of coffee

ABOUT COFFEE

9 "Mocha" is both the name of a kind of coffee bean and the name of the port in **Yemen** that was the center of the coffee trade from the 15th to 17th centuries.

10 In the mid-1600s coffee was brought to **New Amsterdam** (now New York, U.S.A.) by Dutch traders. A hundred years later coffee surpassed tea as the favorite drink in the future United States.

11 Today a **tall latte** (coffee with milk) is the most popular drink at Starbucks.

12 **Hawaii and Puerto Rico** are the only places in the United States where coffee can be grown.

13 In the Muslim world people drank their coffee **black**. Not until the 17th century did people start adding cream to their cups.

14 Coffee is now grown in 65 countries, and it is the world's second **most traded** commodity after oil.

15 The world's first **coffee shop** opened in Venice, Italy, in 1645. By 1700 there were **hundreds** of coffeehouses in London, England, alone.

1 DESERTS COVERED LARGE PARTS OF the Muslim world. For people living in these dry and hot lands, the use and control of WATER WAS KEY TO THEIR SURVIVAL.

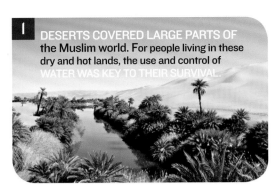

2 People in dry regions used water-raising devices, like the EGYPTIAN *SHADOOF*, a pole-and-bucket system, and the Roman waterwheel, or *NORIA*, and figured out ways to make THEM BIGGER AND BETTER.

3 16TH-CENTURY OTTOMAN ENGINEER TAQI AL-DIN IBN MA'ROUF SAID STEAM COULD POWER A TURBINE ENGINE ABOUT 100 YEARS BEFORE STEAM POWER WAS DISCOVERED IN EUROPE.

4 MUHAMMAD AL-KARAJI, AN 11TH-CENTURY MATHEMATICIAN AND ENGINEER FROM PERSIA (NOW IRAN) DESCRIBED A NETWORK OF UNDERGROUND TUNNELS CALLED *QANATS* THAT COULD CARRY WATER OVER LONG DISTANCES WITHOUT EVAPORATION.

5 TAQI AL-DIN'S 6-CYLINDER **WATER PUMP** HAD ALL THE FEATURES OF A MODERN-DAY 6-CYLINDER CAR ENGINE.

25 WATER

6 *QANATS* are still used to provide water to some areas in Iran and other countries in the Middle East.

7 *QANATS* HAD "MANHOLE" COVERS FOR AIR CIRCULATION AND TO HELP THE WATER FLOW THROUGH THE TUNNEL.

8

9 LARGE **LANDHOLDERS** AND **STATE LEADERS** WERE RESPONSIBLE FOR DIGGING AND CLEANING *QANATS* AND REPAIRING DAMS.

10 SYSTEMS FOR DELIVERING **WATER** TO FARMS AND TOWNS HELPED IMPROVE QUALITY OF LIFE.

LAWS SPELLED OUT WHEN EACH CROP WAS IRRIGATED, HOW TO USE STORED WATER, AND HOW TO MANAGE WATER FOR FARM AND CITY USE.

11 AL-JAZARI MADE THE FIRST MACHINE THAT COMBINED A **CRANK** AND CONNECTING ROD TO CONVERT CIRCULAR MOTION TO LINEAR MOTION.

12 Today crank-rod systems are used in everything from **CAR ENGINES TO TOYS.**

13 THOSE WHO BROKE A WATER LAW HAD TO FACE THE "TRIBUNAL OF THE WATERS," A GROUP OF OFFICIALS THAT DEALT WITH DISPUTES AMONG FARMERS.

14

TEN CENTURIES LATER THE TRIBUNAL STILL MEETS WEEKLY IN VALENCIA, SPAIN.

15

SINCE WATER WAS SO SCARCE,
THERE WERE STRICT RULES ABOUT THE CARE AND USE OF DAMS AND WATERWAYS.

16

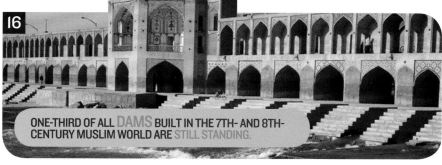

ONE-THIRD OF ALL DAMS BUILT IN THE 7TH- AND 8TH-CENTURY MUSLIM WORLD ARE STILL STANDING.

17

Qanats and *norias* were introduced to

SPAIN

when Muslims ruled Andalusia, the southern part of the country.

18

THE INFLUENCE OF Muslim civilization on

IRRIGATION

in Spain can be seen in certain Spanish and Arabic words. For example, the word for "irrigation canal" in Spanish is *cequia*, and in Arabic it is *sâqiya*.

25

ENGINEERS IN THE MUSLIM WORLD USED TRIGONOMETRY, GEOMETRY, AND PHYSICS TO BUILD ENORMOUS DAMS TO CONTROL FLOODS AND TO PROVIDE IRRIGATION.

FACTS TO TAP INTO

19

In the early

13TH CENTURY

the engineer Al-Jazari, from southern Turkey, developed a brilliant way to lift huge amounts of water— WITHOUT HAVING TO LIFT A FINGER.

20

IN ALL, AL-JAZARI DESIGNED FIVE

WATER-RAISING MACHINES,

including a water-driven pump that sucked water up 39 feet (12 m) into a system that was used to supply water for irrigation and sanitation.

21

The BASICS behind Al-Jazari's pumps led to more sophisticated modern developments, including

ARTIFICIAL HEARTS and BICYCLE PUMPS.

22

AL-JAZARI'S

PUMPS

REPLACED ANIMAL POWER WITH GEARS AND WATER POWER.

23

LEONARDO DA VINCI is often credited with developing and using hydraulics and GEARS, but his work likely benefited from the achievements of earlier mechanical GENIUSES.

24

IN THE VALENCIA AREA OF MUSLIM SPAIN YOU COULD ONCE HAVE SEEN 8,000 NORIAS WATERING RICE PLANTATIONS.

15 WINDMILL FACTS

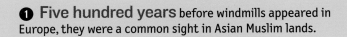

❶ Five hundred years before windmills appeared in Europe, they were a common sight in Asian Muslim lands.

❷ Beginning in the 7th century windmills were used in the Muslim world for grinding grain and pumping water for crops and gardens.

❸ One man's offer to build a mill driven by wind power, an idea that originally developed in Persia, led to the construction of the first known windmill in Arabia around 640 during the rule of Caliph Umar.

❹ Windmills harnessed the power of the steady winds that blew regularly across Persia's dry deserts.

❺ Al-Masudi, a 10th-century geographer, described Persia as a "country of wind and sand."

❻ Wind power soon became widely used throughout Muslim civilization to run millstones for grinding corn, crushing sugarcane, and pumping water.

❼ Early windmills were two-story buildings with as many as 12 fabric-covered, rectangular sails that turned on a vertical axis.

Medieval windmills in Campo de Criptana in Castilla La Mancha, Spain

TO BLOW YOUR MIND

8 Windmills were usually built on top of **castle towers,** hills, or platforms.

9 Wind towers on **rooftops** caught air and channeled it through homes, providing an early form of air conditioning.

10 European windmills looked very different. Instead of turning on a vertical axis, sails rotated on a horizontal axis like most do today.

11 You can still see the remains of ancient **vertical windmills** in Afghanistan.

12 Sails of ancient windmills were made from bundles of **palm leaves.**

13 Today **wind power** is a popular source of clean energy.

14 The biggest wind turbines generate enough **electricity** to supply about 600 U.S. homes for a whole year.

15 Modern windmills—called **TURBINES**—can be as tall as a **20-STORY BUILDING** and have three 200-FOOT (60-M)-LONG blades.

Chapter One

A Northwest Legacy

When I was growing up, Bothell was a small, rural town. It seemed miles away from bustling, urban Seattle. In Bothell, my dad ran a five and dime store, where I started working at the age of 12. It was always an exciting time when my brothers, sisters, and I climbed into the car to drive to Seattle so my dad could buy things for the store. Today, Bothell itself is a bustling, urban community in its own right. Like all of King County, it's retained the things that make it a special place to live and raise a family.

100 Words by
Patty Murray
Senator
United States Senate

A NORTHWEST LEGACY

You are here. . . The Washington State History Museum draws you and other visitors into historical millennia. It opens with a digital display of the state's awe-inspiring landforms; its volcanoes, river basins, beaches and tide pools, inlets, rivers, rain forests, wetlands, plains, and irrigated desert. You see a land molded by the elements—the flow of fire, water, and ice.

Voices of greeting from various Native tribes call to you in the Chimakum, Wakashan, Salishan, Chinookan, Shaptin, Athapaskan, and Nicola language families. You approach a wilderness scene where human-sized historical figures tend to campfires, and animal pelts and venison dry on wooden stands. You learn that in early days, two beaver pelts could be traded for a hatchet or a powder horn, and that a prime beaver pelt could go for two deer hides, four marten pelts, a pound-and-a-half of Virginia tobacco, a pound-and-a-half of gunpowder, or a yard of flannel cloth.

As you continue your tour, totem poles, plank house photos, and artifacts capture your attention. You inspect a simulated coal-mine tunnel and read about the all-too-common mining accidents. Another exhibit features the "prairie schooner" wagons that carried pioneer families west along the 2000-mile Oregon Trail. You peek inside a mock general store, complete with original signage, that stocks axes, wall clocks, and pitchers, among other necessities.

Along with other museum-goers, you walk to where a train chugs around a miniaturized landscape. You observe Native American basket weaving and then pause to watch a movie about the settling of the great Columbia River. Nearby, you peruse kiosks that pay homage to the Native peoples of Washington state and their traditions. And as you step back into the present, you carry with you a piece of Northwest history.

Masks are an important part of the Burke Museum's ethnology collection.

No one knows exactly when the Pacific Northwest was first settled. Some anthropologists speculate that the Native peoples originally descended from today's Mongolia and Siberia regions. They may have crossed a temporary 1,000-mile-wide grassland steppe or bridge between Asia and North America, dubbed "Beringia," during the Ice Age. It is believed that plants and animals moved in both directions across this vast steppe. Beringia was named after Vitus Bering, the eighteenth-century Danish explorer commissioned by the czar of Russia.

Native Americans are believed to have existed in the continent since 3000 B.C., although some experts say evidence suggests that

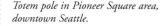

Totem pole in Pioneer Square area, downtown Seattle.

Initially, loggers used oxen to haul logs out of the woods. Horses eventually replaced oxen because they were easier to handle. The logs were pulled down "skid roads" to a river or railroad line. Skid roads were built of logs laid across or along the track. The logs were often greased to ease transport.

This painting is of Seattle's waterfront in 1874. Civic leaders were frustrated when Tacoma was chosen over Seattle to be the terminus for the Northern Pacific Railroad in 1873. However, it did not stop private investment in local railway lines that brought coal from the Eastside coal mines to the waterfront. The subsequent growth was phenomenal through the 1880s and after the Great Seattle Fire of 1889. Finally, the Northern Pacific incorporated a locally owned railroad and began service to Seattle in 1896. The photo on the upper left demonstrates what a few short years and a railroad can do to change the face of a city.

Courtesy of Seattle Museum of History & Industry, Lantern Slide Collection, 2002.3.483

their history dates back as far as 12,000 years ago. No established numbers exist for estimates of the Native American population before the coming of Euro-Americans, according to historian Carlos A. Schwantes. (36) Tribes of the greater King County area include the Suquamish, Duwamish, Twana, Squaxin, Sahhewamish, Steilacoom, Puyallup, Muckleshoot, Sammamish, and Nisqually. Tribes throughout the rest of Washington state are the Clallam, Makah, Ozette, Quilleute, Hoh, Queets, Quinault, Copalis, Humptulips, Whiskah, Wynoochee, and the Satsop along the Pacific Coast. (Ruby and Brown 116-117)

DISCOVERIES

Various maritime explorers representing different countries probed the Pacific Northwest, beginning in 1592 with Juan de Fuca (né Apostolos Valerianos) from Greece. Sailing for Spain on behalf of the Viceroy of Mexico, de Fuca claimed to have discovered the strait that bears his name today. In 1774, another Spanish expedition, under the command of Juan Perez, sailed from San Blas and proceeded to the 54th parallel. Along the way, Perez discovered a harbor that he named Port Lorenzo (later renamed Nootka Sound), where the Spaniards started a colony in 1789.

In 1775, when the Viceroy of Mexico sent out Lieutenant Bruno Heceta on a ship and Spanish Commissioner Don Quadra on a schooner, they sailed by the mouth of the Columbia River and the Strait of Juan de Fuca without noticing either. Heceta failed to find the strait because ". . . he did not examine the coast one degree farther north. Continuing southward, in the latitude of the mouth of the Columbia River, he discovered an indentation in the coast which he named Assumption Inlet, and he gave Spanish names to the headlands on both sides of it." (Hanford 39-40)

In 1778, Captain James Cook, the famous English navigator, discovered and named Cape Flattery. In 1787, Captain Charles Barkley (after whom Barkley Sound was named) rediscovered the Strait of Juan de Fuca, as reported to fellow British navigator Captain John Meares. At this time, a royal charter gave British fur trading rights to two monopolies. Meares managed to sidestep this problem in 1788, when he and his crew sailed from China to Nootka aboard vessels flying the colors of Portugal.

In 1790, Spaniards explored the interior waters. In 1792, an American, Captain Robert Gray, discovered the Columbia River and named it after his ship. The *Columbia* was the first American ship to circumnavigate the globe, from Boston via Cape Horn to Nootka, then to China and back to Boston. (Hanford 45)

*The Klondike gold rush kept the
shipyards busy, which was yet another
economic boon to the Seattle area.*

*In the spring and summer of 1898,
the docks on the Seattle waterfront were
crowded with dreamers struck with
Klondike fever. The ship passage was
only the first part of the long voyage to
the Klondike gold fields.*

In 1803, President Thomas Jefferson sent Captain Meriwether Lewis and Lieutenant William Clark west of the Mississippi to explore the territory for commerce. Their expedition lasted two years, 1804 to 1806, and sparked widespread interest in these lands.

FRIENDS AND FOES

European and Russian traders ventured to this region of the world to trade for animal pelts. The British Hudson's Bay Company, founded in 1670, made inroads in the fur business and dominated the industry for generations.

The European traders found the Native Americans of the Pacific Northwest to be established traders, some tribes using dentalium (tooth-shaped mollusks) or blankets as money. Items that were traded included whale bones and oil, seal oil, mountain sheep horns, dried herring roe, mountain goat meat, red ocher for cosmetics and war paint, shells, tools, copper, carved chests, baskets, beads, carving knives, masks, and clothing.

While conflicts between the Native peoples and European settlers cost lives on both sides, a majority of Native American deaths stemmed from their lack of immunity to illnesses brought by white settlers in maritime visits, the inland fur trade, and agricultural settlements. In 1775, the first epidemic of smallpox resulted in a full third of the Indians from the lower and middle Columbia River succumbing. Between 1830 and 1833, an outbreak of malaria at the Hudson's Bay Company's Fort Vancouver headquarters resulted in the deaths of 90 percent of the Chinookin tribe. In 1847, measles hit, and in 1853, smallpox broke out again. During WWI, the Columbia Plateau Indians were severely affected by the Spanish influenza. (Washington State History Museum)

BORDERS. With the sale of the Louisiana Territory to the U.S. by France in 1803, efforts were made to establish the boundary between the Columbia River country and that region claimed by Great Britain. In its negotiations with Great Britain in 1804, the United States claimed the 49th parallel as the boundary. The U.S. argued on the grounds that it had been adopted and definitely settled in 1713 as the dividing line between the French possessions of western Canada and Louisiana to the south, and the British territories of Hudson's Bay to the north. (Snowden 31) In 1853, Congress approved the creation of the Washington Territory.

In 1907, about 400 people lived in North Bend and were employed in the timber industry. This photographic postcard, which was created between 1907 and 1912, shows a boomman standing on a huge log at the edge of a log pond near North Bend. He uses his long pole to sort the logs in the pond and direct them toward the sawmill.

Courtesy of Museum of History & Industry, Postcard Collection, Photo by Siegrist, 1997.20.4

HOMESTEADERS

Settlers began pouring into the Pacific Northwest, initially lured by publicity from the Lewis and Clark expedition with their "Corps of Discovery." The opening of the Oregon Trail in the 1840s and the laying of the Northern Pacific Railroad tracks through Stampede Pass, completed in the 1880s with the help of 11,000 Chinese laborers who dynamited their way through the Cascades, also attracted settlers from the East. "On May 10, 1869, Irish-born immigrants working westward for the Union Pacific met Chinese immigrants working eastward for the Central Pacific at Promontory Point, Utah. Four symbolic spikes—two gold, one silver, another made of gold, silver, and iron—were tapped into position." (Kaplan 107-110) With the availability of rail service to the West, the mountainous terrain was much less of a barrier for new settlers, and within a decade, Washington's population quadrupled.

DEVELOPMENT

In 1851, explorers John C. Holgate and Colonel Isaac N. Ebey made separate trips to explore the territory around Elliott Bay. "The first settlement within the present boundaries of Seattle was on the prairie in Duwamish River Valley, bout [sic] three miles from Elliott Bay, that was John Holgate's first choice for a land claim. In the spring 1851 Luther M. Collins, Henry Van Asselt, Jacob Maple and Samuel Maple located there and planted gardens and fruit trees. Mr. Collins' wife and daughter were the first white women to arrive and become domiciled in King County." (Hanford 73-74)

In December of 1852, King County was created by an Act of the Legislature of the Oregon Territory. The county seat was located in Seattle.

By 1885, the city of Renton had nine saloons, one of which was the Eagle Saloon, pictured here circa 1900. The men who worked in nearby mines, mills, and logging camps came to town on Saturday and Sunday to catch up on news, shop, and drink with their friends. Saturday nights were frequently noisy and rowdy.

Courtesy of Seattle Museum of History & Industry, SHS 16.026

GOLD FEVER

The Klondike Gold Rush from 1897 to 1898 brought tens of thousands of gold-struck speculators from around the U.S. through Seattle on their way to the Canadian Yukon. It is estimated that millions of dollars of equipment, steamship tickets, pack animals, and supplies were purchased for the trip north. Each prospective gold rusher was required by the Canadian Mounted Police to bring one ton of goods, deemed to be a year's supply.

As the influx of immigrants grew, stores, missionary schools, and log-cabin churches (with circuit-riding preachers) were established. While the land itself was rich in natural resources, pioneers engaged in the hard labor of growing crops; mining for coal, gold, and minerals; extracting timber and forest products for building and export; fishing; hunting; and building construction.

IMMIGRATION AND DEMOGRAPHICS

From early days through the present, immigrants from foreign countries as well as from other parts of the U.S. have settled in Washington state. *Peoples of Washington* details the cultural lives, social issues, and contributions of the people of Native, European, African, Middle Eastern, Asian, and Hispanic decent, as well as others of various ancestries from around the world. "According to the 1980 federal census records, there were over one hundred ethnic communities in Washington," writes Sid White, co-author of *Peoples of Washington* (White and Solberg xvi).

In 2000, the U.S. Census Bureau reported 18.9 percent non-white residents in Washington state. The bureau reported 24.3 percent non-white residents in King County, including 10.8 percent Asian Americans, 5.5 percent of Hispanic or Latino origin, 5.4 percent African Americans, .9 percent American Indians and Alaska Natives, and .5 percent Native Hawaiian and other Pacific Islanders. Another 2.6 percent of respondents reported "Other" and 4.1 percent reported two or more races. ("State and County QuickFacts: King County, Washington")

GEOGRAPHICAL ADVANTAGES

Mirroring its diverse population, the geography of the Pacific Northwest features highly varied mainland areas: the Olympic Mountains, the Coast Range, the Puget Sound Lowland, the Cascade Mountains, the Columbia Plateau, and the Rocky Mountains. It includes 3,026 miles (4,869.88 km.) of total shoreline, with 157 miles (253 km.) directly along the Pacific Ocean. The climate is temperate, averaging about 64 degrees Fahrenheit (17.7 Celsius) in the summer and 38 degrees Fahrenheit (3.3 Celsius) in the winter. Washington state is split down the middle, from the north to the south by the Cascade Range, resulting in a rainy, temperate climate in western Washington and more extreme temperature variations in the drier eastern half of the state.

One of the most appealing features of Washington state is its plentiful water supply. Not only does rain keep much of the state green year-round, the numerous lakes and rivers, and extensive shoreline along Puget Sound and the Pacific Ocean, give the region a special beauty. There is an economic benefit, as well, to the abundance of water. By the early twentieth century, Seattle residents approved a hefty $590,000 bond issue to develop a hydroelectric facility on the Cedar River, marking the beginning of public power in the city. (Seattle City Light "A Brief History")

While exploration and development have long played key roles in the settlement of Washington state, this region's beauty and abundance of natural resources continue to lure immigrants to this day. Indeed, the pioneering spirit that invigorates each new generation of "settlers" originally laid the groundwork for building Seattle and King County into economic powerhouses and centers of international trade.

Railroad cars carried coal from the mines that lie east of Lake Washington to the Seattle waterfront. The coal was offloaded and stored in bunkers, then loaded onto ships.

Before coal companies began to use electric engines, mine operators used mules to haul the coal cars out of the mines and do other heavy work. This photo, taken around 1910, shows the mule drivers with the mules that they worked with and cared for.

Sealth, known to settlers as Chief Seattle, became the leader of the Suquamish and Duwamish people sometime around 1810. When settlers began to move into the Elliott Bay area during the 1850s, Chief Sealth was friendly and urged his people to remain so as well. The city of Seattle was named for the Chief, but it is said that he felt uneasy about his name being used in this way.

Emily Inez Denny, the eldest child of early settler David Denny, drew numerous pictures of Seattle's early settler life. This sketch by Ms. Denny is of early settlers bargaining with Native American traders at the Alki Point settlement in 1851.

Courtesy of Museum of History & Industry, SHS 16,468

Native American tribes in the Puget Sound region built large, seaworthy canoes that could be paddled or sailed. In this photo, circa 1911, several Native people leave the shore of what may be Elliott Bay. Their sail is folded in the bow. The canoe was built in the Nootkan style, which was common in western Washington.

FOCUS: MODERN POTLATCHES AND COMMUNAL SHARING

"Potlatch" comes from the Chinook words for "to give away" that were adopted from the Nootka word patshatl, *which means "gift." These were traditional gatherings of Native Americans, often held in their painted long houses, to commemorate important events such as marriages, births, deaths, ceremonial naming, and the transfer of power.*

"The movements of dances, the words of songs and their beat, the costumes and regalia, the audience reaction to dramatic performances, all are central to the Northwest Coast Indian life. All are intertwined with potlatching, which specifically refers to the distribution of gifts to pay an audience for serving as witnesses. In general usage, however, the term includes the entire ceremonial program that culminates with the actual potlatching. Such occasions are sociable, but their fundamental purpose always has been to express relative ranking and group relationships." (Kirk 30)

Washingtonians celebrate the region's Native American community and heritage through modern potlatches, canoe races, cedar canoe-building projects, and museum exhibits. Tillicum Village on Blake Island (believed to be the birthplace of Chief Sealth) offers tours from Pier 55 in downtown Seattle to the island. Guests are treated to a hearty salmon meal served in a traditional longhouse, along with traditional dances and storytelling of the Northwest Coast tribes.

Other events in communities throughout the state celebrate the Native American heritage. Some tribes have built lavish gaming and entertainment centers on their lands. Modern maps of the state are dotted with Native American tribes' names as well as words and phrases from their languages. Today, there are 23 Native American reservations and communities in Washington state, according to the Bauu Institute: the Confederated Tribes of the Chehalis Reservation, the Lummi, Makah, Muckleshoot, Quileute, Samish, Puyallup, Shoalwater Bay, Squaxin, Tulalip, and Upper Skagit Indian Tribes of Washington.

Chapter Two

DIVERSITY AND A NEW ECONOMY

Few regions provide more opportunities for individuals to pursue their personal and professional potential than King County.

Whether in agriculture or aerospace, King County and its neighboring cities boast the best of the new and old economy. Beyond internationally known companies like Microsoft and Boeing, independent businesses serve as the cornerstone for economic prosperity. Entrepreneurs throughout the globe have made King County their home, and enriched us culturally and financially in the process.

From the depths of Puget Sound to the summit of our mountains there are countless ways for an individual or family to explore their interests and aspirations.

100 Words by
Pete von Reichbauer
Councilmember, District 7
Metropolitan King County Council

DIVERSITY AND A NEW ECONOMY

You are here. . . You are inside the simulator cockpit of a Boeing 737, courtesy of The Boeing Company. Beside you is your co-pilot. In front of you is a multi-panel display of the natural contours and shapes of Washington state at tens of thousands of feet—the greens, the blues, and the browns of nature, the blacks and the whites of buildings below. The organizers have put the simulator in simple mode, with only the steering in your control. Trained pilots would have all the sophisticated equipment functioning in virtual reality—the controls, buttons, gauges, and switches. You start out in the air. The computer simulation is precise. Every move of your steering affects the plane as it comes in for a landing. Your instruments tell you where you need to be, but if truth be told, you're all over this simulated three-dimensional world, and you're coming in for a landing. . . .

. . . Into the real. *Feet firmly planted on the ground, you're visiting the Boeing plants where the company's jetliners are assembled. At the Everett plant, the concrete floors are 20 feet thick, and the building is so stable that in an earthquake only the most sensitive equipment might need recalibration (although all of it is checked). The building itself, at 472 million cubic feet, is the largest in the world in terms of cubic mass.*

Overhead, giant cranes move plane pieces. The Boeing representative talks about the thin durable plane siding that reduces fuel costs. The plant floors are tidy, the workers focused. Small, motorized vehicles zoom by, and bicyclists move from one end of the factory to the other. People wear hard hats and goggles. A group of workers is wiring a portion of the plane. One plant has its own fire station and hospital; it's like a small city.

Eventually, the large hangar doors will be opened for each plane's debut. New models are greeted and admired by an enthusiastic crowd. Each rollout is the result of precision, state-of-the-art building of world-class aircraft.

"Test flight" at the Museum of Flight.

ECONOMIC POWERHOUSE

King County is the largest in land mass of the 39 counties in Washington state. Its residents make up a third of the state's population, and 43 percent of the jobs are located within its borders. ("King County Profile" 1) A manufacturing and banking center, the county owes a great deal of its job growth in recent years to the service sector.

This state exceeded $46 billion in foreign exports in 2001, nearly 75 percent of which were from the central Puget Sound area. Two-way trade through the Port of Seattle exists with over 100 countries,

King County has a rich history in aviation.

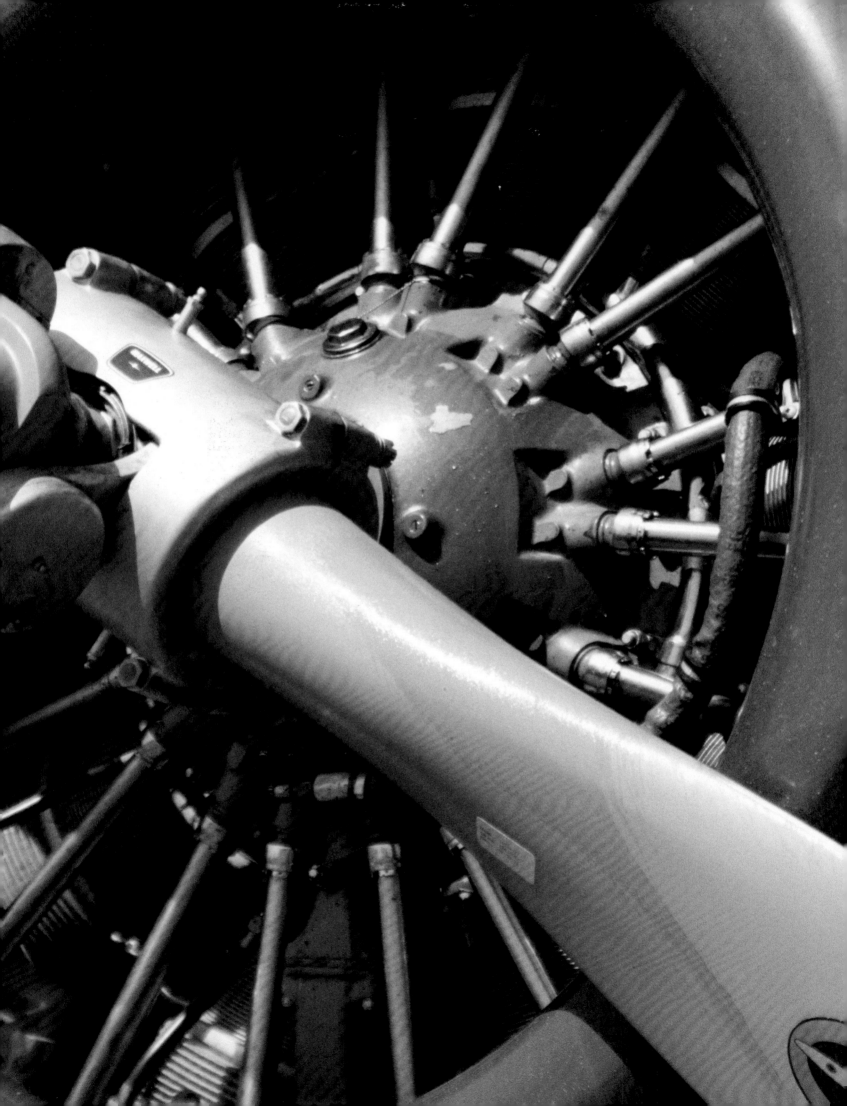

A cargo ship navigates the misty waters of Elliott Bay.

accounting for $106 billion in 1999 according to the Economic Development Council. The top-ten trade partners in 2001, listed in descending order, were Japan, Singapore, China, the United Kingdom, Canada, South Korea, Germany, Taiwan, France, and Saudi Arabia. (Office of Trade & Economic Development) The largest exports are in aerospace, forest products, computer products, and processed food. The Port of Seattle handles seven percent of all U.S. exports and six percent of all imports. A full third of the state's jobs are linked to international trade.

Seattle has consistently been rated one of the best cities in which to locate a business because of its skilled workforce, higher education, transportation infrastructure, high-tech connectivity, access to markets, manufacturing capabilities, government support, low-cost utilities, and business expertise. Its cosmopolitan perspective, with its 20 sister cities (the second most of any city in the nation) and diverse population make it a prime location for business. The quality of life in Seattle has also been well-recognized. The city was rated the "Best City for Work and Family" by *Fortune* (1996), "Best City in the West" by *Money* (1998), and one of the top ten cities by *CNN Money* (2002). Its highly educated workforce and suitability as a business location have also attracted media accolades, for example being named the number one metro region for careers and business in *Forbes'* inaugural list (1999), and the tenth metro region in educational attainment in *Forbes* (2002).

Residents of Seattle and King County take pride in their work. They define their world by actively creating it, through higher education, training, long work hours, and innovations. At the forefront are the scientists, researchers, engineers (software, electrical, industrial, and others), architects, thinkers, and builders who dare to do things differently. They are the ones who think beyond what they are taught, and explore the realm of possibilities. Along with the homegrown innovators, they are workers who arrive from different parts of the nation and world, who speak in diverse languages and probe issues in novel ways. This confluence of talent brings about a powerful synergy and regional advantage.

King County companies continue to leave a significant mark in the national and international business arenas. Nordstrom has redefined customer service in high-end retail. Costco effectively introduced millions of consumers to warehouse shopping. Recreational Equipment Incorporated (better known as REI) targets outdoor enthusiasts with in-store rails and rock-climbing walls. Local architects have created unique Northwest styles of architecture, including mansions built in the high-tech boom of the 1990s.

From the pioneers to industrialists to millionaire "techies," the people of the Northwest have created a diverse, broad-based economic foundation in King County. Following is a partial list of the county's key industries.

Aerospace

Floatplanes descend and take off on Lake Union in downtown Seattle. Boeing jumbo jets grace the skies overhead. Chartered commuter planes hopscotch across the state. Per capita, Seattle may well have more pilots than any other metropolitan area in the country. A love of flight is common to many of the region's residents, not least because a large percentage is employed by The Boeing Company. In fact, generations of families have been employed by the company since it began manufacturing airplanes in 1916.

The Smith Tower as seen through the branches of a tree in winter.

Boeing's industry dominance since its founding in 1916 as Pacific Aero Products Company has lasted because of its ability to meet the changing needs of a globalizing world. It manufactures 60 percent of the world's commercial air fleet. Its design of the B-1 bombers, luxury 80 jets, 307B Stratoliner, commercial jumbo jets (737 and 747), B-52G Stratofortress, and LGM-30 Minuteman, placed it in a class of its own. Boeing's innovations in aerospace include solar orbit vehicles, rockets, and manned and unmanned space vehicles. The company engages in national defense work, airport security, Connexion airline Internet connectivity, and other endeavors. Boeing's planned 7E7 has been touted as the world's most advanced aircraft, given its composition-based structure and unprecedented fuel efficiency.

The Commercial Airplane Group is headquartered in Renton, where the 737 and the Boeing business jets are assembled. Boeing's Commercial Aviation Services—Global Customer Support, Spares and Logistics Support, Maintenance and Engineering Services, Fleet Enhancements and Modifications, and Flight Operations Support—is located in Seattle. The fabrication and aircraft systems and interiors plant is located in Auburn.

Approximately 500 companies work in aerospace in the King County area, with many headquartered in Renton, Kent, and south Seattle. Paccar, Inc.; ELDEC Corp.; Neuvant Aerospace; and Northwest Composites are just a few companies with ties to this industry that accounted for $22 billion in exports in 2001.

Courtesy of Seattle Museum of History & Industry, Seattle Historical Society Collection, SHS11540

William Boeing started his airplane company in this hangar he had built on the shore of Lake Union December 1915. The B & W seaplane, shown here, was named for its designers, Boeing and Conrad Westervelt. It was the first airplane produced at the small factory and only two were ever built.

BIOTECHNOLOGY

Biotechnology, the use of microorganisms in industry and manufacturing, has already improved human lives globally. With post-WWII leaps in molecular biology, the findings of the Human Genome Project, and growing expertise in this field, biotechnology stands at the forefront of new discoveries.

Bioengineered crops have greater production, with heartier strains that ward off viruses, plant diseases, and pests. Human pharmacology has been expanded, and genetic therapies are often used in the treatment of various diseases. In addition, biotechnology has been applied to information storage and computing. The potential applications have barely been plumbed.

The Northwest has attracted increasing worldwide attention for its biotechnology research and development, due in part to its visionary academic and business sector leadership. Amgen's $625 million Helix Project campus started welcoming its 750 employees in early 2004. A new million-square-foot, $150 million biotechnology research building is set to open in 2005 at the south end of Lake Union. The University of Washington was awarded a $70 million biotechnology grant and received a $10 million donation to fund genomics research of diseases in the developing world. With support from local high-tech entrepreneurs and philanthropists like Microsoft founders Bill Gates and Paul Allen, biotechnology may well develop into the next global powerhouse industry.

Biotechnology includes proteonomics (the study of all the proteins in a cell or tissue), genomics (the study of genes), bioinformatics (the application of computer technology to the management of biological information), nanotechnologies (controlling individual atoms and molecules to shrink or "miniaturize" processes), and environmental engineering. According to the "2002 Washington Biotechnology & Medical Technology Annual Report," federally funded research at the University of Washington, Washington State University, Fred Hutchinson Cancer Research Center, Battelle/Pacific Northwest National Laboratory, Pacific Northwest Research Institute, and Virginia Mason Research Center has had a far-ranging impact on the field of biotechnology. According to the report, "Nearly one-half of the more than 190 biotechnology and medical device firms in the state are founded on technologies developed at these institutions." From 1980 to 2002, the research institutions cited brought more than $19.3 billion in revenue to the state.

In 2001, an estimated 18,500 Washingtonians worked in the biotechnology sector. According to the Washington Biotechnology and Biomedical Association, 115 local companies participate in

The Kenworth Motor Truck Company got its start building heavy-duty trucks for the timber industry. During World War II, the company participated in many war-related production contracts. Beginning in 1943, Kenworth began making components for Boeing. This 1944 photo shows female Kenworth employees posing with an airplane fuselage. During World War II, many industries employed women in traditionally male jobs in order to keep up with war-related production. Of Kenworth's 507 Seattle employees at this time, 415 were women.

Courtesy of Seattle Museum of History & Industry, PEMCO Webster & Stevens Collection, 1983.10.14851.16

The vineyards outside Chateau Ste.
Michelle Winery.

Courtesy of Wyndham Images

Courtesy of Wyndham Images

Seattle Coffee Company, the makers
of Seattle's Best Coffee, has played a
key role in the development of the
specialty coffee business in the Puget
Sound region.

Downtown Bellevue has become a center for corporate business.

Courtesy of City of Bellevue

biotechnology, with 54 percent focused on research and development, 26 percent on diagnostics, 11 percent on contract manufacturing and genetic testing, six percent on plant, agriculture, and animal research, and three percent on natural resources. Various non-profit organizations have sprung up to promote this burgeoning field, such as the Washington Biotechnology Foundation and the Washington Biotechnology & Biomedical Association, among others. A few of the local companies engaged in biotechnology are Cell Therapeutics, Inc.; ZymoGenetics; Corixa Corp.; ICOS Corp.; and Rosetta Inpharmatics, Inc.

SOFTWARE

The mystique of 0s and 1s—much of the coding and back-end directions that help computers to store information, communicate, provide entertainment, offer secure financial transactions, trade goods, and calculate grocery purchases, happen here in King County. Washington state is one of the epicenters of computer coding.

Microsoft Corporation, the world's largest software company, is located in Redmond. Started by two "local boys made good," Bill Gates and Paul Allen, it is one of over 4,200 local companies that create custom software or related services. With its ubiquitous Microsoft Office Suite, X-box games, mobile devices, and business applications, Microsoft has created a distinctive place for itself in the fast-changing world of high-tech and software. Its Redmond campus is headed for more expansion as its world-class innovators and designers create next-generation technologies.

Founded in 1975, this company has a hand in much of the philanthropic and community development efforts around King County and beyond, donating computers and software to local schools, giving generously to the arts, and nurturing political leadership within its hard-working ranks.

This industry sector is estimated to contribute $5 to $10 billion in export revenues. Companies that create business software, data storage, and computer games all fall into this industry category. In addition to Microsoft, leaders in the software industry include Itron; Attachmate Corp.; RealNetworks, Inc.; Sierra Entertainment, Inc.; Onyx Software Corp.; and Captaris Inc.

E-COMMERCE

In the 20 years of the "dot-com" era, electronic commerce has come a long way. E-commerce has matured and begun to deliver on its promises of efficient customer relations and service delivery, increased telecommuting, technology maximization, and the globalization of companies. Online auctions, shared online workspaces, database management, e-mail, blogs (Web logs), and other products and practices now work in concert with online retail tools to enhance e-commerce.

Amazon.com, the online selling site of CEO Jeff Bezos' vision, originated in Seattle in 1994. One of a handful of billionaires in King County, Bezos has seen his company make significant headway towards profitability while becoming the world's largest online retailer with 37 million customer accounts. With improving online security, online micro-payments, affiliate marketing, clearer industry standards, and increasingly savvy shoppers, this multinational corporation has attracted hundreds of thousands of consumers and had sales topping $851 million in 2001.

SPECIALTY COFFEE

An Aged Sumatra Earthy®. Brazil Ipanema Bourbon®. Ethiopia Yergacheffe. Decaf LightNote Blend®. For a town that has hosted a Coffee Fest and counts coffee tasters among its select workforce, Seattle has a special affection for its hundreds of varieties of coffee drinks—hot, cold, sweet, spicy, tall, short, or in-between. Fueled by savvy marketing, quality products, and a sense of Pacific Northwest chic, specialty coffees have become inextricably linked to the wet-and-rainy Seattle lifestyle.

And between sips, Northwesterners want to know that their coffee comes from environmentally sound farming practices. They want to know that Fair Trade Certified prices were paid for the coffee beans to sustain farmers worldwide, and that minority-owned suppliers were used to multiply the fiscal benefits with social ones. All are practices that the Starbucks Coffee Company believes in and has adopted. Since the company started in 1971 at its original location in the Pike Place Market, Starbucks has expanded from its Seattle base (currently headquartered in the SoDo district) to 30 countries worldwide. In North America, Starbucks has 1,600 company-operated stores, and the company is on schedule to meet its long-term goal of operating 25,000 stores worldwide (10,000 in North America and 15,000 in international markets). Annual sales top $3.3 billion, with a net revenue of $215 million in 2002, according to the company's annual report.

Seattle Coffee Company, which markets Seattle's Best Coffee and other brands, has been in the specialty coffee business since 1968 and has played a key role in the development of Seattle's coffee industry. The company has operated under various names, including Wet Whisker, Stewart Brothers Coffee®, and in 1988 SBC, a brand name that was quickly dubbed "Seattle's Best Coffee." Known for the smooth taste of its dark and medium roasts, flavored coffees, and decaf blends, Seattle's Best has served international connoisseurs of coffee for over a quarter-century. The company was acquired by Starbucks Corp. in the summer of 2003.

Tully's Coffee Corp., founded in 1992, sells coffee as a retailer, wholesaler, and roaster. Also based out of Seattle, Tully's has grown rapidly through strong branding. With annual sales of approximately $50 million, Tully's has emerged as a powerful contender in the heated competition for market share.

Telecommunications

The telecommunications industry provides a strong backbone of real-time and virtual communications. Local entrepreneur Craig McCaw started McCaw Cellular in the early 1990s, pioneering cell phone technology and usage. AT&T Wireless acquired McCaw Cellular in 1994, and in turn, Cingular put in a bid to acquire AT&T Wireless in 2004. Together, Cingular and AT&T Wireless would become the largest carrier in the U.S.

Washington state exported $347.1 million in telecommunications equipment to overseas markets in 2001. At this very moment, other innovations are being developed for more efficient worldwide communications. The ultimate goal is complete connectivity around the globe.

Evidence of human activity spans 9,500 years in the Cedar River Watershed. For thousands of years, the watershed acted as a travel route between eastern and western Washington.

An aerial of downtown Seattle, the waterfront, and Mt. Rainier.

Courtesy of Seattle Public Utilities; Photo by City of Seattle Photographers

Courtesy of City of Seattle, Photo by Ian Edelstein

PUBLIC MARKET CENTER

The top of Seattle City Light's Diablo Dam at night, with its 1930s light posts, looks more like an urban boulevard, but is actually located deep in the remote North Cascade Mountains on the Skagit River.

The Pike Place Market sign glows at the west end of Pike Street.

ELECTRONICS

King County companies that produce electronic instruments exported $876 million in electronic equipment and $421 in scientific instruments/measuring equipment in 2001. Semiconductors, computer hardware, marine electronics, monitoring equipment, and scientific instruments demonstrate the range of local output. Emerald City Marine, Protrack Inc., Imaging & Sensing Technology Corp., Novatech Instruments Inc., Cypress Semiconductor Corp., Axcelis Technologies Inc., Interpoint Corp., and Motorola are a handful of local employers in the electronics industry.

ENVIRONMENT/ENERGY

With a sophisticated eco-consciousness, 400 local companies specializing in water treatment, radioactive waste, hazardous waste, and other services exported $189 million in environmental services and equipment in 2000. URS Corp.; RCI Environmental; Hart Crowser, Inc.; Golder Associates; and Earth Tech, Inc. are among these 400 companies, however many more local companies engage in "green design" of everything from homes to equipment and work processes in order to protect the environment. This design approach emphasizes simplicity, the efficient use of natural resources, and maximizing the unique strengths of an environmental niche with the least environmental impact. The key principle is future-focused, sustainable development.

FORESTRY/WOOD PRODUCTS

Weyerhaeuser Company, one of the world's largest forestry products companies, maintains its corporate headquarters in Federal Way and a major research and development center in King County. The company has offices or operations in 18 countries and owns or leases 7.3 million acres of U.S. timberlands. Started in 1900, the company has diversified its interests with investments in transportation and housing, along with its core building products, pulp and paper, and packaging. The company is known both for its responsible environmental stewardship of timber as a renewable resource and for its useful applied research.

In 2001, Washington state exported $843 million in wood and secondary wood products. Other leading companies in this industry sector include Potlach Corp., Plum Creek Timber Company, Simpson Timber, and Rayonier. The fact that petrified wood was chosen as the state "gem" in 1975 indicates that locals clearly have affection for this natural resource.

AGRICULTURE

From pioneer days onward, King County has maintained agricultural ties. While agriculture accounts for only a small percentage of King County's employment ("King County Profile" 23), farmland continues to be protected for its commercial viability as well as to preserve an ancient way of life and connection to the land.

Today, farmers markets are scattered throughout the county to showcase local farmers' products and specialties, like organic herbs, fruits and vegetables, honey, dairy and meat products, greenhouse foods, nursery plants, and flowers. Practicing sustainable farming to protect the environment and promote biodiversity, many local farmers rely on the savvy of urban shoppers for their livelihood.

The King County Agriculture Commission (KCAC) includes ". . . producers of agricultural commodities as well as persons with demonstrated knowledge, experience and interest in such support activities as agricultural real estate, food and feed processing, wholesale and retail marketing, produce buying, direct marketing, supply and finance." It encourages community support for local farmers through "Puget Sound Fresh," a publicity campaign the KCAC initiated to encourage wholesalers, retailers, restaurants, and consumers to purchase locally grown products. Statewide, Washington is a primary producer of dairy products, apples, cattle and calves, potatoes, wheat and grains, and hay. Its top agriculture exports include fruits, vegetables, wheat and related products, and live animals, with a combined value of nearly $1.8 billion in 2002. (U.S.D.A.)

ZymoGenetics is now located in what was once the "old steam plant" on Lake Union.

Courtesy of Wyndham Images

King County maintains its agricultural ties. Today, farmers markets showcase local farmers' products and specialties.

Pacific Galleries has served as Seattle's Auction House since 1972. Located downtown on Third Avenue, it handles fine art, antiques, jewelry, carpeting, furniture, china, and figurines. On the auction floor, several dozen would-be buyers have gathered for the final day of a three-day auction. Dealers, couples, individuals, and families all clutch catalogs of goods that they have thoroughly reviewed. They also carry laminated cards with their unique numbers for the bidding.

Once the bidding starts, it is raw, acquisitive energy, similar to a game of poker. The auctioneer is a young woman whose lively intonation keeps the proceedings moving at a brisk clip. Beside her is a man who keeps written records of the bids and results. An organized group of employees moves the objects onto the stage according to lot numbers. The auctioneer observes unique aspects of the items briefly, mentions any absentee bids, and then takes bids from the floor. She begins some bids at $5, but those items that have received phone bids begin much higher, in the hundreds of dollars. She will intersperse the rising numbers with comments like, "We're way in the money, now," or "Would you like to come in at $350? Do I hear a $350?"

The parade of items continues: a film trunk, antique mirrors, bed frames, dressers, a Chippendale sofa, a diamond necklace. Five men carry out a large hand-woven carpet. Others wheel out sewing machines, coffee tables, chaise lounges, and piano benches with practiced efficiency and care. The smaller items are featured on an overhead camera for the best effect. The audience is on a buying binge, with or without planning or deep knowledge. Some attendees have made notations in their catalogs about how high they will bid before giving up.

A casual atmosphere pervades this event, even though some bidders have seemingly dressed for opening night at the opera. A black dog wanders in with one patron who has been searching a back room filled with antiques. A nervous bidder smokes in the rear of the auction house and gallery. The auctioneer knows some audience members by name. At one point, she asks a grizzled onlooker, "Roger, what number are you?" to keep her records straight. People move in and out of the room over several hours, timing their entry for the items they wish to acquire.

Courtesy of Wyndham Images

Courtesy of Wyndham Images

Courtesy of Seattle Public Utilities; Photo by City of Seattle Photographers

Seattle's historic waterfront remains an active part of the city's life.

A red schoolhouse desk from the early twentieth century. A mahogany octagonal candle stand with a tripod base. A six-inch cloisonné vase with an Avian scene. A Louis XV-style seven-drawer, marble-top lingerie chest with inlay and ormolu mounts. The bidding wars escalate sometimes without warning, starting in the low tens and moving quickly into the hundreds. No items last more than 30 seconds on the stage. The bidding goes fast, and if an item fails to bring bids, it is quickly moved backstage.

These items may have come from private estates, individual sellers or consignors, or elsewhere. Part of the mystery and fun of antiques shopping is tracking the provenance of the pieces and ascertaining their value. There is a sense of gamesmanship, with individuals and business owners outbidding each other. Who knows what conversations or horse-trading may have occurred before the auction itself, but there is only muffled talk once the items start moving. The auction's fine arts offerings include a piece by Dale Chihuly, a Mark Tobey painting, a Delacroix, and Asian antiquities. One seasoned dealer explains that some cherished and valuable items may never be seen in public except for such private sales held through auctions.

Among Seattle's well-heeled, only a subset may be interested in collecting a particular artwork or piece from antiquity, and those are the people who will bid up a piece and cherish it. Such goods belong to the wealthy connoisseurs, one dealer explains, because only they will truly love a piece. He tells the story of a jade dealer in Hong Kong: A rich woman had entered the shop and bought a carved jade brooch that cost $6,000. After examining it, she put it into her purse and moved on to other pieces. The jade dealer, however, asked for the return of the piece because she felt the purchaser was too careless in the handling of it; the customer would not appreciate it as much as the dealer herself did.

Auctions held at Pacific Galleries are sometimes charitable events to support such causes as world aid or cancer research. Whatever the occasion, this auction house serves as a place for easy acquisition and disquisition of quality goods. It is one small part of the larger Pacific Northwest economy. It is also part of a larger community of people who share a love of valuable things.

Courtesy of City of Seattle

Bicyclists enjoy a ride in Myrtle Edwards Park against a dramatic backdrop of the Port of Seattle and Mt. Rainier.

Chapter Three

THE GATEWAY

In 1854, when a fledgling Seattle occupied only 400 yards of waterfront, a reconnaissance hydrographic survey of Duwamish (Elliot) Bay and Seattle Harbor first opened the Pacific Northwest to worldwide shipping.

Seattle's forefathers recognized the vast opportunities afforded by Puget Sound and forged a jewel in the frontier territory. Today, Seattle and King County enjoy a thriving, diverse and vibrant economy due in large to its location on the Pacific Rim and its excellent transportation and communication infrastructures. As free trade in the world continues to increase, so will the prosperity and well being of King County and its cities.

100 Words by
Captain John C. Clary
National Oceanic and Atmospheric Administration

THE GATEWAY

You are here. . . You are leaning on the railing of one of the many ferries that ply the waters of Puget Sound. As you gaze out at the steely gray ripples of Elliott Bay, absent are the cares of the day, left behind in the big-city high-rise offices that flash with the orange and gold shimmers of sunset.

As the engines churn the waves, seagulls cut through the air overhead and call out to each other. Occasionally, a horn sounds as the ferry moves through a fogbank. Glimpses of local islands, covered with trees and dotted with homes, tantalize your curiosity. Time seems to have slowed. The sea wind ripples through your hair and pulls at your windbreaker.

From the deck, you look through the ferry's panoramic windows to where other passengers are eating hot foods at the onboard diner and children are playing videogames. Those who don't want to brave the mercurial weather stay inside and admire the view from their tables. A few tourists snap photos and talk in excited tones. The island regulars work on their laptops. Others read books or magazines.

You duck back inside to explore the other levels of the ferry. You're at home on the water.

Photo by Toni Kerr

Cleat on a Seattle waterfront pier.

A package arrives on a container ship that has docked in Seattle. From there, the package is promptly picked up by a truck or a train and brought to the airport, where it is loaded onto an airplane and whisked away to its final destination thousands of miles inland. All along the way, its progress is tracked digitally on a computer network. In real time and in real space, the package has just traveled a segment of the Pacific Northwest's efficient transportation network.

BY SEA, BY LAND, BY AIR

The first settlers to the Pacific Northwest came by sea. They came by land. And as air travel progressed, they came by air. The Pacific Northwest appeared on local and national maps first as it became more central to the local economy, then as it became significant to the national economy. Today, it holds an important place in world commerce. King County's strategic location serves as the connection to the Pacific Rim countries of Asia and also offers access to inland markets as well as to Alaska and British Columbia. Exports to over 100 nations flow through King County seaports and airports. Fully $7.2 billion in world exports move through Washington state. The state's

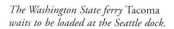

The Washington State ferry Tacoma *waits to be loaded at the Seattle dock.*

Courtesy of Wyndham Images

top trade partners are Japan, Canada, China, Singapore, Australia, the Netherlands, South Korea, Britain, Taiwan, and the United Arab Emirates. (Dunphy E1)

The central infrastructure of an economy relates to how efficiently people, goods, services, and resources—the lifeblood of a strong economy—may be transported. In the days of the later settlers, that meant a bustling shipping seaport, railways, trucking, and horses. Today, it means same-day worldwide air delivery of packages, massive container ships, thrumming rail lines, a 24-hour airport, and efficient use of satellite, Internet, and telecommunications.

WATERWAYS AND SEA

Marine Services and the Seattle Harbor

Many steamship and barge companies operate from Seattle's waterfront. The fifth largest container port in the nation, the Port of Seattle ranks as one of the largest in the world as well. Its waterfront functions with state-of-the-art equipment and well-trained longshoremen, freight forwarders, and other personnel. Each year, $36 billion in products are processed through these docks.

The Seattle waterfront has come a long way in a century. It was developed in the mid- to late-1800s as "thousands of trees [were] cut and driven into the sea bed to make pilings to support the piers, buildings, and railroad tracks forming the waterfront." (Puget Sound Maritime Historical Society 10) Seattle has a long maritime history, from its first settling in 1851 at Alki Point, to its present ocean-going freighters, pleasure boats, ferries shuttling between the islands of Puget Sound, tugboats guiding oil tankers, and cruise ships.

According to the Economic Development Council of Seattle & King County, harbor services and functions include an on-dock, intermodal railyard; sea-to-air transfers; 152 acres for general cargo; five container terminals and four break-bulk terminals; a grain terminal with a 4.2 million bushel capacity; 1.5 million square feet (4,572,000 meters) of distribution warehouse space; freezer facilities; dry-dock facilities; and moorage for 1,550 ocean-going boats up to 130 feet (40 meters) in length.

The Port of Seattle is the fifth largest container port in the nation and ranks as one of the largest in the world.

Pier 66 offers an expanded cruise ship terminal for luxury liners. The Terminal 30 Cruise Facility also accommodates cruise ships. In 2003, Seattle hosted an estimated 100 port calls and 400,000 passengers. Terminal 18 on Harbor Island is under construction and will become the largest container terminal in the Pacific Northwest. Fisherman's Terminal, homeport for the U.S. North Pacific fishing fleet, offers comprehensive support services. The nearby Maritime Industrial Center adds "vessel moorage, storage, re-supply, maintenance and repair facilities." ("Seattle Datasheet: Transportation")

Washington State Ferries

Washington State bought out Puget Sound Navigation (PSN) in 1951 to create the Washington Toll Bridge Authority (later known as Washington State Ferries). Beginning in the early 1900s, PSN used small steamers for navigating Puget Sound. Increasing labor costs after WWII made the operation of the ferry system difficult. When the State Highway Department failed to approve a 30 percent fare increase for PSN, this private company halted operations. That incident highlighted the region's growing reliance on ferries. In the ensuing years, a fleet of ferries was built up to serve the region.

Today, an estimated 26 million passengers and 11 million vehicles, from eight counties in Washington and British Columbia in Canada, use the toll ferry system each year. Its 29 vessels run 10 routes

The busy Port of Seattle processes $36 billion in products annually.

between 20 terminals. From Elliott Bay, commuters and tourists may take a ferry to Bainbridge Island, Bremerton, Vashon Island, and even to Victoria, British Columbia, on the friendly Canadian island to the north. Ferry service also runs between West Seattle, Southworth, and Vashon Island, and between Edmonds and Kingston.

LAND

Highways and Byways

Washington is among the top ten states in tonnage carried by trucks, and nearly 13,000 trucking companies are located here. Some 3,700 local trucking companies offer interstate shipping.

Three main freeways intersect King County, with many smaller ones feeding these main tributaries: Interstate 5, Interstate 90, and Interstate 405. These are the main arterials for both commercial trucking and commuter transportation. With 1,200 King County Metro buses and 700 vans in the largest vanpool fleet in the nation available to them, numerous commuters take advantage of the region's convenient public transit. A ride-free zone exists in downtown Seattle for convenience and efficiency. For interstate bus travel, bus lines out of Seattle connect with major U.S. cities, Canada, and Mexico.

High Occupancy Vehicle (HOV) lanes are enforced throughout King County. The state's 1991 Commute Trip Reduction law affects workplaces with 100 or more full-time employees who arrive at work between 6:00 a.m. and 9:00 a.m. Participating employers and organizations must develop and implement programs to help simplify the commute. One such effort is the innovative Flexcar program that promotes car sharing. Increasingly, companies encourage telecommuting or subsidize the fees for commuters who use Metro's vanpool program.

As a portal for world trade and access to the lucrative American marketplace, King County has long focused on strengthening its transportation capacities. Sound Transit (Central Puget Sound Regional Transit Authority) has been working with Snohomish and Pierce counties to establish express bus routes within and between the three counties, and commuter rail between Seattle and Tacoma. The connections between bus and rail services aim for networking convenience. Currently, Sounder Transit Express buses carry more than 24,000 passengers every weekday on trans-county routes. Sounder commuter trains carry 12,000 people per week. Long-range goals involve full Sounder commuter rail service between major cities, light-rail lines between urban commuter points, the building of additional transit centers and park-and-ride lots, and easy pedestrian access to all transit hubs.

Pioneer Square Station is part of the Metro bus tunnel system that has provided ease of access for commuters and vastly improved the flow of vehicles in the streets above.

Facilities such as Metro's Bellevue Transit Center make commuting much more convenient.

Courtesy of City of Bellevue

The Seattle Monorail.

An elevated bridge for trains near the Ballard locks draws open and waits for boats to pass beneath it.

Monorail

The Seattle Monorail, a full-scale elevated train, runs along a two-minute, mile-long route from the Seattle Center station to Westlake Center Mall. Built in 1962, the Monorail system includes two original Alweg trains with four cars each. These are the only Alweg trains in operation in the world today. These cars, featuring large, scenic windows and the occasional "train wrap advertising," run on 62 pre-stressed concrete piers that hold the concrete beams and tracks. The trains may run at top speeds of 50 miles per hour (80.5 kilometers/hour), which makes them the fastest full-sized monorail trains in the nation. Seattle voters have approved plans to expand the Monorail by 14 miles to other parts of the city for fast, pollution-free, and scenic commuting.

Railroads

King County receives transcontinental rail service by the Burlington Northern Santa Fe (BNSF) and the Union Pacific Southern Pacific (UPSP) railroads—with double-stack container trains. Existing spur lines enable railroads to deliver nearly any type of load. With over 4,000 miles of track around Washington, goods are moved easily throughout the state and the nation. Passengers may take Amtrak trains to major cities while rapid transit trains move commuters and tourists between points of interest.

AIR

King County International Airport: A Hub for General Aviation

Located just five miles south of Seattle is a 594-acre airport that hosts some 500 aircraft, 150 businesses, and one of the country's premier air and space museums, the Museum of Flight. King County International Airport (KCIA), also known as "Boeing Field," has been serving the local area since 1928 and is one of the busiest airports in the nation, but has often been overshadowed by Sea-Tac International Airport to the south.

KCIA serves commercial and recreational aviation, passenger, and freight transportation. Its 375,000 flights each year involve numerous types of aircraft: recreational airplanes, helicopters, jets, cargo carriers, Boeing planes, military aircraft, and others. The airport's tenants include passenger airlines (Helijet International, North Vancouver Air, and West Isle Air), cargo companies, flight schools, helicopter services, hangar leasing, retail services, and government agencies. Emergency medical flight services are also based here. In addition, educational opportunities for high school and college students are available.

The Montlake Bridge near the University of Washington is a draw bridge that spans the Montlake Cut. The Cut links Lake Washington and Lake Union and is the site for crew races and the Opening Day of Boating Season.

Courtesy of Wyndham Images

Financed by fees paid by those who use the airport, KCIA does not receive any tax dollars for its maintenance or activities. This airport has hosted the President of the United States and Air Force One a number of times, and has received many other dignitaries, too. It recently celebrated its seventy-fifth anniversary with the renovation of its passenger terminal.

Seattle-Tacoma International Airport
Rated one of the top five airports in the nation by the International Airline Passengers Association, and one of the 20 busiest cargo airports, Sea-Tac International Airport accommodates 30 airlines and six cargo-only carriers, services numerous international and domestic destinations, and offers competitive shipping rates. The airport has 40 weekly nonstop flights to Asia and 10 weekly nonstop flights to London. In 2000, more than 28 million passengers and nearly a half-million metric tons of cargo passed through this airport. These figures made Sea-Tac the seventeenth busiest U.S. airport in total annual passengers and the twentieth busiest in take-offs and landings. Three-fourths of the passengers are "origin and destination passengers," meaning they begin or end their trips there.

The Port of Seattle has been working to strengthen and expand the airport with the development of a third runway (to allow for landing at two runways simultaneously in most weather) and additional terminal and air-cargo facilities. These improvements will be completed by 2010. While King County has a number of regional airports and airfields, Sea-Tac is the only commercial airport serving the Seattle area.

OTHER WAYS OF GETTING AROUND
In King County, getting from point A to point B involves some refreshing methods. Bicyclists, unicyclists, tandem cyclists, skateboarders, roller skaters, motorized-scooter riders, and strollers are all in motion around the county. Water taxis cruise Elliott Bay. Private motor- and sailboats are a common sight on lakes and in the Sound. Canoes and kayaks slice through the waters of the region's lakes and rivers. Crew teams practice on Green Lake. Floatplanes, helicopters, custom-built aircraft, and hot-air balloons fill the skies, especially in the summer when Seattle's wet winter weather gives way to blue skies and sunshine.

Courtesy of Wyndham Images

The King County International Airport, also known as Boeing Field, hosts approximately 500 aircraft, 150 businesses, and one of the country's premier air and space museums, the Museum of Flight. The photo at left shows the tail ends of Blue Angel jets that were guests of Boeing Field while performing during SEAFAIR. These planes are acrobatic biplanes.

Courtesy of Wyndham Images

A LOOK AT SEATTLE MARITIME HISTORY: LIGHTBOATS, SUBMARINES, AND YACHTS

Shaping the Land. *While King County is endowed with a variety of natural land formations, its residents have also actively shaped the land for ease of transport. As historians have noted, hills have been lowered, streets regraded, tidal flats filled in, water diverted, and canals dug. A 1910 plan, approved by agreement between the federal, state, and local governments, "called for the lowering of Lake Washington nine feet to the level of Lake Union. The water level in Salmon Bay east of the locks would be raised a like amount. The Cedar River to the Southeast was diverted into Lake Washington so that there would be a continual supply of water to the canal system. The Lake Washington Ship Canal was finally opened for traffic from the salt water to Lake Washington and dedicated in 1917. Four bascule bridges, Ballard, Fremont, University, and later, Montlake, were constructed over the canal. The two high-level bridges came much later." (Puget Sound Maritime Historical Society 21)*

Frontier Seattle opened with wooden side-wheel steamers carrying homesteaders and settlers to this rugged new land. Various steamers would move people and freight (coal and wood) up and down the coast. In addition, boats were used for whaling, seal-hunting, and fishing for salmon, halibut, and many other types of fish. Local shipbuilders created and launched a number of ships for the Navy and area businesses. Fire boats were also created in the late 1800s. The Klondike Gold Rush of 1897-1898 industrialized the Seattle waterfront with the building of "shipyards, foundries, and machine shops." (PSMHS 22)

Courtesy of Wyndham Images

STERN LINE FIRST
FOR
SAFETY FIRST

ERIN NICOLE

SEATTLE WA

GLACIER BAY

The Ballard Locks are among the most popular tourist attractions in the Puget Sound area. Vessels of all sizes, large and small, commercial and pleasure, travel through the locks on a daily basis.

The first steel vessel built on Puget Sound was the United States Revenue Cutter Service (U.S.R.C.S.) tug Golden Gate in 1897, for use in San Francisco Bay. (PSMHS 19) With the nation's entry into WWI in 1917, many more steel-hulled boats began to be built. U.S. Navy boats included cutters with hulls able to withstand ice, deployed for search and rescue missions, medical assistance, the transport of officials, and other naval duties. In 1941, the Seattle-Tacoma Shipbuilding Corporation received a $76 million contract to build 30 C-3 cargo ships. Twenty-five destroyers were already in the works. (Strong 219) In 1913, Moran Shipyard launched the submarine USS H-3. A total of nine submarines were constructed in Seattle before the end of WWI.

The nation's entry into WWII spurred the boat-building industry in new ways. In 1944, two new minesweepers were launched in Puget Sound. Seaplane tenders that serviced Navy seaplanes, used for reconnaissance and rescue, were launched in the early 1940s. (PSMHS 90) Currently, King County shipyards maintain and repair tugs, barges, ferries, and ocean-going ships. New ships are built here too, and launched into the Pacific Ocean.

Pacific Northwesterners have long maintained a love affair with boats, which number one for every five people in the region. The Seattle Yacht Club has hosted the opening day of boating season since 1895 with a parade of private boats, a Coast Guard cutter, and a city fireboat through Portage Bay and into Lake Washington. Sailboats, yachts, and speedboats parade through the Montlake Cut while onlookers watch from the shore and anchored boats. For many residents, the best part of Seafair, an annual festival held in early August, are the hydroplane races on Lake Washington.

A NOAA research vessel cruises past Gasworks Park.

Sailing on Lake Union.

Chapter Four

EDUCATION AND RESEARCH

Since 1910, Swedish has provided the highest quality health care to our community. Today, that commitment extends far beyond the walls of our three campuses through our expansive education and research efforts.

Every year, Swedish offers hundreds of classes to community members and medical professionals and manages a nationally renowned health-education center. In addition, Swedish is a major clinical research site with more than 500 research studies being conducted in areas ranging from perinatal medicine to cardiovascular disease to oncology. Investing I research allows us to give patients access to emerging medical breakthroughs and to improve their quality of life.

100 Words by
Richard H. Peterson
President and Chief Executive Officer
Swedish Medical Center

EDUCATION AND RESEARCH

You are here. . . The school's band is playing loudly. Friends and relatives crowd the stands. Feeling breathless, you are wearing your graduation cap and gown, waiting in the over-heated hall for the ceremony to begin. At last, you march in alongside your fellow classmates. Your professors file in after all the soon-to-be graduates are seated. Their colorful hoods reflect their field of study, their institution of higher learning, and their level of highest degree earned: professional degrees, masters, and doctorates.

You settle in for the commencement speaker who shares life experiences, pieces of wisdom, some jokes, and advice as you go into the working world. Selected students talk of their academic, job, health, and economic struggles during their years of study, and you also hear about their academic achievements: scholarships awarded, internships served, certificates won, and job offers accepted. This day, you will all graduate together.

As you approach the stage, you hear your name called on the loudspeaker. Under the hot stage lights, you see the professional photographers videotaping and digitally photographing the event. The school president smiles, shakes your hand, and gives you your diploma.

After all your friends and peers have also walked across the stage, there is a ceremonial shifting of the tassels on the mortarboards to signify the graduates' change in status. The mortarboards are tossed into the air. Confetti flies. People congratulate each other with thumps on the back, handshakes, joyful tears, and ear-splitting shouts. Balloons are released, and the band strikes up again amidst the cheering of family and friends. Groups separate from the mass to attend the dinner gatherings and parties that follow.

The graduates are stepping forward.

C ommencement represents one of the most significant achievements in formal higher education and, for most, only the beginning in terms of career attainment and contributions. Many of these graduates will return one day to school for additional degrees and further learning.

A full third of Americans have earned undergraduate degrees, and this national passion for education is especially evident in King County. Washington's higher-education institutions grant 50,000 degrees and certificates annually. In the 2000-2001 school year, more than 26,000 associates degrees were earned at the two-year college level; 23,695 four-year bachelor degrees; 7,756 masters; 1,193 professional; and 675 doctorate degrees. ("Key Facts about Higher Education in Washington" 70).

Bike riders take advantage of the pathways throughout the University of Washington.

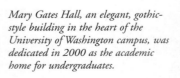

Mary Gates Hall, an elegant, gothic-style building in the heart of the University of Washington campus, was dedicated in 2000 as the academic home for undergraduates.

There are three figures above the west entrance of University of Washington's Suzzallo Library—they are Thought, Inspiration, and Mastery. These figures represent the phases in the way one thinks.

Drumheller Fountain sparkles with Mt. Rainier in the background.

A Long History of Respect for Education

The first school in what is now Washington state opened back in 1832 at Old Fort Vancouver to teach the children of employees of the Hudson's Bay Company. Washington's public school system was started in 1895. The first institution of higher education was Whitman College, a private school founded in 1859.

Education for all has been a central tenet of the state's constitution from the beginning. Article IX of the Washington State Constitution reads: "It is the paramount duty of the state to make ample provision for the education of all children residing within its borders, without distinction or preference on account of race, color, caste, or sex." The framers of the constitution clearly recognized that a strong primary and secondary school education helps to shape cultured citizens and encourage all to achieve their full potential. Higher education has been an important value from the beginning, too. By the time Washington achieved statehood in 1889, the University of Washington (1861), Gonzaga University (1887), and the University of Puget Sound (1888) already existed.

Economic demands on graduates continue to grow. With the globalization of the economy, those who wish to be competitive need cutting-edge knowledge in a variety of fields, transferable skills, high-tech savvy, cooperative teaming skills, and critical thinking abilities. Washington's institutions of higher education have risen to the challenge, offering hundreds of degree programs and proven track records of turning out original thinkers and innovators.

Community Support

Local philanthropists have donated generously to Washington's research universities for new buildings and research centers, libraries, endowments, academic chairs, and student scholarships. Washington families contribute through volunteer hours at the various schools, the Parent-Teacher Associations, fund-raising, and contributions to college savings accounts to the tune of nearly $200 million in 2002.

Research and Industry

Research and development often leads companies and industries to uncharted territories and nearly inconceivable possibilities. Innovations change people's attitudes and expectations, lifestyles, working lives, and the trajectory of the economy. The global ripple effect takes innovations around the world.

This photo of the Alaska-Yukon-Pacific Exposition, held on the University of Washington grounds, was taken from a balloon a quarter of a mile high in 1909.

At National Oceanic and Atmospheric Administration Science Camp at Sand Point on Lake Washington, young minds are introduced to oceanography, *marine biology, marine mammals, weather prediction, oil spill trajectory prediction, nautical charting, and diving operations.*

Courtesy of NOAA

Many of the professors and the students at Washington state universities contribute insights in numerous fields in the arts and sciences. World-class scientists and their graduate students study health issues. Theoretical mathematicians explore the complexities of abstract connections. Biotech experts discover ways to apply biological and other sciences in practical ways.

K-12

Washington has been working to provide over a million youth (ages 6-18) with foundational learning in a safe environment. Overseeing 296 school districts, the Office of Superintendent of Public Instruction (OSPI) is the primary agency responsible for kindergarten through 12th grade education.

In 1993, the state passed the Basic Education Act with four learning goals for all students. The first is for students to read and write with skill and to communicate effectively in a variety of settings. Students need to know and apply the core concepts and principles of mathematics; social, physical, and life sciences; civics and history; geography; arts, and health and fitness. They should think "analytically, logically, and creatively, and [be able] to integrate experience and knowledge" to form reasoned judgments. Lastly, they need to understand the importance of work and how their effort, performance, and decisions will affect their future opportunities. ("Preparing Washington Students for the 21st Century" 21)

The OSPI published a five-year plan to support students' success in academia and in their careers. It encourages the partnering of schools with students, families, and communities to create a "safe, civil, healthy, and engaging environment for learning." The plan spells out the state's commitment to provide sufficient state resources to promote innovation in learning. This educational reform is expected to bring about groundbreaking improvements.

COMMUNITY AND TECHNICAL COLLEGES

The state's 34 community and technical colleges have an excellent reputation of flexibility in offering job training, worker retraining, and high-demand programs, depending on the vicissitudes of the economy. Such institutions are to "offer an open door to every citizen, regardless of his or her academic background or experiences, at a cost normally within his or her economic means," according to state law. [RCW 28B.50.020(1)]. Washington's community and technical college system is the fourth largest in the nation.

According to the Washington State Board for Community & Technical Colleges, "Washington's first junior college was started in 1915 in Everett when 42 students began a one-year college program on the top floor of Everett High School.... Centralia College, the state's oldest existing community college, opened in 1925. It was followed by Skagit Valley College in 1926, Yakima Valley College in 1928, and Grays Harbor College in 1930."

Eleven community colleges serve King County residents: Seattle Central (1966), North Seattle (1970), South Seattle (1970), Seattle Vocational Institute (1987), Shoreline (1964), Bellevue (1966), Highline (1961), Green River (1965), Lake Washington (1949), Renton (1941), and Cascadia (1994). In addition to the community college system, a variety of proprietary schools operate in Washington state. These are privately owned schools that focus on applied skills, such as computer graphics production, real estate, paralegal work, cosmetology, and massage therapy. And since the late 1990s, WashingtonOnline Virtual College has served as a portal for higher education learning via the Internet.

RESEARCH AND COMPREHENSIVE UNIVERSITIES

Washington state spends $6.4 billion every two years on higher education. The nation's sixteenth-largest state, with close to 6 million residents, Washington hosts six public baccalaureate institutions and a number of connected branch campuses. Its foremost research universities are the University of Washington (Seattle) and Washington State University (Pullman); these offer bachelor's to professional degrees. Its comprehensive universities include Central

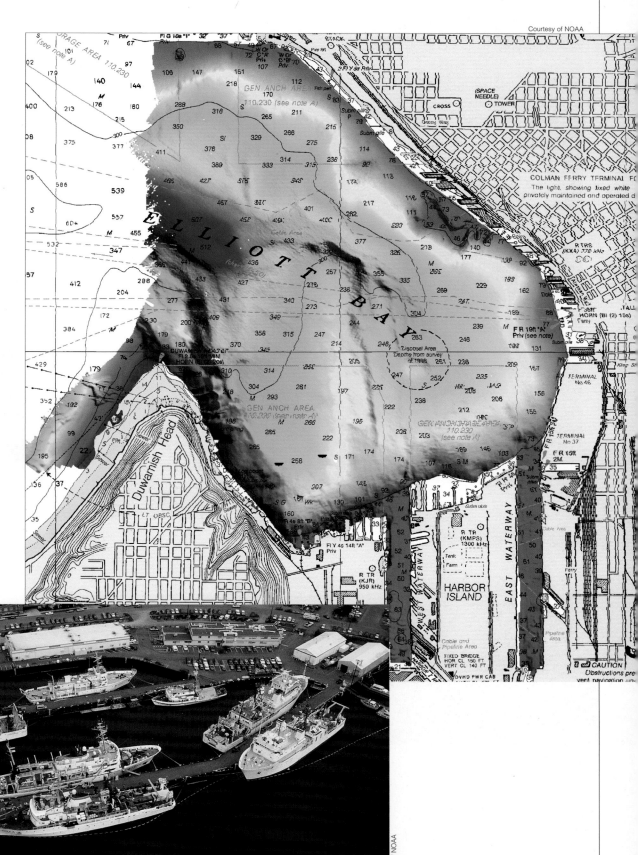

A hydrographic survey of Seattle's Elliott Bay that was conducted by NOAA Ship Rainier.

NOAA Marine Operations Center on Lake Union.

Courtesy of City of Bellevue

Courtesy of City of Bellevue

King County Library's Bellevue branch.

Washington University (Ellensburg), Eastern Washington University (Cheney), The Evergreen State College (Olympia), and Western Washington University (Bellingham); these schools offer baccalaureate and masters-level programs.

Washington's education system not only supplies the region with a well-educated, cutting-edge workforce, it also exports locally educated scholars around the globe. Graduates go into the public, private, and non-profit sectors. Washington schools also work with industry to solve in-field research challenges and questions.

PRIVATE UNIVERSITIES

Private universities serve thousands of local and international students. Seattle University, a prestigious private university, offers under-graduate degrees, masters, and doctorates in law and educational leadership. Seattle Pacific University, a renowned Christian university, also features world-class in-city education. Based in Kenmore, Bastyr University, a world leader in natural health sciences, has trained undergraduate and graduate students for over 25 years. City University, a private non-profit institution of higher education with several branch campuses, offers courses for professionals in career development, networking, and mentorship. Other private institutions focus on art, business, religion, engineering, high technology, video-game production, and other fields of study.

The Northwest has been home to innovators in numerous fields, from high technology to architecture, to biotechnology, to the arts. By fostering open, continual learning and diverse talents, the educational system of this state is building for a fluid future.

WHERE WASHINGTON STATE STUDENTS GO TO LEARN

In 2001, well over 250,000 students attended community and technical colleges; 67,686 attended public research institutions; nearly 43,000 attended independent, four-year institutions (both public and private); and 36,763 attended public comprehensive institutions. The age distribution of students in institutions of higher learning range from 19-year-olds and under to 50-year-olds and above. At public four-year institutions, 70 percent of the students are 24 years old or younger, while 25- to 34-year-olds, 35- to 49-year-olds, and 50-year-olds and above represent the remaining 20 percent, 8 percent, and 2 percent, respectively.

Foreign students have long attended these schools, often on merit scholarships and teaching assistantships. They contribute greatly to the cutting-edge research and discoveries in many fields.

Courtesy of City of Bellevue

Bellevue Community College.

Courtesy of Wyndham Images

Courtesy of Wyndham Images

Drumheller Fountain, in the center of Frosh Pond, was a gift from Regent Joseph Drumheller for the university's centennial in 1961. Originally, the pond was known as Geyser Basin and was a focal point for the Alaska-Yukon-Pacific Exposition in 1909. That same year, it became known as "Frosh Pond" after a group of well-organized sophomores captured a number of less-experienced freshmen and tossed them into Geyser Basin. A legend was born and the landmark has been called Frosh Pond ever since.

SPIRIT OF INQUIRY

The spirit of research—inquiry in a complex universe—drives the ambitious and curious on. At a school the size of the University of Washington, with 41,300 students in 2001 and over 100 departments, research takes many forms. A recent glance at some of the higher profile projects at this venerable institution revealed a new biotechnology center, a $50 million federal grant to explore ways to protect against biological warfare agents and new infectious diseases, and an $8.6 million National Institute of Health grant for the university's Autism Center. Additionally, the university is involved in an international effort to create a network of undersea observatories in the Pacific to study marine mammal populations and earthquakes, an Intelligent Transportation Systems development project (melding electrical, civil, and environmental fields to apply computing and communications technology to travel), and a project with NASA Discovery to send an unmanned mission to capture comet particles.

In fiscal year 2002, the University of Washington brought in over $800 million in sponsored research. Current and emeritus faculty members have included five Nobel laureates, five Lasker Award winners, four Medal of Science recipients, and 37 members of the Institute of Medicine. Research can be arduous and challenging, and often involves years of struggle, with only incremental discoveries, carried out in anonymity. Yet, researchers build on the work of their predecessors and leave a legacy. The University of Washington, a world-caliber research university, draws on this spirit of collaboration and innovation, melding human learning from various fields for applied uses, probing the edges of the unknown, and bringing new findings to light.

Courtesy of Wyndham Images

Chapter Five

THE CITIES

I grew up in Seattle. After living in Utah, Mississippi, Colorado, and California, I came home in 1976 and settled six children and myself in Woodinville, where my community activism blossomed.

With the help of local friends and neighbors, I started a newspaper in my garage—*The Woodinville Weekly*—the first of several. I love my community and became involved in Teen Northshore, The Woodinville Community Band, Woodinville Farmers Market, Annual All Fools Day Parade, Basset Bash, and The Woodinville Wine Festival, and Woodinville Chamber of Commerce.

Community involvement has been the best, most rewarding experience I could have imagined.

100 Words by
Carol Ann Edwards
Publisher
The Woodinville Weekly

THE CITIES

You are here. . . *You are visiting a place of Northwest lore, a town with a romantic name but a gritty past. Your drive takes you 35 miles southeast of Seattle, on two-lane roads past bingo halls and U-pick lavender fields. The welcome sign posted at the city limits reads, "Black Diamond: Village with a View." You note that the town has a community center, library, amphitheatre, fire department, police station, and a couple schools. Businesses include a bow-shooting range, a nursery, a rock quarry, a small bank, a paintball field, an auto body shop, a consignment-clothing store, a bed and breakfast, and mom-and-pop types of shops.*

As you wander through the community, you pick up a bit of history. For example, Black Diamond originated in 1882, a few years after the Black Diamond Coal Company of California discovered a major vein there. At the time, approximately 3,500 people lived in the town, which was the top producer of coal for King County. You learn that after WWI, due to the increased use of oil and electricity in the late 1920s, the mine was shut down, and a new site was mined south of Renton. In 1959, the city was incorporated into King County.

The renovation of historic Black Diamond began, you discover, with the founding of the Black Diamond Historical Society in 1976. In 1982, the Black Diamond Historical Museum opened in the former 1883 Columbia-Puget Sound Line depot. This is your first stop, where you take in exhibits of nineteenth century antique machinery, a Western jail, a replica of a country doctor's office, a coal-mine entrance, and a coal-train car.

After a tour of the museum, you browse through a nearby gift shop then follow your nose to the bakery where an old-style oven is still in use. Along historic Railroad Avenue, you see a sign reading, "Black Diamond 1920 No. 1 1946 Fire Station," posted on a small, graying shack. The Old Town post office sits nearby. A sign on another historic building reads, "Pacific Coast R/R 1916-1951," referring to the train that transported Black Diamond's coal to Seattle.

As you hop in your car to leave, you decide to tour the vicinity. Much of the area around Black Diamond, you realize, is still wooded with giant pines. Its local parks, Flaming Geyser State Park, Green River Gorge Conservation Area, and the Kanaskat/Palmer Recreation Area, are set in lush, wooded wilderness. Lake Marjorie, Lake Sawyer, Mud Lake, Jones Lake, and Black Diamond Lake are located in or near Black Diamond, and Rock Creek and the Green River run through the town.

Black Diamond's sign welcoming newcomers to the city is actually a coal car filled with coal.

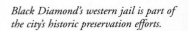

Black Diamond's western jail is part of the city's historic preservation efforts.

Carillon Point, located on the shores of Lake Washington in Kirkland, is home to a marina, a luxury hotel, several restaurants, a variety of retail stores, and office space.

Sunset at Meydenbauer Beach Park.

Photo by Somaly Hoy

The 39 incorporated cities of King County embody the strengths of specialization and the local flavors. With 2,128 square miles (3,424.70 sq. km.) of landmass, King County has a population of approximately 1.7 million people, according to the U.S. Census Bureau's 2000 report. It serves as the engine for economic development of the state, with its high concentration of companies, industries, and workers. The median household income in King County is $53,300.

NORTH END

Bothell (1909)—Originally a logging and farming town, Bothell has become a hub for biotechnology firms, high technology parks, and the state's 34th and newest community college, Cascadia Community College (co-located with the University of Washington's Bothell branch). Half of Bothell lies in King County, and the other half in Snohomish County. Its total population was 30,470 in 2001.

Lake Forest Park (1961)—This wooded city at the north end of Lake Washington had a population of 12,860 in 2002, with a majority working in finance/services, retail, government, and construction. The Great Harvest Bread Company, Shoreline School District, and a variety of shops are located in this municipality, with many clustered around the Lake Forest Park Towne Center.

Shoreline (1995)—This young and growing city lies in the northwestern part of King County. With a population of 53,250 (2002), its main industries include finance/services, retail, government, and wholesale/utilities. Shoreline Community College, the Shoreline School District, Sears, GTE Northwest, Pan Pacific Development, and Crista Ministries are the main employers in this area.

Skykomish (1909)—Located in the far northeast corner of King County, Skykomish is a rural town with 215 residents in 2002. Its citizens work in retail and government. The Skykomish Historic Commercial District showcases this historic railroad community, with buildings dating from the late 1890s and early 1900s.

Woodinville (1993)—This city is home to well-known wineries and ale breweries set alongside the scenic Sammamish River. Its citizens work in manufacturing, construction, finance/services, and retail. One of the newer cities in King County, it features new homes situated in a laid-back rural environment.

The Historic Train Station in Issaquah is part of the city's efforts to preserve its heritage.

Courtesy of City of Issaquah

EASTSIDE

Beaux Arts Village (1908)—In 2002, only 295 residents lived in this exclusive 51-acre enclave of lakeside homes. Located on wooded land along Lake Washington, this former art colony was started by members of the Society of Beaux Arts, "a school of every art and craft." It's the smallest town in King County and often is not included on maps.

Bellevue (1953)—With 117,000 residents in 2002, Bellevue is the fifth most populous city in the state. It serves as the financial, retail, arts, and business center of the Eastside. Microsoft, The Boeing Company, and numerous other businesses have offices here. A majority of residents work in finance/services, retail, wholesale/utilities, and manufacturing, according to the Economic Development Council of Seattle & King County (EDC). Notable places to visit include the Bellevue Art Museum and Bellevue Botanical Garden. Bellevue has had sister-city relationships with Yao, Japan; Hualien, Taiwan; Liepaja, Latvia; and Kladno, Czech Republic.

Carnation (1951)—This former dairy town was originally incorporated as "Tolt" in 1912. Located between the Tolt and Snoqualmie rivers in the lush Snoqualmie Valley, Carnation has 4,397 residents (2002), most of whom are engaged in government work, or the manufacturing and service industries.

Clyde Hill (1953)—This city of 667 acres includes some of the most elegant homes in King County. A majority of its 2,895 residents (2002) hold bachelor's degrees and a full third have masters and/or professional degrees.

Duvall (1913)—Founded by James Duvall, this city located in the northeast corner of King County offers idyllic, pastoral views. Its 5,190 residents (2002) work in finance/services, retail, and government jobs.

Hunts Point (1955)—Hunts Point lays claim to some of the area's most stately homes. In 2002, over 450 residents called Hunts Point home.

Issaquah (1892)—Due east of the Cougar Mountain Wildlife Park, Issaquah has grown significantly in recent years because of its prime location on the Interstate 90 business corridor. Home to Boeing Computer Services; Price/Costco, Inc.; and Zetec, Issaquah had a population of 13,790 in 2002. That number is expected to grow exponentially with the expansion of local high-tech companies. Issaquah celebrates its unique Salmon Days Festival to honor the return of spawning salmon. Attractions include mountain trails and state parks, a zoo, and the boutiques and specialty shops at Gilman Village.

Kenmore (1998)—One of the newer cities to be incorporated into King County, Kenmore lies at the north end of Lake Washington. In 2002, more than 19,000 residents lived in Kenmore, and a majority worked in finance/services and retail. This city has many beautiful parks, like St. Edward State Park, Moorland Park, and the Kenmore Rhododendron Park.

Kirkland (1905)—Just 15 minutes from Seattle or Bellevue, this Eastside city combines corporate headquarters with light manufacturing and high-tech businesses. It is the second-largest city on the Eastside, with a population of 45,790 in 2002. Art galleries, upscale boutiques, and restaurants dot its six miles of Lake Washington shoreline. Totem Lake Mall, the Woodmark Hotel, and Evergreen Hospital are located here. Residents work in finance/services, wholesale/utilities, retail, and government.

Piper's Creek in Carkeek Park.

*The masts of sailboats rise from a
marina at Lake Union.*

Sailing on Lake Washington.

As one seaplane lands, another takes off from Lake Union.

Courtesy of Wyndham Images

Courtesy of Wyndham Images

Medina (1955)—Surrounded on three sides by Lake Washington, this exclusive neighborhood's most well-known citizen must be Bill Gates, co-founder of Microsoft and the world's richest man. With a population of 3,010 in 2002, Medina's citizens mostly work in finance/services and government. This area was first settled in 1891.

Mercer Island (1960)—With a population of 22,036 in 2000, this six-mile-long island city offers the best of suburban living, with modern housing, a peaceful community, and easy access to the state's two main interstate highways. The island was named after one of the three Mercer brothers (Thomas, Asa, or Aaron), but historians are unsure which.

Newcastle (1994)—This municipality, formerly incorporated as Newport Hills in 1994, is located on the Eastside, north of Renton and east of Mercer Island. Its 8,205 residents (2002) work in finance/services, retail, government, and wholesale/utilities. Major employers include Valley Medical Center, Bartells, and Mutual Materials.

North Bend (1909)—Situated at the east end of King County, North Bend is named for its location where the South Fork River bends toward the north. In 1889, the town was known as Snoqualmie, and later as Mountain View, before being renamed North Bend. It serves as a gateway to Snoqualmie Pass's nature trails, camping, skiing, and sightseeing. Its 4,735 residents (2002) work in retail, finance, and government jobs. Major employers in the city include Factory Source of America, Nintendo, and Thriftway.

Redmond (1912)—This Eastside city was put on the international map by Microsoft Corporation. Other major companies hailing from Redmond include Nintendo of America, Inc.; RAF Technology; and Primex Aerospace Co. Its 46,040 residents (2002) work in high-tech, finance/services, manufacturing, retail, and wholesale/utilities. Once an agricultural and logging town, Redmond now boasts an economy based on high-tech innovation.

Earthworks Park, located on Kent's Scenic Hill, is an award-winning combination of passive park and aquifer recharge area.

Courtesy of City of Kent

Renton (1901)—The sixth-largest city in King County with 53,840 residents (2002), Renton is where Boeing's 737 and 757 aircrafts are built. The Boeing Company is the city's main employer. IKEA, Valley Medical Center, PACCAR, and ER Solutions, Inc., are other large employers. Most jobs are in manufacturing, finance/services, retail, and government.

Sammamish (1999)—The newest incorporated city of King County lies on the eastern shore of Lake Sammamish. Many of its residents work in the Eastside's high-tech industry. In 2002, 34,660 called Sammamish home. The main employers here are retail, finance/services, government, and wholesale/utilities.

Courtesy of Wyndham Images

This horse and rider fly through an equestrian event, which took place in Marymoor Park, Redmond.

Snoqualmie (1903)—This former timber town on the prairie lies 30 miles east of Seattle at the foot of the Cascade mountain range. Locals and travelers alike visit Snoqualmie to see the spectacular Snoqualmie Falls, where the Snoqualmie River cascades 268 feet. Photographers, skiers, tourists, and extreme cyclists enjoy the area for its scenery and access to outdoor activities. Major employers include the City, its school district, Salish Lodge, and Weyerhaeuser Company. Snoqualmie's population was 4,210 in 2002. Its major businesses are in the finance/services, government, retail, and manufacturing sectors.

Yarrow Point (1959)—In 2000, just over 1,000 people lived in this exclusive community on a narrow peninsula west of Bellevue. The area, which is known for its scenic views, was first homesteaded in the 1880s.

WESTSIDE

Seattle (1865)—Seattle is the oldest and largest city in King County. It is the hub of international trade, with a worldwide reputation as an end-destination for tourists. It has a strong economic base with major companies and institutions such as The Boeing Company, Port of Seattle, University of Washington, and others. In 2002, Seattle had 570,800 residents—with a majority working in finance/services, government, retail, wholesale/utilities, manufacturing, and construction. (Please see the above section for more details.)

SOUTH END

Algona (1955)—This city, located near the Pierce County line, surrounds a noted wetland. Its main economy involves manufacturing. In 2002, it had approximately 2,500 residents.

Auburn (1891)—Auburn is a center for shopping, with its Supermall of the Great Northwest. It is also the home of the Emerald Downs Thoroughbred Racetrack, popular among horseracing fans. Many of its citizens work in manufacturing, finance, and the service industry. In 2003, Auburn's residents numbered about 44,000.

Black Diamond (1959)—This former mining town of "black gold" or "black diamonds" had a population of 4,015 in 2002. Most residents are employed in government, construction, and retail work. Black Diamond offers camping opportunities at the Flaming Geyser Recreation Area, Kanaskat/ Palmer State Park, and Nolte State Park. Interestingly, a small amount of coal is still being mined here.

Fishing in Phantom Lake, Bellevue.

View of the Space Needle, downtown Seattle, and Mt. Rainier.

The arches of the Pacific Science Center, Seattle.

Burien (1993)—The number of Burien residents in 2003 was 31,810. This city is home to Highline Community Hospital, a farmers market, and various shopping outlets.

Covington (1997)—This recently incorporated city in southeastern King County has 14,395 residents (2002), who primarily work in retail, finance/services, and government. Its vision is to create a city that is "family-oriented, safe and pedestrian-friendly" and which celebrates its "small town character and natural environment."

Des Moines (1959)—The city of Des Moines, which lies directly south of Sea-Tac International Airport, features a 900-slip marina. Located on the eastern shore of Puget Sound, with six miles of shoreline, Des Moines boasts several waterfront parks and a popular boardwalk. Highline Community College and a variety of senior care facilities are located here. In 2002, Des Moines had 29,510 residents who mostly worked in finance/services, government, and retail.

Enumclaw (1913)—This town was named "Enumclaw"–meaning "strong wind" or "thundering noise"–by a group of Native Americans who camped nearby and were buffeted by strong winds that kept them awake. Homesteaded in 1879, Enumclaw stands at the foothills of the singular and awe-inspiring Mt. Rainier. Its 11,195 residents (2002) work in finance/services, retail, and government. Major employers in the area include Weyerhaeuser Company, Fugate Ford/Mazda, and city offices.

Federal Way (1990)—This city's name comes from the federal highway that was built through the region in 1929. As one of the state's largest cities, Federal Way had 83,850 residents in 2002, making it the most populous city in south King County. Centrally located to Interstate 5 and highways 18, 99, 161, and 509, this city offers easy access to the ports of Tacoma and Seattle, as well as to Sea-Tac International Airport. Sears, St. Francis Community Hospital, DeVry University Seattle, and World Vision are all located here. Attractions include Dash Point State Park, Pacific Rim Bonsai Collection, Rhododendron Species Botanical Garden, and West Hylebos Wetlands State Park.

Kent (1890)—Kent's economy has evolved from farm- and light industry-centered to one of the largest warehouse, distribution, and manufacturing centers in North America. (EDC) With 84,275 residents in 2002, this city ranks as the seventh largest in the state. Its business-friendly reputation is enhanced by having no Business & Occupations tax. The Boeing Defense and Space Group, Mikron, Recreational Equipment Inc., and the Starbucks coffee roasting plant are located in Kent. Its residents work in manufacturing and whole-sale/utilities, as well as finance/services and retail.

Maple Valley (1997)—This up-and-coming city of 15,040 residents (2002) revels in its rural lifestyle. Its proximity to Mt. Rainier gives Maple Valley residents easy access to Mt. Rainier National Park. In addition, the city's Lake Wilderness Park offers canoeing, fishing, baseball, tennis, and swimming. The Cedar River runs through the city, and hiking, cycling, and horseback riding along its banks is popular. Maple Valley's workforce is employed in retail, finance/services, and government positions.

Due to its temperate climate, the Puget Sound region is ideally suited to rhododendrons. They are the heralds of spring, and one can count on seeing different bushes blooming from March through June, depending on the variety.

Milton (1907)—A third of this city is within King County, and two-thirds lies in Pierce County. In 2000, over 800 residents lived in the King County section. Residents in both counties numbered 5,820 in 2001.

Normandy Park (1953)—This "Wonderful World of Woods and Water" in southwestern King County began as a planned residential community on Puget Sound. The Seattle-Tacoma Land Company initiated the project in the 1920s, and homes in the city still reflect the distinctive French Normandy style popular then. In 2002, Normandy Park had a population of 6,395.

Pacific (1909)—Crossing both King and Pierce counties, Pacific has a population of 5,405 living in King County (2002). Its citizens work in government, manufacturing, wholesale/utilities, and finance/services. Major employers include the City of Pacific, trucking companies, homebuilders, and the Webstone Water District.

SeaTac (1990)—As the home of the Seattle-Tacoma International Airport, Sea-Tac features world-class hotels and hospitality services for business travelers, tourists, and convention attendees. Its 25,320 residents (2002) work in wholesale/utilities, finance/services, retail, and government jobs.

Tukwila (1908)—Tukwila is a major retail and manufacturing center at the southern junction of Interstates 5 and 405. Major employers here include The Boeing Company, Metro Transit, Bon-Macy's, Tukwila Warehousing, and Kenworth Trucking. Tukwila's Southcenter Mall draws shoppers from throughout the region. In 2002, well over 17,000 people resided in Tukwila, which has had a sister-city relationship with Ikawa-Cho, Japan, for many years.

*An aerial of the Cedar River Watershed,
the source of Seattle's drinking water.*

These interesting characters from the mural across the street seem to have taken a table at their favorite trattoria in Seattle. There is a seat waiting at the counter for them.

Photo by Cindy Cooke

Photo by Cindy Cooke

Pike Place Market is a huge tourist draw for downtown Seattle, but it is also where people do their day-to-day shopping for the freshest fruit, vegetables, meats, and fish.

SEATTLE NEIGHBORHOODS

Within Seattle lie many evocative neighborhoods. A former mill town, Fremont (the self-declared Center of the Universe) has been remade with its high-tech businesses (such as Adobe), outdoor art (its troll under the Aurora Bridge, the "Waiting for the Interurban" sculpture, the seven-ton Lenin statue from Slovakia), and its esoteric, funky neighborhood culture. Ballard, incorporated by Captain William Ballard in 1888, originated with a strong Norwegian community. It hosts the Nordic Heritage Museum and a parade on Syttende Mai (May 17), Norway's Constitution Day. Wallingford is an easy stroll from the University of Washington, with its mix of intellectuals, students, scientists, researchers, and artists. Duwamish, with its metalwork artisans, interior designers, and day laborers, features manufacturing and heavy industry.

The downtown core offers world-class art, performances, dining experiences, and a vivid nightlife. Belltown features trendy clubs and boutiques. Pioneer Square showcases antiques stores, art galleries, and nightclubs. Visitors may explore the Underground Tour and Klondike Goldrush National Historical Park in this neighborhood. Phinney Ridge boasts the 92-acre Woodland Park Zoo with its renowned horticultural collection and state-of-the-art natural exhibits.

The Seattle waterfront includes Pike Place Market, a Soviet submarine, the Seattle Aquarium, island-hopping ferry rides throughout the Sound, luxury ship tours, whale-watching excursions, and dining cruises. The Seattle IMAX® Dome shows films on a 180-degree domed screen for an exciting film experience.

Some of the older, more upscale neighborhoods of Seattle include Laurelhurst, Madison Park, Magnolia, Montlake, Windermere, and the historic Queen Anne Hill.

Seattle's neighborhoods are a mixture of settler moxie, planned growth and development, happenstance, and foresight. Its residents, informed and passionate, participate in neighborhood and regional governance to help shape their collective futures.

Chapter Six

Sports and The Great Out[door]

On this last day of school, Liberty High School stude[nts]
tions are abuzz with summer plans. As the school's pr[incipal]
glad that besides summer jobs, they are making time [to]
ski, ride horses, attend camps, hike, camp, boat—eve[n]
the sunshine at home. Our students in King County [are fortunate]
to have easy access to activities that keep their bodies [strong and]
their minds quick. The link between healthy mind an[d]
body is obvious to those of us who work in schools a[nd want our]
students to grow strong mentally, physically, socially,

100 Words by
Kevin Davis
Principal
Liberty High School

SPORTS AND THE GREAT OUTDOORS

You are here. . . *As the massive machine glides quietly over the rink at Key Arena, the ice smoothes out and turns transparent. While courtside at a Seattle Thunderbirds game, you scan your fellow spectators that have all but settled into the inner and upper bowls of the stadium. Flaunting their Thunderbirds green, blue, and white jerseys, fans clutch their hot dogs, candies, sodas, and nachos and look to the ice in anticipation. The referees speed onto the ice and circle the rink before the teams emerge in their bulky gear. After live performances of the anthems for the American team and their Canadian challengers, you brace yourself for a heart-stopping game.*

The puck is dropped, and the teams go at it with ferocity. Combining the grace of ice skaters with the aggression of football players, the teams maneuver the puck with finesse and brute strength. One moment, the T-birds are on the offensive, and a split second later it's all about protecting the goal. The hockey players smack the puck against the glass walls surrounding the rink or the rim, so it skitters harmlessly past the goal and to the waiting scoop of a teammate's blade. The goaltenders take on defensive postures in front of their cages as the puck whizzes by. A red light and buzzer signal a successful score.

The hockey players smack full bore into opposing team members as they hustle for the puck. Occasionally, fights erupt and the players throw off their helmets and gloves and go at it bare-fisted. The refs stand back until the fighters have exhausted some of their steam, and then order the players involved to leave the ice for a forced time-out. The fans erupt into cheers and shouts when a breathtaking play is made or when a thunderous crash occurs on the glass. All is constant motion, speed, and grace, a kaleidoscope of patterns, and colors, and noise, until the final buzzer sounds.

B reath comes in jagged intervals. The jogger's heart is pounding, and a heat flush rides high around his eyes. Sweat cools his forehead as the ache begins in his calves and moves up to his thighs and upper arms. Athletics in the Pacific Northwest is not just about vicarious thrills via spectator sports. It is about "personal bests" at the track meet. It is about the day-in-day-out discipline to train in the off-season for the explosive, graceful, or nuanced performance during competition.

It is about teamwork—knowing one's peers well enough to read their movements, understand their strengths and weaknesses, enhance their skills, and cover their flaws. It is about team spirit and loyalty to

Courtesy of City of Seattle, Photo by Ian Edelstein

Ichiro at bat in Safeco Field.

Courtesy of City of Seattle, Photo by Erik Stuhaug

Safeco Field with Qwest Field immediately behind.

Kayakers paddle in Lake Union.

Courtesy of Wyndham Images

SEAFAIR Archive

*Spectators enjoy the hydroplane race and
air show on the SEAFAIR Logboom.*

your local sports heroes. It is about high sportsmanship—ethical play, physical sweat and preparation, intense mental focus, and respecting others and oneself. It is about celebrating human potential and ambition, athletic grace and form, the love of the game and its heroes and heroines (and champions-in-the-making). It is about the will to win . . . fairly.

COMMUNITY SPORTS

King County not only has professional basketball, football, baseball, soccer and hockey teams, it also has college teams, high school teams, and training camps for youth. These teams engender as much passion as the fevered stadium games of the athletes in the big leagues. Fans dress in school colors, they paint their faces, and they arrive ready to cheer their teams on to victory.

Community centers offer classes in more traditional fields, such as dance, karate, and gymnastics. They also host community teams for children and adults who share a love of organized sports or intramural games like flag football. Community-sponsored, star-studded athletic camps bring out the limos, sports icons, photo opportunities, and free jerseys and sports gear for the up-and-coming youngsters. Non-traditional games are also popular with locals—activities like disk golf, geocaching ("trinket" treasure hunts in mountain locations based on GPS-readings), and fusions of dance and martial arts. King County's geography and weather allow for creative mixes of athletics and recreational pleasure.

FOR ALL SEASONS

Seattle Mariners—Seattle had a minor-league baseball team, the Seattle Rainiers of the Pacific Coast League, for years until 1968 when the Pilots franchise joined the American League. The Pilots lasted for a season and then dissolved due to financial challenges. Then, in February 1976, the Seattle Mariners franchise joined the American League.

In 1977, the Seattle Mariners professional baseball team was established, but it took 15 years to post their first winning season. In 1995, the team won its first AL West title, and since then has had its sights set on a World Series championship. The Mariners, with their charismatic lineup that includes Ichiro Suzuki, one of the most recognizable players in major-league baseball today, have drawn fans from all around the world.

Courtesy of Wyndham Images

Windsurfers breeze across the shimmering waters of the many lakes in King County.

Seahawks Stadium, now known as Qwest Field is the exciting new venue for the Seattle Seahawks.

Courtesy of Wyndham Images

For 13 years, the Mariners played in the Kingdome, the American League's first indoor stadium, which was imploded in 2000. That same year, the Mariners began playing out of Safeco Field, or "The Safe" (2000), with its signature retractable roof and local sculptor Gerard Tsutakawa's glove sculpture.

Seattle SuperSonics

The Seattle SuperSonics (1967), a National Basketball Association team, plays in the Key Arena ("The Key") at the Seattle Center. The team selected its name through a public contest that resulted in over 25,000 submissions. More than 200 submittals were for the "SuperSonics," named after a proposed plane by The Boeing Company, the SuperSonic Transport.

The team, which made the NBA playoffs for its first time in 1974, has turned out a number of major superstars—"Downtown" Freddie Brown, Jack Sikma, Gary Payton, Nate McMillan, and Lenny Wilkins among them. This team has inspired generations of basketball players, from young school-yard players to the pros. Squatch, the Sonics' mascot (a Sasquatch who hails from the Cascade Mountains), entertains the fans with his acrobatic dunks and crowd-pleasing antics.

Seattle Sounders

The Seattle Sounders originated in 1974 as a North American Soccer League expansion team, first playing out of Memorial Stadium at the Seattle Center and later in the larger Kingdome because of sell-out crowds. In 1977, the team advanced to the North American Soccer League Soccer Bowl championship, where they lost to the New York Cosmos 2-1. In 1980, they achieved a team-best record of 25 wins and seven losses. In 1982, they again played for the NASL championship but were denied once again by the Cosmos, this time by a score of 1-0. The team was sold in 1983 and folded shortly thereafter. In 1994, the Seattle Sounders were brought back as an A-League team, and in 1995 captured the league championship. In 2002, the team moved into its new home at Qwest Field and again won the regular season A-League Championship.

Seattle Seahawks

The Seattle Seahawks (1976), of the National Football League, began their 2003-2004 season at the new Qwest Field (2002). With a 67,000-seat capacity, Qwest Field lends a distinctive touch to the Seattle skyline.

Seahawks admirers dress in their Hawks gear—their greens, blues and whites—to show their team spirit. They yell and cheer from the seats at particularly skillful plays. They follow their favorite team members' statistics and public lives. Children may rally the team along with Blitz T. Seahawk, the team's bird mascot. In fact, the Seattle fans have contributed so much to the team in terms of loyalty and spirit that collectively they have been dubbed "the twelfth man." In honor of the twelfth man, the Seahawks retired the number 12 in 1984.

Seattle Thunderbirds

Starting out as the Seattle Breakers in the Western Hockey League in 1977, the Seattle Thunderbirds changed their name in the 1985-86 season. In 1997, the team won the WHL's Western Conference Championship, and in 2003 the T-birds won their first U.S. Division Championship. The team posted its best regular season record in 1989-90 with 52 wins. Each season during the past 10 of 11 years, the T-birds have attracted more than 200,000 fans. Playing out of the Key Arena at the Seattle Center, the Seattle Thunderbirds maintain a busy year-round season. The faithful hometown crowd rallies around their T-birds, with the help of team mascot, Cool Bird.

The Junior SeaGals ready a cheer for the fans at the Seattle Center.

Courtesy of Wyndham Images

Courtesy of City of Seattle, Photo by Ian Edelstein

The Seattle Seahawks take on the Kansas City Chiefs.

Golf courses have become more and more prevalent in King County and throughout the Puget Sound region. From the Cascade foothills area of Snoqualmie to the urban area of Bellevue, from municipal courses to country club venues, the region offers a challenge for every golfing preference.

Courtesy of Wyndham Images

Courtesy of City of Bellevue

Several sailboats take a turn during a regatta on Lake Washington.

Courtesy of Wyndham Images

Seattle Storm

The Seattle Storm franchise started when the Women's National Basketball Association selected it as one of four expansion teams to begin play in the 2000 season. Just two years later, in the 2002 season, this young team made the playoffs.

The Storm has brought great pride to Washington with their "Bring it" attitude and history-making performance. Doppler, the team's furry mascot, entertains the rapidly growing crowds of loyal Storm fans. The popular team is led by three-time Olympian Ann Donovan, who in 2003 picked up where Linn Dunn, the team's highly respected first coach, left off. Among the Storm's standout players is Sue Bird, a point guard who is arguably one of the best players in the WNBA today.

AT HOME IN THE OUTDOORS

Residents can take their pick of recreational sports and fitness activities. Tennis courts, indoor and outdoor, abound. There are dozens of golf courses with lush greens and clubhouse amenities. The Emerald Downs Racetrack in Auburn beckons thoroughbred horseracing fans from throughout the region. Pacific Raceways in Kent, formerly the Seattle International Raceway, draws fans of drag racing, motocross, hotrod racing, and other motor sports to its 2.25-mile course. On local lakes, Northwesterners water-ski, jet-ski, wakeboard, and wind-surf. For water polo, swimming, and aquacise classes, Bellevue Aquatic Center and Weyerhaeuser King County Aquatic Center are two notable facilities among many, in addition to the popular salt-water pool in West Seattle's Lincoln Park.

For many King County residents, off-work hours mean time to explore the great outdoors—rock climbing, scuba diving in area lakes and Puget Sound, extreme cycling, hiking, golfing, camping, and myriad other outdoor activities. With its many green spaces and waterways, lush woodlands and public beaches, King County offers numerous places to recreate and relax. The Cascade and Olympic Peninsula mountains are only a short drive or ferry ride away.

Fall is a popular time for camping. In the winter, snowboarders and skiers enjoy the local mountains, as do snowshoers, cross-country skiers, and snowmobilers. In spring, white-water rafters, mountain climbers, wind surfers, canoeists, and kayakers take on the water and the rock. Local rivers and lakes beckon outdoor enthusiasts for sport fishing and fly-fishing during the fishing season and other recreation during the off-season. In the summer, residents head to their cabins

for communing with nature and relaxing with friends and family. They may hike the local trails with camping gear in tow, or bicycle along paved trails, or go extreme cycling in the mountains.

One historian compares the characteristics of this region to the rugged people who live here. "The landforms of the Pacific Northwest are not matters just of geology and real estate but also of aesthetics and culture. The most repetitive theme in the region's literature is the interaction of people and their natural environment; much of the region's history is played out against a backdrop of dramatic landforms. Not surprisingly, Pacific Northwesterners commonly [translate] their sense of place into a belief that natural environment determined the types of people who settled Oregon, Washington, and Idaho. Rugged mountains and gargantuan trees called forth strong-willed, self-reliant individuals to match them, or so Northwesterners have often claimed." (Schwantes 6)

Whether the land made the people, or the people attracted to the land were of a hardy type, Pacific Northwesterners work hard and play harder.

*Kayaking beside the Burke Gilman/
Sammamish River Trail. The trail ends
along the side of Marymoor Park.*

Courtesy of Wyndham Images

*A climber scales the challenging
climbing facility at Marymoor Park
in Redmond.*

Courtesy of Wyndham Images

The windmill is a landmark at Marymoor Park.

Courtesy of Wyndham Images

RIDING THE BURKE-GILMAN/SAMMAMISH RIVER TRAIL

One of the most common sights on King County streets is that of cyclists—commuters, bicycle messengers weaving through downtown traffic, friends tandem-cycling, or students with their helmets and backpacks. With the popularity of cycling, most residents have eagerly supported the development and maintenance of special bike trails throughout the area.

The Burke-Gilman/Sammamish River Trail (1978) begins humbly enough at the railroad tracks and business yards of Ballard. It curves past Gasworks Park, the University of Washington's main campus, and Matthews Beach Park. Hugging Lake Washington's northwestern edge, it wends its way to Tracy Owen Station Park, through Blyth Park in Bothell (where it becomes the Sammamish River Trail), then to Woodinville's Jerry Wilmot Park, Sixty Acres Park, and finally to Marymoor Park, 27 miles later, in Redmond.

The paved path and gentle grade offer many pleasures for a day ride. The trail captures some of the most memorable sights of King County: a weeping willow beside a bridge, streams, golden fields, lakeshore beaches, waterfront homes, and expansive parks. The trail also winds through wetlands, a natural resource protected by Seattle Parks and Recreation and the Seattle Department of Transportation.

The Burke-Gilman/Sammamish River Trail is only one of dozens in King County totaling over 100 miles of paved and 70 miles of unpaved trails for bicycling, roller-blading, horseback riding, and hiking. An estimated 750,000 people use the Burke-Gilman Trail each year. An extension with both pedestrian and bicycle corridors is planned from Ballard to Golden Gardens Park on Puget Sound.

King County delights
guished arts organizat
dance, and the visual
our vibrant economy,
celebrating the achiev
and future.

The arts are of vita
beyond ourselves, to u
cultures throughout ti
sorrows, our dreams a
natural beauty are co-

100 Words by
Mimi Gardner Gates
Director
Seattle Art Museum

THE ARTS

You are here. . . *Seated in the front row at a performance of the Seattle Symphony, your sense of anticipation has been excited by the pre-show demonstrations and exhibits. A cellist warms up on stage, and several in the horn section are clearing their pipes. Dressed in their formal best, the musicians take their places. A hush ripples through the music hall. The conductor steps on stage to applause. He says a few words to the audience, and then turns to the symphony. The houselights go down, and the performance begins.*

Fast forward. . . *you mingle with the other guests at the elegant opening of an art exhibit. The walls are hung with watercolors and sumi ink paintings on paper. Some of the colors on the ink paintings are laid on with lotus roots and drips reminiscent of Jackson Pollock. The Francine Seders Art Gallery, which hosts the exhibit, is in a large home fitted with gallery lights. Browsers and friends of the artist circulate the room and comment on the various pieces. "What do you think of this piece?" "Doesn't this remind you of rain in Seattle?" "Why would the artist name this piece, 'When Seeds Get Together'"?*

Fast forward. . . *the University Book Store is crowded with dozens and dozens of patrons as you shoulder your way past them to grab the last empty seat. The author is introduced and you clap with generous enthusiasm, along with everyone else. She approaches the microphone and stands under the spotlight. Before reading from her works, she opens each section with personal anecdotes. Afterwards, a line of eager fans forms around the author. You are breathless with excitement as the author signs her new book (the one you have been eagerly clutching all evening) and exchanges a few words with you, further drawing you into her world of literature and ideas.*

Fast forward. . . *the morning sun begins to warm the cool bay air as you take a lazy stroll in downtown Seattle. You hear the strum and song of a guitarist that performs for a small crowd. A mime follows amused tourists in a merry dance. Plastered on the walls and telephone poles around you are posters of current events—concerts, plays, lectures, dance performances, and films. As you meander through the streets and parks of the city, you encounter some of the county's 1,000-piece public art collection. Indeed, the numerous sculptures, fountains, paintings, gardens, earthworks, murals, and mixed-media artworks add up to one piece of public art for every two square miles in King County.*

You are here. . . *living the art.*

Carrie Imler in Carmen.

Ariana Lallone and Jeffrey Stanton in Lambarena.

Music Director Gerard Schwarz
leads the Seattle Symphony on stage at
Benaroya Hall under the looming
presence of the Watjen Concert Organ.

Courtesy of Seattle Symphony; Photo by Fred Housel

Courtesy of Seattle Symphony; Photo by Fred Housel

At dusk, the luminous beauty of
Benaroya Hall is caught in
glowing pink/red tones of a Pacific
Northwest sunset.

A local culture that values and nurtures art has fostered the growth of numerous world-class artists, including glassblowers, painters, sculptors, and architects. Well-known actors, cartoonists, writers, and poets have also hailed from the Pacific Northwest. Art and sculpture walks, many hosted by local galleries, are available in a number of local cities, neighborhoods, and public parks. The Metro Bus Shelter Mural Program has produced vivid, multi-cultural street art, while Metro buses and the Westlake Center Bus Tunnel feature the poetry and art of locals. Neobohemia lives on in Belltown, Pioneer Square, Capitol Hill, artists' lofts, caffeine-fueled cafés, and clubs throughout Seattle. Musicians perform on their own live Web sites that offer song lyrics, digital poses, and streaming video of concerts.

THE MUSIC SCENE

This $240 million Experience Music Project, commonly referred to as the EMP, opened in 2000 to worldwide attention for architect Frank Gehry's take on the fluidity and unpredictable wildness of music: a building of colorful metals and undulating design. There, too, was the brash vision of billionaire philanthropist Paul Allen who, in tribute to the late Seattle guitarist Jimi Hendrix, created this multimedia wonderland, complete with a Sky Church, interactive displays, and techno-modern installations.

As one of the leading opera companies in the nation, Seattle Opera (1963) has been delighting audiences for generations. Its 2003-2004 season inaugurated the new Marion Oliver McCaw Hall with Wagner's *Parsifal*. The season also included Levy's *Mourning Becomes Electra*, Bizet's *Carmen*, R. Strauss' *Ariadne auf Naxos*, and Puccini's *Fanciulla del West*. Pre-show "Overtures to the Opera" introduce these complex works, and "Opera Unabridged" offers insightful discussions of the music. The Young Artists Program provides opportunities for talented young singers to perform in the community and to produce a fully staged opera.

The Seattle Symphony (1903) celebrated its centennial season in the new Benaroya Hall (2001), the first building in Seattle acoustically designed exclusively for concert music performances. More than 300,000 people attend Seattle Symphony performances annually. This orchestra is one of the most recorded in the nation, representing 10 Grammy nominations and collaborations with more than 80 companies. Known for showcasing works by contemporary composers, the Seattle Symphony attracts music lovers of all stripes.

Courtesy of Seattle Symphony; Photo by Fred Housel

The Samuel and Althea Stroum Grand Lobby in Benaroya Hall beckons visitors with its enveloping warmth.

Ariana Lallone and Olivier Wevers in
The Moors Pavane.

Courtesy of Pacific Northwest Ballet

Here. . . live! The original home of grunge and a dynamic alternative music scene, Seattle offers a variety of clubs and live music venues. There are a handful of underage clubs as well as dozens for the adult crowd, with techno, house, fusion, funk, reggae, alternative rock, jazz, folk, swing, country, and culture-based music. Trend-setting hipsters define the music for their generation from their garages and the clubs down the street.

Live rock, country, jazz, rhythm and blues, and soul concerts are held in outdoor venues, such as the AT&T Wireless "Summer Nights at the Pier" series on Seattle's waterfront, with the stars and moon overhead. In Woodinville, the Chateau Ste. Michelle "Summer Festival on the Green" features blues, jazz, classical, and contemporary artists performing at an outdoor grass amphitheater.

DANCE

The Pacific Northwest Ballet (1972) has maintained a reputation for world-class excellence as one of the five largest companies in the nation. Its 49 dancers present 90 performances a year. The Pacific Northwest Ballet School (1974) has earned acclaim with its comprehensive curriculum as one of the top three ballet training institutions in the U.S. This company offers an extensive repertory of both classic and modern ballets. Ballet Bellevue (1995) is another dance company and ballet school with both classic and modern works in its repertoire. Other local professional dance companies focus solely on modern dance.

THEATER

Theaters of every size and in many neighborhoods, including the downtown core, serve the King County area. The Moore Theatre (1907) is the oldest remaining theater in Seattle, presenting community events, comedy shows, plays, solo performances, beauty pageants, local dance and musical groups, and alternative musicians on tour. The opulent 5th Avenue Theatre (1926) serves as home to the 5th Avenue Musical Theatre Company, and is a popular venue for concerts, lectures, and films, as well as theatrical performances.

The Paramount Theatre (1928) opened as a movie palace. It underwent a major renovation in 1994, thanks to a local philanthropist, and reopened as the Seattle Theatre Group. Its offerings include a range of contemporary theater, dance, poetry, comedy, opera, and music concerts.

The Seattle Repertory Theatre (1963) was awarded the 1990 Tony Award for Outstanding Regional Theatre. "The Rep" focuses on modern and classic dramatic works. A Contemporary Theatre (ACT), which originated in 1965, was the first Seattle theater dedicated to producing new plays. Located near the Convention Center, the theater is housed in the former Kreielsheimer Place building, which is on the National Register of Historic Places. ACT has staged works by Samuel Beckett, Bertolt Brecht, Arthur Miller, Edward Albee, John Steinbeck, Harold Pinter, James Thurber, and Tennessee Williams—as well as contemporary playwrights like Philip Glass, Joyce Carol Oates, Neil Simon, Stephen Sondheim, Lanford Wilson, and David Hare. The Intiman Theatre (1972) at the Seattle Center combines classics with new works by contemporary authors. Since 1973, the Empty Space "Uncommon Theatre" has been showcasing works that challenge aesthetic conventions; it is known for premiering new plays.

The University of Washington's Meany Hall for the Performing Arts (1975) offers a full schedule of international dances, speeches, university events, concerts, chamber-music performances, and theatrical events.

Kaori Nakamura in Serenade.

The entrance to the Experience Music Project.

Courtesy of Wyndham Images

Courtesy of City of Bellevue

The Bellevue Art Museum.

Fusao Kajima leads the Bellevue Philharmonic Orchestra.

Several theaters serve a younger audience. The Northwest Puppet Center (1986) creates professional, touring puppetry theater for youth and family audiences. The Seattle Children's Theatre (1975) located in The Allen Family Pavilion at the Seattle Center since 2000, presents quality, age-sensitive works based on children's literature.

King County's discerning and appreciative audiences, known for their receptiveness to new works, draw performers from around the world to these and other venues.

LITERARY ARTS

Local bookstores, cafes, non-profit literary organizations, and university lecture halls host visiting and local writers. The Seattle Arts & Lectures series draws world-class authors to the region for public readings and discussions. Reading clubs, organized by individuals as well as booksellers, promote a thriving life of the mind, mixing the solitary nature of reading with the social sharing of literary discussions and discoveries. Pacific Northwesterners have the highest literacy and per-capita book-reading rate in the nation.

ART GALLERIES, MUSEUMS AND CENTERS

The Seattle Art Museum (affectionately known as "SAM" by locals) serves as a fulcrum for the arts in King County. Its permanent collection of over 23,000 objects includes artifacts from Africa; ancient art from Greece, Rome, Egypt, and the Americas; an extensive Asian collection; decorative arts from Europe and America; European paintings, sculptures, and prints; Native American artworks; and American and European contemporary art. The exhibits are invariably insightful and sensitively presented — reflecting the expertise of the museum staff, as well as local and international academicians. Artist Jonathan Borofsky's "Hammering Man," one of a series of such sculptures, stands outside the museum entrance at First Avenue and University Street. The museum's second venue is the Seattle Asian Art Museum, which features an extensive collection of art and artifacts. The Seattle Art Museum is expected to open its third venue, the 8.5-acre Weiss/Manfredi-designed Olympic Sculpture Park, on waterfront property in Belltown in 2006.

The University of Washington's Henry Art Gallery (1927) has a reputation for challenging the intellect through provocative new works. This gallery has a permanent collection of 20,500 objects that includes "late 19th and 20th century paintings, the extensive Monsen Collection of Photography, and a textile and costume collection, along with a burgeoning collection of cutting-edge works in new media." This was the first public art museum in Washington state. A 1997 renovation by architect Charles Gwathmey, using glass and stainless steel, increased the size of the museum to 40,000 square feet. The facility now includes an auditorium, multi-media gallery, bookstore, café, and sculpture court. The museum also hosts a film and lecture series.

The Frye collection of art, which later became the basis for the Frye Art Museum (1952), originated when Charles and Emma Frye, part-owners of a meat packing company, settled in Seattle in the 1800s. Their fortune was made in the Klondike Gold Rush, and the couple ultimately collected some 230 pieces, including nineteenth and twentieth century European and American representational works (particularly paintings of the Munich School). The works of Mary Cassatt, John Singleton Copley, Thomas Eakins, Robert Henri, Winslow Homer, John Singer Sargent, and Andrew Wyeth are part of this superb collection. The museum offers a quiet, reflective environment and is free to the public.

The Pratt Fine Arts Center (1977), located in Seattle's vibrant Central District, commemorates Edwin T. Pratt, executive director of the Seattle Urban League (1961-1969) who was assassinated by unknown assailants. This center brings together culturally diverse artists and students for workshops in glass, sculpture, drawing, printmaking, jewelry design and metalsmithing, artist books, and paper sculpture.

In 2001, the Bellevue Art Museum (1947) moved into its new Stephen Holl-designed angular, modernist building. Since then, it has offered some ground-breaking displays and installations. This museum is a key part of Bellevue's new civic core.

The Kirkland Arts Center (1962) is a focal point of the arts on the Eastside with an exhibition gallery, arts studio, and educational facility. The center organizes Summerfest at Marina Park, an annual event that attracts over 35,000 visitors with its arts and crafts booths, musical entertainment, hands-on arts activities, and artist demonstrations. The Kirkland Arts Center's original name was the Creative Arts League, formed by a group of citizens and artists concerned with preserving the Peter Kirk building (now on the National Historic Register) and providing local arts opportunities.

MUSEUMS

Numerous King County museums focus on unique topics. The Children's Museum (1981) offers educational workshops and displays at their Seattle Center location. The Museum of Flight (1964) , the region's premiere air and space museum, hosts an extensive collection

The Miss Budweiser races to victory on Lake Washington with Mt. Rainier looming in the background.

(19,000 items) of aerospace artifacts, including 131 historic aircraft; designs, drawings, photographs, videos, and documents; models; instruments; engines; armament; tools; and oral histories. It recently was chosen by British Airways to display a retired Concorde, the first supersonic jet. The Nordic Heritage Museum (1979) and Wing Luke Asian Museum (1967) offer special perspectives on the settling of the Pacific Northwest. The University of Washington's Burke Museum (1885), the only major museum of its kind in the Northwest, focuses on natural and cultural history. Its anthropology, geology, zoology, and botany collections include more than five million specimens. The Museum of History and Industry (1914) focuses on the cultural, social, and economic history of the Pacific Northwest.

FESTIVALS AND FAIRS

The King County area hosts many dozens of festivals each year. The annual Seattle International Film Festival brings movie buffs from around the region for intense days of film viewing and meeting renowned directors, actors, and others involved in the film industry. Children learn about the world's cultures through the Seattle International Children's Festival. Bumbershoot celebrates books, music, dance, foods and togetherness. The Bite of Seattle brings restaurateurs from around the region to showcase the cuisines of practically every country around the globe. The annual Seafair celebration includes a torchlight parade, the landing of the "Seafair pirates" at the Seattle waterfront, hydroplane races on Lake Washington, the Miss Seafair scholarship competition, and a riveting air show with the Navy's Blue Angels.

Patriotic festivals abound, such as the Family Fourth at Lake Union, which includes music and mega-fireworks displays to celebrate the nation's founding. Regional festivals celebrate salmon runs, various seasons of the year, the performing arts, dance, ethnic heritage and culture, audio arts, choir, jazz, literature, athletics (marathons and bicycle races), maritime culture, and folk life. Throughout the summer, street fairs highlight farmer-raised produce, local arts and crafts, the talents of local performers, and locally designed jewelry.

The King County Fair, also held in the summer, draws many to Enumclaw to watch a professional cowboy rodeo, complete with bull riding, saddle bronc riding, bareback riding, team roping, steer wrestling, calf roping, and barrel racing. Local and national musicians perform at this venue. Fair-goers may join in the fun of hog calling and logrolling, along with enjoying the typical fair foods such as hot dogs, hamburgers, snow cones, cotton candy, and other favorites.

The Navy Blue Angels perform over Lake Washington at the 2004 SEAFAIR Hydroplane Race and Air Show.

SEAFAIR Archive

SEAFAIR Archive

Looking south, high above the SEAFAIR Hydroplane racecourse.

GLASS LIKE WATER

One comes upon glass art like a revelation—with the element of chance, this explosive mix of fire and sand captures the frailty of form, at once coaxed by the touch of an artist's hand and shaped by an artist's life-giving breath. Unnatural blooms of eye-piercing colors play with the light and change moods, like a surprise-find in the ocean depths or like a mysterious, layered rock found on a salty beach.

These are sea anemones that will play wild music to the touch. These are baskets so frail they can just barely hold their own. The red glass fruits float on the water of an outdoor installation, moved by the breeze, elusive beyond the protective electronic eyes of the museum's security system. Here is a glass teapot. And here, pieces of glass dangle like a waterfall of a million pieces of light. These are masterfully created works of art pretending to be found in some parallel universe, in nature.

Glass art comes in many forms—finely etched vases and containers, representational sculptures, large architectural installations, and textured shapes. The creation of the pieces is full-sensory, physical, both individual and collaborative. To manipulate these red-hot orange glass blobs and create the form and colors with precision is to know the substance with intimacy. It should come as no surprise that glass artists work without gloves as they handle the gathering irons, tweezers, and blowpipes, because glass art requires finesse.

The "hotshop," as the central workspace is called, is a hive of purposeful activity, with simultaneous flameworking and glassblowing, the layering of powdered colors, and the heating and re-heating, shaping, and working of the molten glass in the furnaces. Timing is everything. The frailty of these glass forms plays with the conceit of permanence.

Seattle Center Ferris wheel.

Courtesy of Wyndham Images

Courtesy of City of Seattle, Photo by Ian Edelstein

Roller coaster excitement at the Seattle Center.

A glittering Winterfest is celebrated in Seattle Center.

Courtesy of City of Seattle, Photo by Erik Stuhaug

Chapter Eight

A UNIQUE CULTURE

As a citizen this great region between the Mountains and the Sound, I too treasure it. You cannot live in this special place without every day being reinforced in spirit by our natural blessings and in heart through the diversity of our people. As we continue to grow and prosper, we are blessed by an outstanding quality of life that will continue to nourish our hopes and dreams. We have demonstrated through our collective successes that we can grow and change, while still sincerely at peace with our Northwest values and while always nurturing the things that must remain timeless.

100 Words by
Bob Drewel
Executive Director
Puget Sound Regional Council

A Unique Culture

You are here. . . *As the cafe door opens onto the street, you gratefully welcome the smell of the coffee, pastries, and chocolates, and the rush of warmth that enfolds you. The lighting is intimate, as if you walked into a cozy house at dusk. The fireplace is roaring, and around you people are reading newspapers and books, chatting, and word-processing on Wi-Fi (wireless fidelity) laptops.*

You walk to the counter and ask for "thunder thighs" or a "skinny." The barista calls you by name, asks about your work, and takes your order precisely. By the time you make it to the serving counter, your coffee is ready to go in a cup with "legs" (cardboard handles). In King County, it's hard to do without your preferred mochaccino or café ristretto, whether it's with or without cream, a dash of caramel or cocoa, or a sprinkle of cinnamon.

Fortunately for you, stopping in for a fast hot or iced drink is easy enough. The coffee shops are ubiquitous, slipped into a mall next to the ice cream shop or tucked in the back of the mega-bookstore. You have your favorite miniature roadside and parking-lot espresso stands, with baristas in coats and sweaters when the weather turns cool. There are also the free-rolling carts in public parks, on jogging paths, in university building atriums, and in courtyards.

With drink in hand, you head for the newspaper racks and are lucky enough to find a comfortable leather chair. In short order, you'll be ready to face the day.

P acific Northwest culture is a refreshing combination of creative independence and civic-mindedness. The Northwest is a place where entrepreneurial genius and giving back to the community are equally valued. Northwesterners have long defined themselves by their freethinking, an approach to life that is the result, quite possibly, of living in the so-called hinterlands.

Lives Lived In Community

Local residents care about their fellow citizens, whether they define "neighbor" as the person next door or those several continents and seas away. Residents have donated many millions toward health services, higher education, the arts, and research and development for industry. This giving extends globally to the continents of Africa, Asia, and other regions of the world, from which many King County residents hail.

Coffee shops and cafes are a ubiquitous sight in the Puget Sound area.

A boat glides into the sunset on Lake Washington.

Courtesy of City of Seattle, Photo by Ian Edelstein

Mapes Creek in Kubota Gardens Park.

Courtesy of Wyndham Images

A colorful canna.

Not only is King County the home base of the Bill & Melinda Gates Foundation, which is noted for some of the largest private donations in history, but residents and businesses here make charitable gifts to non-profit organizations, public and private schools, charities, and political groups. This sense of largesse and sharing has been infectious and ongoing. Residents donate more than cash; they give land, stocks, vehicles, and other items.

They share their time and expertise, too. Many residents volunteer on school committees. They attend city council meetings to share their insights with elected leaders. They form community organizations to advocate for particular issues. They join political parties to shape their governance on the local, state, national, and international levels.

It is common for Northwesterners to view contentment as complacency. With a mix of idealism and compassion, young college graduates head off to years of service in developing countries. Others will put in 40- to 50-hour workweeks and then pitch in for weekend nature trail cleanup, or garbage pickup duty on the freeways, or serving cookies and juice to donors at the local blood bank.

Community meeting places are scattered throughout King County neighborhoods. Neighbors work side-by-side in public gardens. They gather at community centers for friendly sports competitions, salmon bakes, arts-and-crafts fairs, second-hand sales, and school fundraisers. Groups organize around shared passions that run the gamut from classic car collections, to knitting or quilting, to volunteering for search and rescue missions. It is not unusual for sympathetic residents to rally support around stray killer whales to make sure they get reconnected to their pods. Their engagement with the world is about rolling up their sleeves to make a difference.

A bike rider pauses to enjoy the comings and goings at the Ballard Locks.

SHARING THE ENTREPRENEURIAL SPIRIT

Why go to work simply to follow a set regimen? Northwesterners bring personal passions into play at their workplaces. With so many at the cutting edge of the technology, biotech, engineering, and software industries, locals know their 9-to-5 is not about business as usual, but rather, it is about new ways of achieving.

Some residents' days are spent telecommuting from home offices with a view—or in downtown high-rises that overlook Elliott Bay—or on desktop computers with a digital virtual blue sky. Northwesterners are into flex-time, overtime, and 24/7 time.

Courtesy of City of Seattle, Photo by Ian Edelstein

Even those who have retired early stay active and intense. They may turn personal obsessions into businesses, like starting a winery from scratch, designing golf courses, funding historical preservation projects, or developing start-up companies. They may exercise their minds by creating new board games, inventing robots for televised competitions, or funding emerging branches of applied science research. They may buy the local basketball or football franchise. They may save historic buildings and theaters from razing. They may start a new nonprofit agency to improve others' lives and financial opportunities. Some retirees enter the teaching profession, while still others head back to school as students to explore the integration of disparate academic disciplines for innovative solutions.

LIVES LIVED IN WATERCOLOR

This same energy and creativity spills over into the pursuit of fun. Locals are into gaming and translating virtual games into real-life play-acting at local parks, in full fantasy gear. They are into paintball in the woods. They take to the community theater to perform on stage. They sit by fireplaces and play board games, many of them invented locally, such as Cranium, Cool Studio's "Burn Rate," Uberplay Entertainment's "New England," Wizards of the Coast's "Magic: The Gathering," and Screenlife's "Scenelt?" (Cook D6)

Urbanites in King County live hip and energetic lives. Their nights are spent in the glitter of local clubs and dance raves. They are spent in ties and tuxes or shawls and evening dresses at the opera, symphony, or ballet. They are spent in sporty little two-doors, Range Rovers, and Hummers. They are spent under umbrellas or bareheaded in the rain. They are spent in art galleries and warehouse spaces transformed into artists' lofts.

DIVERSE CULINARY PALATE

The Pacific Northwest's cold waters, temperate climate, and location have inspired a style of cuisine that is unique to this corner of the country and reflects the area's status as a global crossroads. It is a style that may be as influenced by Asian cuisine as it is Native American. Northwest chefs use fresh local ingredients and, naturally, a bounty of seafood, and combine them in non-traditional ways that borrow from recipes and flavors from around the world. Traditional recipes from countries such as Mexico, France, or Japan are transformed into an epicurean's delight as local produce, meats, and fish are incorporated. Northwest cuisine has gained national and international attention and has been celebrated by world-class chefs.

Residents of King County know how to appreciate a diverse culinary palate. That appreciation enthusiastically extends to international cuisine. *Pho. Souvlakis. Injera. Phad Thai. Koatgaetang.* The sheer variety of restaurants—Greek, Italian, Indian, Chinese, Vietnamese, Thai, Japanese, Korean, Filipino, Mediterranean, Mexican, and African—speaks to the international palate. Not only are Northwesterners willing to try almost any style of cuisine, they are apt to make non-native foods a part of their regular diets. They will search various neighborhoods to find shops that sell the exotic spices and ingredients of their new-found culinary discoveries.

The area's numerous organic and natural food outlets make it apparent that locals care about what they eat and their overall nutrition. The labels avowing fair wages paid to farmers attest to Northwest consumers' political consciousness and sense of fairness, while the affection for local farmers' produce, offered at open-air markets, reveals their community involvement and concern.

Revelers march in the Fremont Solstice Parade.

A couple looks to the future with joy and possibilities.

The Bradner Gardens P-Patch veggies are tenderly cared for in the Mt. Baker neighborhood.

A Clean Seattle Initiative Work Party takes on a project in Golden Gardens Park.

Courtesy of City of Seattle, Photo by Ian Edelstein

Courtesy of City of Seattle, Photo by Erik Stuhaug

SHOPPING

Residents also enjoy variety in shopping. Westlake Center, University Village, Bellevue Square, Pacific Place, Northgate Mall, Southcenter, and other local malls offer major chain stores as well as local retail shops. High-end boutiques and specialty stores throughout King County attract shoppers for those special purchases. Family-owned supermarkets, shops, restaurants, and other businesses add richness to this selection. Northwesterners enjoy the hands-on aspect of hunting for the deal. One interesting example is Recreational Equipment Incorporated (better known as REI), which offers a unique shopping experience that includes signature entries via "hiking" trails, an indoor climbing rock, and store-sponsored adventure trips.

MEGA-STORES

Costco Wholesale Corporation, headquartered in Issaquah, showcases another popular type of shopping: the discount warehouse approach, which appeals to local bargain hunters. With more than 300 stores across the nation, Costco sells quality foods, housewares, equipment, and services at highly discounted rates. King County is also home to Auburn's Supermall of the Great Northwest, one of the nation's largest indoor malls.

VIRTUAL, TOO

Northwest residents have also readily adopted online shopping: fast, efficient, and customized, with a broad selection and deliveries made right to their doorsteps. Shopping for efficient gifts, such as gift cards, is a favorite. Those maintaining households order groceries through mouse clicks. They solicit car bids online. They scout out esoteric computer parts through various vendors. Some pursue the thrill of the live auction via eBay. Fashionistas and aficionados of all stripes locate items using Internet tools.

COSMOPOLITAN

Locals purchase much of their food, clothing, furniture, and other basics from international sources. Their tastes range from the simple mix-and-match furniture of IKEA to the more exotic flavors and home furnishings of Uwajimaya and Pier 1 Imports. Many discerning customers send their home decorators to the Seattle Design Center for creative ideas on interior design, including every style from suburban sophisticate to modern condo cool to rustic island retreat.

After all, the vision's the thing.

Photo by Karen Wilson-Heunisch

Many Northwesterners are avid gardeners, spurred on by the temperate weather and kind growing conditions.

A "houseboat neighborhood" as viewed through the frame of the Montlake Bridge.

Houses Afloat

From the beginning, Seattleites have taken the concept of "living on the water" literally. Workers at logging camps built mobile, one-story wooden structures on rafts. In the 1920s, the affluent built houseboats as summer homes on Lake Washington. Mill hands, longshore workers, fishermen, and boatmakers built permanent houseboat homes on Lake Union. The Great Depression of the 1930s fueled more houseboat construction, as these makeshift dwellings could be built with ease. In the 1940s, at the peak of Seattle's houseboat community, more than 2,000 houseboats existed on Lake Union. In the ensuing years, houseboat residents have maintained a running "battle for survival," in competition with over-the-water apartment developers, rising moorage fees, and environmental and zoning laws, according to the Seattle Floating Homes Association, founded in 1962. (Means and Keasler)

Today, there are approximately 490 houseboats on Lake Union and in Portage Bay. This small neighborhood attracts some unique residents. "For all kinds of reasons—thrift, beauty, escape, expedience, convenience—life afloat on Seattle's rivers, lakes, and bays [attracts] some of the city's most unconventional people," Seattle native and historian Howard Droker observes. (7) A news article in 2003 placed the value of houseboats at around $89,000 to $1.2 million, in a city with average home costs of approximately $280,000. High-end houseboats have underwater cellars and multiple stories, and range in size from about 250 square feet to 2,500 square feet.

Houseboat living offers a closer tie to nature. ". . . The sensations of being on the water convey the outside environment gently, sometimes forcefully. Rippling water reflects shimmering patterns of light and shadow onto the walls and ceiling. The house sways easily with the lake's swells, and water gurgles under the floor boards." (Droker 8) Some residents cultivate flower and vegetable gardens in wooden boxes on their decks. Others fish off their decks. Houseboat residents say the camaraderie among neighbors is closer than usual and the sense of freedom—being away from big-city concrete structures—is invigorating.

It takes a person with a special sort of spirit to live a houseboat lifestyle.

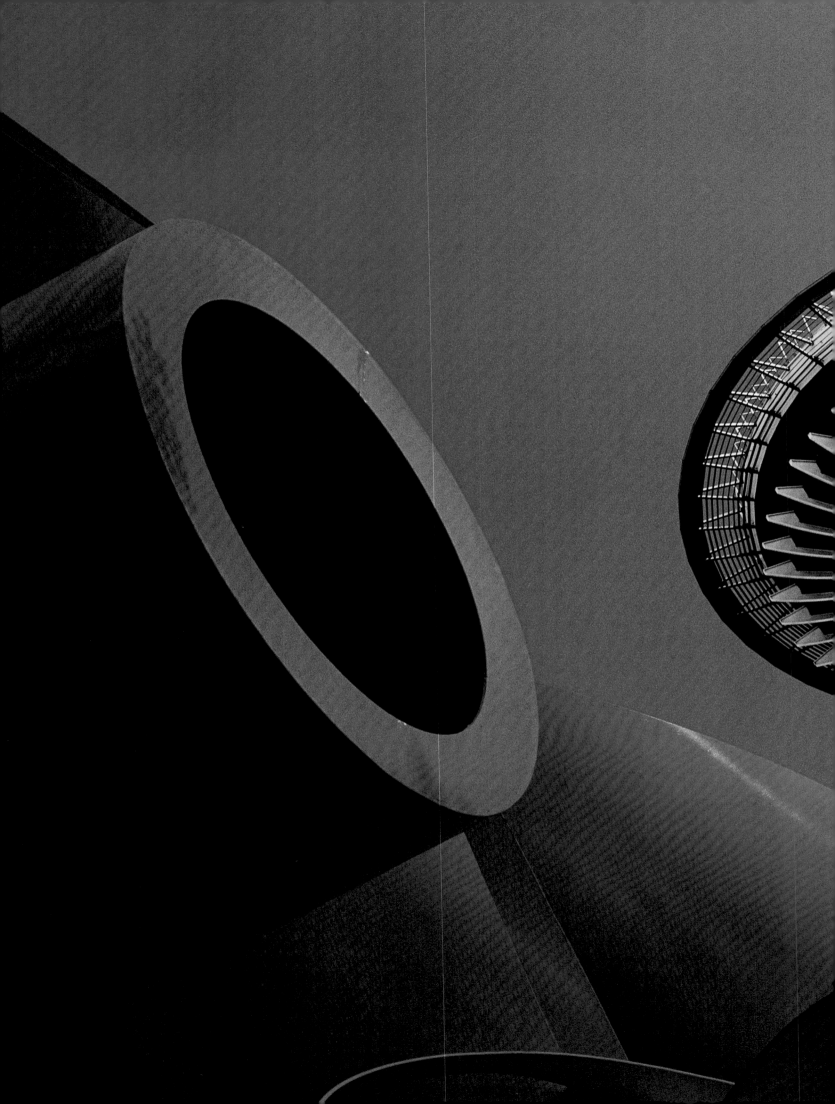

KING COUNTY INTERNATIONAL AIRPORT

FLIGHTS OF FACT AND FANCY
King County International Airport is proud to be the airport of record for Air Force One on presidential visits to the Pacific Northwest. Every president since Harry Truman has visited there at least once, and the county is proud of its long and flawless record of receiving and sending off the nation's leaders.

The arrival and departure of Air Force One, though, tells only one of the thousands of stories about the airport's importance to the region. The airport began as a dream of the citizens when they voted by a margin of 86 percent to spend $500,000 to build the airfield. Officially dedicated in 1928, and named after Boeing Company founder William E. Boeing, King County International Airport (KCIA), also known as Boeing Field, began offering service for

Pacific Air Transport and West Air Transport, to Portland and San Francisco, that same year.

As travel demand grew, so did the dimensions of the airport, in a series of expansions and improvements that included a new 5,825-foot runway in 1941 and a War Department-

funded expansion project in 1944. The airport has grown by stages to its present dimensions and is now one of the nation's busiest general aviation airports. As a general aviation airport, King County International serves commercial and private business, corporate jets, and helicopters. The airport features a 10,000-foot main runway, a 3,710-foot small-aircraft runway, and airport hangar complexes totaling 82 bays. It also has a Lighted Taxiway Guidance Sign system and a state-of-the-art Instrument Landing System.

Courtesy of King County International Airport, Photo by Ned Ahrens

The graceful arches of the 1930 Terminal building have welcomed visitors to King County International Airport for seventy-five years.

Courtesy of King County International Airport, Photo by Ned Ahrens

Small aircraft provide recreational opportunities and flight training for local flying enthusiasts.

Rotary and fixed-wing aircraft make up the more than 300,000 yearly operations.

To meet today's advanced security requirements and ensure smooth operations as well as the safety of all its customers, visitors, and employees, the airport's Terminal building is equipped with full Department of Homeland Security immigration and customs services. The airport is also home to the outstanding Museum of Flight, including the historic "Red Barn" where the Boeing Company was first established. The museum showcases aircraft spanning the entire history of manned flight, from the first Boeing plane to one of the legendary British Airways' Concordes to examples of current craft used for space flight. It also maintains an extensive library of aviation and aerospace resource materials and is the venue for countless educational activities. It is not uncommon for school children to meet an astronaut, or combat veterans to relive the days of World War II, or avid aviation fans to explore rare artifacts at this world-class facility on any day of the week. Many visitors arrive by air and after landing at the airport, taxi right to the Museum's entrance. The airport has a rich history that has helped shape what it is today.

The airport now handles more than 300,000 takeoffs and landings annually, is home to 486 fixed-wing aircraft and 54 helicopters, covers 614 acres, and has 150 tenant businesses. Scheduled passenger flights bound for regional destinations also operate out of the recently renovated 1930s airport passenger terminal. Upgraded to meet the demands of today, the terminal building retains its historic charm and, filled with a wide variety of artworks created by local artists, is a gracious facility for passengers arriving and departing Boeing Field. Located close to downtown Seattle and adjacent to the interstate freeway, the airport is ideally located for both passengers and cargo and maintains its importance to the nation's aviation system after more than three-quarters of a century. King County International Airport/Boeing Field was designated in 2001 by the National Air Transportation Association as one of the "100 Most Needed Airports" in the United States. In 2003, Boeing Field ranked thirteenth in the nation for the total number of general aviation operations.

The Terminal building, renovated in 2003, melds the charm and elegance of a historic building with modern safety, security, and technology features.

One of the busiest airports in the country, Boeing Field occupies 614 acres just minutes from downtown Seattle and is home to a wide variety of aircraft.

Courtesy of King County International Airport, Photo by Ned Ahrens

But those are just the statistics. The naked eye tells the same story in a more colorful fashion. One can see at a glance that the airport is a bustling place serving many specialized and general aviation needs. Businesses include commercial airlines, aircraft manufacturing, airfreight companies, aircraft service and repair, flight schools, charter operations, and helicopter services. Every day, the latest models of private jets land and take off from the airport, carrying corporate executives, entertainment and sports celebrities, and domestic or foreign government dignitaries. Major League Baseball's Seattle Mariners, the National Football League's Seattle Seahawks, and the National Basketball Association's Seattle SuperSonics all fly in and out of the King County International Airport, as do many of their competitors. And every year, the tarmac is crowded with the jets of the world's top corporate CEOs, in town for the annual CEO Summit hosted by Microsoft co-founder Bill Gates.

Courtesy of King County International Airport, Photo by Ned Ahrens

Comfortable waiting areas, featuring artwork by local artists, create a quiet atmosphere for visitors as they await their flight or welcome travelers.

THE BOEING CONNECTION

The airport was originally built by the citizens of King County as a means of encouraging The Boeing Company to establish its headquarters in this region. It has since become a point of pride in the Northwest to be "the birthplace of modern aviation." New Boeing aircraft models are tested at Boeing Field and the airport is a delivery center for many airlines. Many of the company's historic milestones were achieved at Boeing Field, as when the company made commercial aviation history in 1954 with the first flight of its 707 "Dash 80" prototype, which landed at King County International Airport after taking off from the company's nearby Renton assembly plant.

From its beginnings, the airport has had broader purposes than just the Boeing connection, however, and they have grown more diverse over the years. King County International was the primary passenger terminal for the Puget Sound region until 1947, when Seattle-Tacoma International Airport opened. In the following years, the airport turned its attention to general aviation and to growing along with The Boeing Company and other aviation businesses. The airport is now home to 150 tenants, including flight schools, air taxi services, the King County Sheriff's Guardian 1 Helicopter, and major air cargo operators such as United Parcel Service, BAX, and Airborne/DHL.

Today, Boeing Field records over 300,000 operations (take-offs and landings) annually, 26,000 involving air cargo, and the airport's master plan projects that by 2020 the number will exceed 397,000.

The oldest airport in the region, King County International Airport/Boeing Field works to preserve the past and meet the needs of today while planning for the future.

THE AIRPORT AS ECONOMIC ENGINE

King County International Airport is not only a historic and industrial asset; it is also a significant economic asset to the region. Although the airport itself employs only 54 people, it provides support to businesses and services providing more than 3,900 direct jobs. KCIA generated more than 10,000 total jobs in King County in 2002, was responsible for sales of $1.6 billion by King County businesses, and supported the earnings of a half-billion dollars in labor income. Nearly $39 million in state and local taxes were generated as a result of economic activity at the airport.

The Boeing Company maintains a presence on the airfield originally named to honor William E. Boeing, company founder, with a testing and delivery center for their latest commercial aircraft.

King County International Airport does not receive any general tax dollars and is totally self-supported by user fees such as rents, fuel flowage, and landing fees. Truly an economic engine, KCIA/Boeing Field is one of the region's best public investments.

PRESERVING THE PAST AND SERVING THE FUTURE

Safety, security and infrastructure improvements are key to the airport's focus for the coming years. Placing emphasis on advanced technology at KCIA is an ongoing commitment that influences all programs and services at the airport. Technology improvements are evident in the modern FAA control tower, operated 24 hours a day, seven days a week, and pilot-navigation aids, safety and security efforts, noise-monitoring systems, along with facility upgrades and new construction.

KCIA recently launched a "Fly Quiet" program for pilots operating out of the airport. That outreach effort includes mitigation and pilot education to reduce aviation noise in local communities. The program complements efforts already in place that encourage residents in nearby communities to help KCIA effectively monitor and

Airport cargo activities are vital to Puget Sound businesses, contributing $1.6 billion annually to the regional economy.

Courtesy of King County International Airport, Photo by Ned Ahrens

Courtesy of King County International Airport, Photo by Ned Ahrens

More than half a million visitors a year visit the Museum of Flight. Located on the southwest side of Boeing Field, visitors can arrive by airplane to begin a tour of this recently expanded facility.

identify noise problems. The airport is also committed to identifying ways to mitigate impacts on affected residences and schools within high-noise areas.

Community outreach efforts have been blended with local interests in a variety of public events and education programs. For example, KCIA staff and tenants support educational institutions such as Aviation High School and Opportunity Skyway to expose students to job, career and recreational opportunities in aviation. Members of the United States Navy Blue Angels precision flying team visit the students of the various aviation programs each summer to encourage future careers in aviation.

The airport constantly conducts a comprehensive review of airport operations and financial

plans to better position itself to meet the region's future aviation needs. Despite the challenges to the aviation industry in the wake of 9/11, KCIA continues to see an increasing demand for airport facilities. The airport is now looking to what the future may hold to evaluate how it can best meet growing demand and guide airport development. King County International Airport's goal is to provide the broadest mix of aviation uses, while allowing flexibility to respond to changing needs and promoting efficient use of scarce airport property.

Whatever the future holds, King County International Airport/Boeing Field is committed to continuing the dream of the early citizens of the region who created the airport more than seventy-five years ago.

Courtesy of King County International Airport, Photo by Ned Ahrens

Conveniently located close to many world-class medical facilities in Seattle, Boeing Field helps to provide life-saving services for patients daily.

Courtesy of King County International Airport, Photo by Ned Ahrens

Every president since Harry Truman has landed at Boeing Field during visits to the Pacific Northwest. Air Force One projects a majestic presence as it arrives on the airfield.

KING COUNTY DEPARTMENT OF TRANSPORTATION

When moving through Seattle's heavily traveled downtown bus tunnel, the city's dual-power transit vehicles convert from diesel power to electricity.

ON THE ROAD

King County's Road Services division is charged with providing residents and visitors with safe, efficient, and reliable transportation for all modes of travel. Road Services maintains an infrastructure that includes 1,875 miles of paved roads, 55 miles of unpaved roads, 222 bridges, and 62,000 traffic-control signs that directly or indirectly help keep vehicles moving around the county. In 2002, the department coordinated 48 capital improvement projects, and installed 6,000 linear feet of guard rails while overseeing repairs and maintenance on another 7,000 feet of railing. Its task of maintaining and ever expanding King County's transportation system is anything but simple, and the geography of the region adds to the complexity.

THE BRIDGES OF KING COUNTY

Because the Pacific Northwest is crisscrossed by rivers and dotted by innumerable lakes, King County's transportation infrastructure includes numerous bridges that vary significantly in size, shape, and design. One bridge, spanning the Green River, is 154 feet above the water's surface; another, the South Park Bridge, is 1,285 feet long. Bridges of every description are found throughout King County, from rural areas with only unpaved roads to population centers with major highways. They range in age from the oldest, built in 1913, to the newest, built in 2003.

The number and age of King County's bridges, together with the region's tendency toward earthquakes, keeps Road Services extremely busy just maintaining its inventory. Bridges built before 1970 have timber supports, and many are wearing out. All the county's bridges have been undergoing "seismic retrofitting" to bring them up to current earthquake-safety standards. Furthermore, Road Services is gradually replacing its oldest bridges with new spans of modern design.

Seattle's antique waterfront streetcars are among the city's most visible—and beloved—icons.

At Seattle's Northgate Transit Center, a traveler gets real-time route information from a Metro kiosk. Seattle is finding more and more ways to deliver electronic up-to-the-minute transit information to its customers.

PRESERVING HISTORY

While facilitating transportation for the ever-increasing population of King County, Road Services works hard to improve and maintain its transportation infrastructure with sensitivity to preserving regional history. For example, the division collaborated with local Native American tribes and a variety of public agencies to develop the Archaeological and Historic Resources Program. The program was initiated in August 2000 to address the effects of road building and road maintenance on significant archaeological and historic resources. It includes training for design engineers and maintenance field staff, and the development of powerful technological tools to find, identify, and preserve artifacts found on transportation project sites.

Preserving the historic and aesthetic value of the county's bridges is a priority, as well. One bridge slated for replacement, the Meadowbrook Bridge near Snoqualmie, is being reconfigured from two lanes to a one-lane bridge with traffic controls at either end in order to preserve its Pratt-parker steel truss, one of only two remaining in the county. Another, the Preston Bridge, was designed to look as much like the previous bridge as possible, without its predecessor's vulnerability to damage and collapse caused by the rushing river below. Through diligence and innovation design, the bridges of King County will complement the region's natural beauty as well as provide safe and reliable passage for transportation.

CONSERVATION AND TRANSIT ALTERNATIVES

Preservation of the region's natural beauty and resources is also a significant driver in the policies and structure of King County's Metro Transit division. Metro's 2,586 drivers moved 1.7 million people (who took 99 million trips) around King County in buses, trolleys, vans, and streetcars in 2002. The transit infrastructure, designed to move people as quickly as possible between homes and major employment centers, now includes 243 transit routes running through 12 transit centers, 9,557 bus stops, 113

King County's famed Novelty Bridge combines an old-style look with a sleek, modern design and up-to-date safety features.

park-and-ride lots, and the downtown Seattle transit tunnel. The tunnel, designed to accommodate both bus and rail traffic, is 1.3 miles long and has four stations, each designed to reflect the city's history and heritage.

Metro has settled on an "electrification" program as the best way to move residents and visitors around King County with minimal impact on the environment. Many Seattle transit routes are trolley routes, with 67.5 miles of overhead electric wire powering the 100 trolleys that operate downtown. Five waterfront streetcars, particularly popular with tourists, are also electrically powered.

Additionally, Metro operates 216 dual-power buses—diesel buses that convert to electric power for running through the downtown Seattle transit tunnel. The year 2002 saw deployment of Metro's first hybrid bus, a diesel hybrid-electric vehicle that stores electric energy when it runs on diesel fuel, then runs "electrically" for as long as possible. Metro plans to phase in use of hybrids as it phases out its fleet of dual-powered coaches. The new hybrid buses can run on electricity without resorting to use of overhead electric wires.

Metro devoted 2002 to operating its test hybrid bus in simulated revenue service 20 hours per day, seven days a week. The bus was filled with water containers equal to a 130-percent passenger load for the first few months of testing, as it operated on five existing routes throughout King County, providing it with a distribution of freeway, urban streets and trips through the downtown transit tunnel. The coach averaged 14 trips through the tunnel every 20 hours, and accumulated approximately 400 miles per day. After three months of testing, covering 30,000 miles—equal to one year of wear and tear—the hybrid began carrying passengers. Now that testing is completed, Metro is beginning

to phase in an entire fleet of hybrid buses, 200 in all. As a result, Metro will be moving ever-larger numbers of passengers throughout King County while consuming less fuel, making less noise, and helping to preserve the region's environmental splendor.

The picturesque bridge over the remote North Fork of the Snoqualmie River is among the newer bridges in King County.

The Green River Gorge Bridge is King County's highest, and affords one of the region's most spectacular water views.

THE WOODINVILLE WEEKLY

CELEBRATING 28 YEARS OF
COMMUNITY SERVICE
The Woodinville Weekly, independently owned and operated, has proudly served Woodinville for 28 years. The first edition of *The Woodinville Weekly* was printed in publisher/owner Carol Ann Edwards' garage on a tabletop press on November 1, 1976. As the community has grown, so has the newspaper. After Edwards started *The Woodinville Weekly*, she began five other newspapers in King County. Edwards' daughter, Julie Unruh, now runs three of the papers from her Woodinville office.

The Woodinville Weekly, *The Northlake News*, and *The Valley View* have a combined circulation of 32,000. With direct mail to Woodinville, Duvall, Carnation, and Fall City, the papers are counter-topped in various establishments throughout Bothell-Kenmore. Serving Northshore and the Lower Snoqualmie Valley, just 25 minutes outside of Seattle, the papers have chronicled the changes in the area from its original rural character to the upscale suburban area it is today, with large commercial and retail developments. As Washington's first newspapers on the Internet, the three papers are known for pioneering a new medium for community new.

Courtesy of The Woodinville Weekly

Another Wednesday in Woodinville and eager residents of all ages gather to see what is in the latest Woodinville Weekly *that came in the mail.*

Edwards and her staff were instrumental in the creation of what are now established community activities such as the Woodinville All Fools' Day Parade and Basset Bash, the Woodinville Community Band, and The Woodinville Wine Festival and Art Walk. Edwards, believing in the importance of participating in the community, has served as president of the Woodinville chamber of Commerce, and as board member of the Northshore YMCA, Shoreline Community College Foundation, and other local organizations. She was a founder of Teen Northshore, a non-profit organization.

SEATTLE PUBLIC UTILITIES

Seattle's skyline exemplifies The Emerald City's unique environment in the Pacific Northwest.

Courtesy of Seattle Public Utilities; Photo by City of Seattle Photographers

Seattle Public Utilities (SPU) provides high-quality drinking water to 1.3 million people in the Seattle King County area and provides Seattle residents with a one-stop shop for other utility services including water, drainage, sewage, flood control, garbage, and recycling services. SPU is renowned for its protected and pristine watersheds, leading the region with innovative approaches to drainage and wastewater systems; solid-waste programs that focus on waste reduction, recycling, and reuse; and habitat protection plans that protect and help the recovery of threatened northwest salmon and other wildlife. SPU's customers are among the national leaders in water conservation and recycling.

Most of the region's water originates from the Cedar and Tolt watersheds in uninhabited areas of the Cascade Mountains. SPU maintains a water supply system of several dams, thousands of miles of distribution and transmission pipelines, pump stations, and reservoirs. Recently, SPU completed a new, one-of-a-kind ozonation and filtration plant for the Tolt River and has a second ozonation and ultra-violet treatment plant under construction for the Cedar supply. Not only do these projects enhance the water supply, their unique design, construction, and operating model significantly reduce the costs to customers.

SPU contracts for and manages Seattle's garbage, yard waste, and recycling services for nearly 150,000 residential and 10,000 commercial customers. Seattle's garbage is compacted and sent to a private landfill in eastern Oregon, while recycling and yard waste go directly to local processing facilities. Recognizing that making less waste in the first place is the least expensive and most environmentally sound option, SPU is also leading the way to reduce waste and promote stewardship and sustainable building practices.

SPU provides drainage services to address storm water within Seattle. The utility also maintains and operates Seattle's sewer pipes and pump stations to protect public health and the environment and to prevent property damage. SPU has begun to implement a "natural system" approach to managing storm water that improves drainage while benefiting the local environment.

Looking ahead, SPU has implemented an aggressive program to evaluate its assets and make investment decisions based on maximizing productivity and service levels in the most cost-effective manner. SPU is proud of its many environmental achievements but continues its focus on stewardship of the region's natural resources to ensure the quality of life of the community, for now and for future generations.

Courtesy of Seattle Public Utilities; Photo by City of Seattle Photographers

The Cedar River Watershed, settled within the forests of the Cascade Mountains, provides the Seattle area with a reliable water supply.

The 90,546-acre watershed is owned by The City of Seattle and is uninhabited with limited public access in order to maintain this pristine water supply.

SEATTLE CITY LIGHT

The scenic Diablo Dam, one of three dams on the Skagit River in the North Cascades.

Between 1925 and 1955, City Light built three dams on the scenic Skagit River in the North Cascades. The utility's largest hydro project, Boundary, was completed in 1967 near the Canadian border in the northeastern corner of Washington state. City Light's other sources of power include a 20-year contract for the Stateline Wind Project in southeastern Washington and several other firm contracts in Washington, Oregon, and Idaho.

City Light is nationally and internationally recognized for its energy conservation programs and for maintaining healthy salmon populations downstream of its dams. The utility began conservation programs in 1978 and has since worked with hundreds of thousands of residential, commercial, and industrial customers to reduce energy use while saving money for both customers and the utility.

In 2003, its Skagit Project—aimed at preserving the Skagit River's massive salmon runs—was certified "Low Impact Hydropower" by the Low Impact Hydropower Institute (LIHI), a nonprofit organization that endorses environmentally sound, low-impact facilities nationwide. Today, the Skagit River is home to one of the healthiest salmon runs in the continental U.S., and draws upwards of 700 bald eagles to its gravel bars annually to feed on the spawning fish.

As one of the nation's finest models of renewable energy, City Light is proud of its heritage of conservation and environmental stewardship, accomplished while maintaining service rates that fall well below the national average.

Serving more than 355,000 commercial and residential customers, Seattle City Light is one of the nation's largest municipally owned utilities. Its century-long record of providing clean, affordable, reliable electric power to businesses and households began in 1905 with the Cedar Falls hydroelectric plant. Located east of Seattle in the foothills of the Cascade Mountains, the Cedar Falls facility was the nation's first municipally owned power plant.

Seattle City Light line worker in the shadow of the Space Needle. City Light provides power to more than 350 thousand residential and commercial customers.

PACCAR Inc

Kenworth's T300 was designed to be a medium-duty customer's best investment. It combines Kenworth's Class 8 heritage with maneuverability, visibility, and versatility. PACCAR has doubled its North American medium-duty truck market share in the past four years.

PACCAR Inc is a global leader in the design, manufacture, and customer support of high-quality light-, medium-, and heavy-duty trucks produced under the Kenworth, Peterbilt, DAF, and Foden names. PAC-CAR also provides financial services and distributes truck parts related to its principal business, as well as manufactures winches under the Braden, Gearmatic, and Carco brands.

Founded by William Pigott in 1905, PACCAR is ranked among the largest Fortune 300 companies and IndustryWeek 100 manufacturing companies. Originally located in Seattle, the company continues be a leader in King County. Its corporate, finance, and lease company headquarters are now in Bellevue, while the Kenworth headquarters are in Kirkland, the PACCAR Parts headquarters are in Renton, and the PAC-CAR Technical Center is headquartered in Mount Vernon.

Kenworth's Renton plant has been praised by *Fortune* magazine as one of "America's Elite Factories." It is recognized for utilizing the latest ergonomic and environmental concepts and technology to create a productive workplace. With a workforce dedicated to the highest levels of product quality and durability, the company builds to its customers' exact specifications, offering more than 6,500 options to produce the right truck for the job. In addition, Kenworth's new Research and Development Lab provides a world-class environment to accelerate product design and development.

PACCAR's Information Technology Division (ITD) also has been recognized for its innovation and advanced technology. ITD includes the Electronic Dealership of the Future, featuring wireless customer recognition, web-based parts catalog searches, wireless Tablet PC service writers, and automatic links to dealership business systems.

PACCAR's local leadership has been acknowledged by the United Way of King County; Independent Colleges of Washington; and transportation, environmental, and workplace safety agencies. In addition, the company was honored as the "Business of the Century" by the Renton Chamber of Commerce.

PACCAR has expanded from its King County origins to become a global company. Today, customers buy PACCAR's products and services from more than 1,700 service locations worldwide. Kenworth has plants in the U.S., Canada, Mexico, and Australia and exports trucks throughout the world. Peterbilt,

Peterbilt's aerodynamic conventional Model 387 delivers best-in-class technology and serviceability performance while remaining—first and foremost— a driver's truck. With uncompromising reliability and safety, superior ride and handling, low cost of operation and serviceability, the Model 387 is as efficient as it is distinctive.

DAF's complete product line features the LF, CF, and XF models. Their excellence is frequently recognized: the LF was International Truck of the Year and German Import 7.5 Tonne Truck of the Year, and the CF won the UK Motor Transport Fleet Truck of the Year.

Courtesy of PACCAR Inc

Courtesy of PACCAR Inc

with factories in Texas and Tennessee, delivers quality vehicles to meet the unique needs and job challenges of its customers with a full line of medium- and heavy-duty trucks. DAF, headquartered in the Netherlands, is the most successful truck manufacturer in Western Europe measured by the quality of its products, increasing market share, and profitability. In the United Kingdom, Foden designs and builds trucks to excel in the most arduous operating environments.

PACCAR's success is based on being the customer satisfaction and quality leader in every aspect of its business. PACCAR's heavy-duty trucks received the highest ranking in four segments of the prestigious J.D. Power and Associates Heavy Duty Truck Customer Satisfaction Survey, and Kenworth or Peterbilt have earned the highest medium-duty conventional truck ranking over the past four years. DAF trucks have been named Truck of the Year in Western Europe twice in recent years, as well as being acclaimed as Best Import Truck in Germany and Fleet Truck of the Year in the U.K.

Chairman and Chief Executive Officer Mark Pigott notes, "A constant focus on improving every element of the business, rigorous cost controls, and the highest quality standards have contributed to PACCAR's position as a leader in the transportation and financial services sectors. PACCAR's commitment is to provide its customers with superior products and services that create value."

PACCAR's operating success has made it the world's most profitable truck company. It has earned a positive net income since 1939 and has paid a dividend every year since 1941. The fundamental elements contributing to the success of this vibrant, dynamic company are quality products, geographic diversification with 50 percent of revenues generated outside the U.S., modern manufacturing and parts distribution facilities, innovative information technology, comprehensive financial services, a superb balance sheet, enthusiastic employees, and the best distribution networks in the industry.

The company's heritage, since its founding in 1905, has positioned PACCAR to maintain the profitable growth its shareholders expect, by delivering quality products and services that have made the company a leader in the markets it serves.

"PACCAR TRUCKS AWARDED HIGHEST CUSTOMER SATISFACTION"

—J.D. Power and Associates Heavy-Duty Truck Customer Satisfaction Study.

Kenworth: "Highest in Customer Satisfaction among Pickup and Delivery Segment Class 8 Trucks." Peterbilt: "Highest in Customer Satisfaction among Over-the-Road Segment Class 8 Trucks," "Highest in Customer Satisfaction among the Vocational Segment Class 8 Trucks," "Highest in Customer Satisfaction with Heavy-Duty Truck Dealer Service."

J.D. Power and Associates 2003 Heavy-Duty Truck Customer Satisfaction Study SM. Study based on

2,675 responses from principal maintainers of two-year-old heavy-duty trucks. Over-The-Road Segment includes all those vehicles that have a sleeper but are not defined as Vocational. Vocational Segment is defined as heavy-duty trucks operating in typically rugged business environments such as construction, sanitation/ refuse, forestry, mining or utility services. Also included in this segment are dump trucks, concrete mixers, cranes, and other related vehicles. The Pickup and Delivery Segment is defined as day cab vehicles that are not defined as vocational. The Heavy-Duty Truck Dealer Service Segment defined Heavy-Duty Trucks as Gross Vehicle Weight Class 8 trucks. www.jdpower.com., Kenworth Truck Company, and Peterbilt Motors Company are divisions of PACCAR Inc.

WASHINGTON MUTUAL

Courtesy of Washington Mutual; Photo by Preston Spencer

Washington Mutual Family Fourth at Lake Union lights up the summer sky.

On a hot day in June 1889, after a long dry spell in Washington state, a burning pot of glue touched off a fire that blackened Seattle's business district and engulfed buildings across 25 city blocks. Four months later, the company that would later be named Washington Mutual opened for business to help the city rebuild.

Today, Washington Mutual remains headquartered in the heart of Seattle, continuing its century-long tradition of community-focused investment, lending, and involvement everywhere the company does business. WaMu (as it's known to customers and throughout the industry) is a retailer of consumer financial services, providing diversified products and services to consumers and small- to mid-sized businesses throughout the nation. Its promise of "great value and friendly service for everyone" has helped make it one of the fastest-growing financial services companies in the U.S.

In turn, helping the communities it serves to grow and prosper – both because it's good business and because it's responsible corporate citizenship – is central to the WaMu philosophy. For example, the company teamed with the Seattle Mariners in 2002 for a "Grand Slam Summer" promotion to support education. The program was developed to reward good reading habits and promote the importance of education. All summer long, Seattle-area students took part in reading projects, met with Mariners players, worked on the ballpark crew, drew portraits of favorite players, and received free tickets to a Mariners Back-to-School Rally.

Supporting affordable housing is another priority at WaMu. The company participates in such local projects as the Village Square development in Seattle's International District, a senior housing development that includes a health care clinic, early childhood education center, and counseling and referral center.

In addition, WaMu is the major sponsor for one of the nation's top five fireworks shows

as rated by *Newsweek.* The annual Washington Mutual Family Fourth at Lake Union is a remarkable display preceded by a full day of free family activities at Gas Works Park, just north of downtown Seattle.

WaMu looks forward to continuing its support of this vibrant community and welcomes you to the Pacific Northwest.

North Bend's Zane Berhold meets Mariners' pitcher, Ryan Franklin, as a prize for winning the Washington Mutual Home Run Reader's program.

Courtesy of Washington Mutual

SKILLS INC.

Skills' state-of-the-art machine shop is complemented by its finish and assembly lines.

Skills Inc. is a non-profit organization whose mission is to change lives by training and employing people with disabilities. The organization was the vision of Earl Fredericks who, after being released from the Firlands Tuberculosis sanitarium in Seattle in the 1960s, recognized the need for a sheltered workshop to help other Firlands patients gain confidence and marketable skills so they could re-enter the workforce.

Inspired by The Boeing Company's philanthropic program to provide meaningful work for the disabled, Fredericks obtained a grant of $4,590 from Boeing's Good Neighbor Fund, and Skills Inc. was born. The year was 1966. Since then, Skills has evolved into a manufacturer and finisher of precision aerospace parts for Pacific Northwest aircraft parts manufacturers, and it has provided employment for thousands of people with disabilities.

Today, Skills has manufacturing plants in Ballard and Auburn totaling over 140,000 square feet. In 2002 the non-profit organization finished more than one million parts, over a quarter-million of which were for Boeing alone. While Skills has relied on its aerospace manufacturing and finishing capabilities to provide training and jobs for its workforce, it has also sought new challenges. The assembly of revolutionary two-speed wheelchair wheels, break-away fishing lures, and other consumer goods have added new training opportunities for Skills employees. Skills has also assisted in producing developmental computer hardware for Pacific Northwest software and hardware manufacturers.

Recently, Skills extended its scope even farther with the creation of a proprietary product line that utilizes its current machinery. The new division, Slliks Design, creates high design furniture, lighting, home accessories, and art. Slliks' unique products provide distinctive design and great value while also fulfilling the Skills mission. The Slliks' retail store is located in downtown Seattle.

From its inception in 1966, Skills has pursued its original goal of providing meaningful employment for as many disabled men and women as possible, without any state, federal, or private funding. The organization's unwavering commitment to its mission and ingenuity in broadening its business scope will continue to serve its employees, customers, and the community well as Skills approaches its fortieth anniversary in 2006.

Skills recently extended its capabilities with a proprietary product line of home furnishings, accessories, and art under the name Slliks Design.

AMERICAN LIFE

Courtesy of American Life

SODO from 4th and Horton by Christopher Martin Hoff.

American Life is a real estate development company based in the SODO (south of downtown) neighborhood of Seattle. Formed in 1996, the company raises capital to acquire property in this high-growth industrial area, which is transitioning to mixed use. It then transforms these properties into functional and appealing buildings that attract occupants as well as investors.

Bordered by Seahawks Stadium to the north, Spokane Street to the south, the Port of Seattle to the west, and Interstate 5 to the east, SODO is becoming an urban hub similar to other former industrial areas, such as Coors Field in Denver, South of Market Street in San Francisco, and the Daiba area in Tokyo. SODO's proximity to downtown Seattle and important infrastructure make it among the most accessible zip codes for commerce

and industry in the greater Seattle area. Also, the SODO area offers the largest and most convenient close-in location to accommodate future growth. The steady growth of the surrounding area increases pressure on SODO to transform from a purely industrial to a mixed-use neighborhood, resulting in increased property values. Companies such as Starbucks, Boeing, and Amazon.com already maintain large offices in the area. Major retailers include Sears, Costco, Home Depot, and Office Max.

American Life's strategy is as unique as it is successful. The company acquires aging industrial properties and renovates them to maximize their current

utility and income while creating a footprint of contiguous properties as a site for mixed-use modern industrial/corporate campuses. It maintains the lowest possible risk by remaining debt-free and owning all its properties outright, without the encumbrance of bank loans.

The company recognizes that its investors seek income, security, and a capital gain opportunity. Some investors also seek immigration status and, in fact, SODO is designated by the government as an area for promoting economic development through investment by those interested in immigrating to the U.S. American Life recognizes that their best sources of new business are referrals from satisfied tenants. The company's successful operating model acknowledges a key principle: that providing superior service keeps buildings rented.

SWEDISH MEDICAL CENTER

The Swedish Health Education Centers offer books, brochures, videotapes, and audiotapes on a wide range of health topics. It also offers a free online research service for more in-depth inquiries about specific health issues.

REDEFINING EXCELLENCE, ONE LIFE AT A TIME

Since its founding by Swedish immigrants more than 90 years ago, Swedish Medical Center has served as the region's model for excellence in health care. What began as a 24-bed facility in a remodeled apartment building on Seattle's First Hill is now the largest, most comprehensive nonprofit medical center in Washington state.

Swedish today spans more than 21 city blocks across three medical center campuses—First Hill, Ballard, and Providence—and is licensed for nearly 1,300 beds. The scope of services available through Swedish now extends far beyond traditional hospital care, and includes a comprehensive home-care program, a network of primary care clinics throughout the Puget Sound region, and numerous affiliations and partnerships with other regional health care providers. More than 2,000 physicians and other practitioners practice at Swedish and more than 7,000 nurses, technicians, and other support staff work at its many facilities.

Patients come to Swedish from throughout the Northwest and beyond, drawn by the reputations of its highly trained and skilled physicians, dedicated nurses, and state-of-the-art technology and facilities. Swedish has earned a reputation as a leading regional referral center, providing the most advanced health care available in virtually every medical and surgical specialty and subspecialty.

LEADING THE WAY IN SPECIALTY CARE

Swedish is perhaps best known for its legacy in obstetrics, having delivered more than 190,000 babies since its inception in 1910. Today, Swedish is still home to the region's most active and advanced birthing program, delivering more than 7,000 babies annually on two medical center campuses. For babies who are born sick or premature, the Swedish/First Hill campus offers a Level III Neonatal Intensive Care Unit (NICU), equipped with the most advanced technology available and staffed by a team of highly trained professionals dedicated to caring for these fragile infants. Each year, nearly 700 babies are treated in the NICU.

Swedish also offers a Level II, or "step down," nursery for those infants who require less intensive care, as well as a service to quickly transport critically ill newborns from other hospitals in the community to the Swedish NICU. While Swedish provides the highest level of care available for moms

Swedish Medical Center is the largest, most comprehensive non-profit health-care provider in the Pacific Northwest. Comprised of three hospital locations, a home-care program, and a network of clinics, Swedish carries a long-standing tradition of medical excellence.

*In a state-of-the-art cardiac catheteriza-
tion lab, Swedish cardiologists delicately
reopen a blocked coronary artery using
the latest technologies.*

each year than any other facility in the state. The nationally recognized program offers state-of-the-art facilities, the most advanced technology, dedicated physicians, nurses, and other care providers, as well as a full selection of personalized treatment options. The Swedish Cancer Institute emphasizes a multidisciplinary system of care that embraces a person's emotional and spiritual needs, along with his or her physical well-being. From prevention and early detection, through treatment, complementary therapies, and support groups, the Swedish Cancer Institute addresses the individual needs of each patient.

Swedish has also garnered recognition for its outstanding cardiac care and is a leading regional referral center. As the state's largest cardiac program, the Swedish Heart Institute offers access to the latest

and babies who need special care before and during pregnancy, the hospital also offers a wide array of other health care services for women.

Swedish continues caring for children as they grow, offering one of the region's most complete pediatric programs. Some of the finest board-certified pediatric subspecialists practice at the medical center, in areas such as orthopedics, neurology, cardiology, and general surgery. Recognizing that children are not simply small adults, the medical center is specially staffed and equipped to meet their unique needs, offering a family-friendly environment that helps children feel safe. If a child must be hospitalized, Swedish provides dedicated pediatric units that are staffed around the clock by in-house pediatricians (hospitalists), trained pediatric nurses, child-life specialists, and other health care professionals who care exclusively for kids. Swedish also offers one of the most advanced Pediatric Intensive Care Units in the region.

Another key specialty is cancer care. The Swedish Tumor Institute opened in 1932 as the first cancer care center west of the Mississippi. Now known as the Swedish Cancer Institute, the program has since grown into the Northwest's largest cancer care program, treating more people for more types of cancer—more than 100 in all—

At Swedish, children are cared for by a highly skilled multidisciplinary team, including child-life specialists who help meet the emotional and developmental needs of hospitalized children.

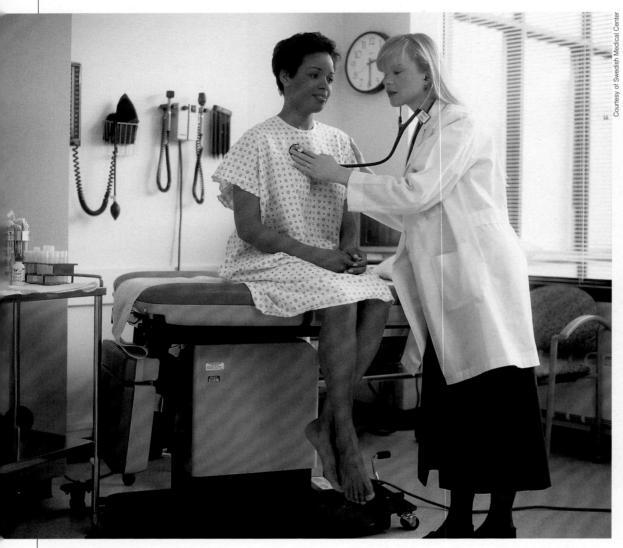

More than 70 health-care providers practice at Swedish Physicians clinics throughout the Greater Seattle area.

region—as many as 37,000 adult and pediatric procedures each year. These range from tonsillectomies, to gallstone removal, to intricate heart and cancer surgeries. Life-saving organ transplants are another specialty, with Swedish's success rates significantly exceeding national averages. Surgeons at Swedish have access to nearly 60 state-of-the-art operating suites, all of which are supported by skilled surgical teams. At the Swedish/First Hill Outpatient Surgery Center, as many as 50 procedures are performed each day. The assurance of advanced resources and the expertise that comes with experience draw surgical patients to Swedish from across the region and around the world.

In orthopedics alone, more than 12,000 inpatient and outpatient procedures are

advances in treatment as well as heart disease prevention, diagnosis, and rehabilitation. Its network of partnerships with hospitals and physician practices in the Puget Sound region brings together experienced cardiologists, cardiac surgeons, and dedicated care teams. Every year, the Heart Institute performs thousands of cardiac surgeries and non-surgical procedures, including special catheterization technologies and treatments, such as leading-edge stent and radiation therapies. As a

national leader in cardiac research, the Heart Institute is typically involved in as many as 50 active investigational research protocols at any one time.

BUILDING ON A
TRADITION OF EXPERTISE
Swedish was founded as a surgical hospital, and that focus continues today. Experienced and highly trained surgeons perform more surgeries at Swedish than at any other hospital in the

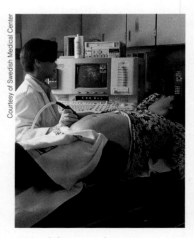

At Swedish, patients have access to the most sophisticated imaging and diagnostic technologies available.

Just minutes after a patient arrives at Swedish with chest pain, an advanced imaging study reveals whether he is actually having a heart attack. Swedish pioneered the use of this study in Seattle.

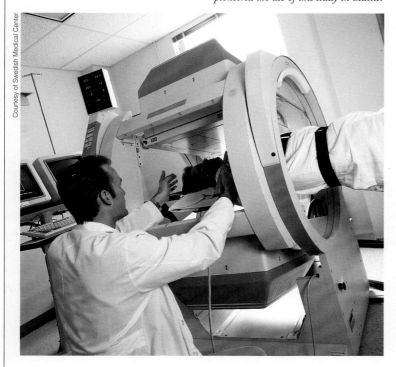

Courtesy of Swedish Medical Center

performed annually, making Swedish a national leader in both volumes and successful outcomes. Swedish orthopedic surgeons pioneered many of the surgical techniques and instruments now used worldwide for joint replacements and other important procedures. Surgeons and orthopedic specialists work with patients of all ages and conditions, including elderly women suffering from osteoporosis and babies born with curvature of the spine or other birth defects. Many of the region's top amateur and professional athletes choose Swedish for their orthopedic procedures and surgeries, relying on the high caliber of its surgeons as well as its reputation for responsive, personalized care and

comprehensive rehabilitation services to ensure a swift return to competition.

That same high level of trust is evident among the more than 12,000 people who each year seek treatment at Swedish for neurological diseases and disorders. They find a full range of services—from sophisticated diagnostics to advanced rehabilitation resources—along with the most progressive medical and surgical protocols in virtually every neurological field. The Swedish Neuroscience Institute provides a comprehensive program that includes a state-of-the-art epilepsy center, and

the region's only full-time neuro-ophthalmology unit. And at the Swedish Sleep Medicine Institute, patients find relief from insomnia, life-threatening sleep apnea, and other sleep disorders.

Neurology patients who are hospitalized at Swedish are cared for in a 30-bed unit devoted exclusively to neurology care and staffed by multidisciplinary teams of neurology-trained nurses, rehabilitation therapists, social workers, and dietitians. As a major clinical-research site, Swedish remains at the forefront of treatment, providing many neurological patients with the opportunity to be among the first to benefit from emerging medical breakthroughs.

The Swedish Cancer Institute provides radiation treatments at its main location and at satellite facilities in Edmonds, Burien, and Northgate.

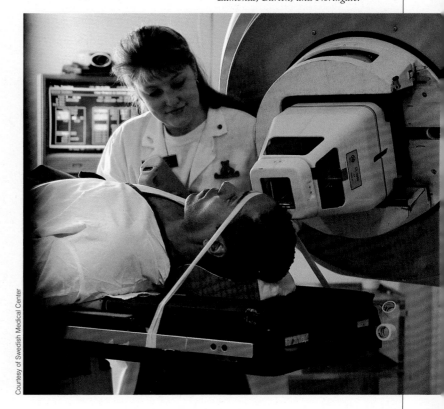

Courtesy of Swedish Medical Center

Whatever the medical need, chances are there is a program at Swedish to help. In addition to its leadership in cancer, heart, surgery, and obstetrics care, Swedish also offers a wide variety of medical and surgical specialties in other areas—everything from behavioral health, to emergency services, to diabetes care, to an advanced bloodless medicine and surgery program.

BEYOND THE HOSPITAL WALLS

While perhaps best known for its hospital-based programs, the scope of services available through Swedish now extends far beyond the walls of its hospitals. For complete primary care for the entire family, area residents can select a health care provider from one of 11 Swedish Physicians clinics. Swedish Physicians is a network

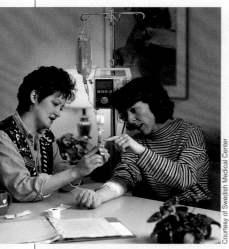

Skilled nursing professionals extend quality of care into the home. Infusion therapy is just one of the many services available through Swedish Home Care Services.

of more than 70 physicians and advanced registered nurse practitioners located at clinics throughout the Puget Sound area. Their primary care specialties include pediatrics, family practice, internal medicine, and obstetrics and gynecology. Patients who choose a provider from a Swedish Physicians clinic are assured of convenient and personal primary care, as well as access to the world-class programs and services at Swedish Medical Center.

Today, the Swedish tradition of excellence also reaches into patients' homes and extends into the broader community. The Swedish home-care program brings skilled nursing, hospice, home infusion, rehabilitation, and private-duty care to more than 5,600 homebound patients annually. And through innovative partnerships with other community hospitals, Swedish brings cardiac and cancer care out into Puget Sound-area communities—closer to where people need it. Swedish is also deeply committed to bringing clinical advances closer to people in need. The hospital actively

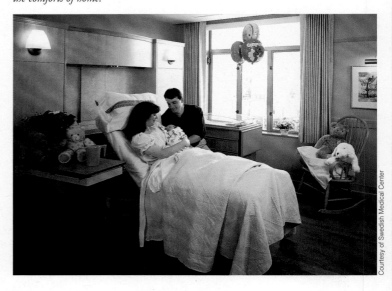

Birthing suites in the Swedish Women and Infants Center offer parents-to-be the comforts of home.

participates in approximately 500 research studies each year, in a wide range of specialty areas, making Swedish one of the nation's leading clinical-trial sites.

LIVING THE MISSION

As part of its community commitment as a nonprofit organization, Swedish is dedicated to serving all members of the community, regardless of their ability to pay. Each year, the medical center provides more than $33 million in charity care and community services. Through its Foundation and other means, Swedish also provides millions of dollars annually to support myriad community-benefit programs. These include offering free flu vaccinations and health-education classes for the public,

as well as providing screening and diagnostic mammography services to low-income women. Swedish also supports medical residents who are part of an extensive training program to care for underserved populations in the region. The residency clinics offer everything from women's health care to elder care to people of all ethnic backgrounds and financial situations. Two of the clinics are located on Swedish campuses—Swedish Family Medicine at Providence and Swedish Family Medicine at First Hill.

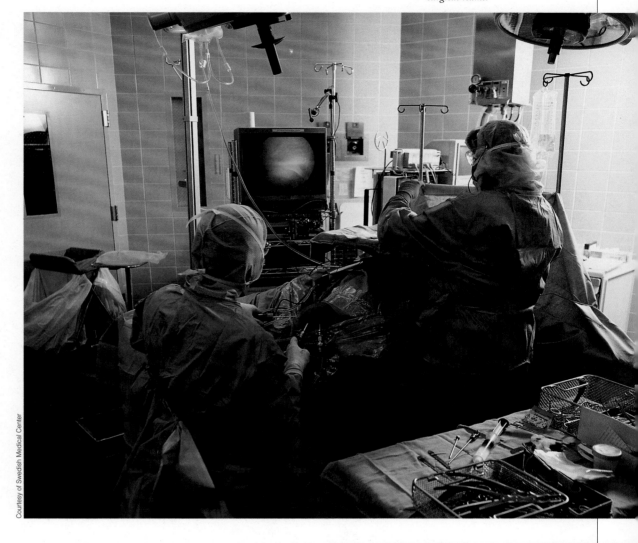

At Swedish, surgeons have access to state-of-the-art operating suites supported by skilled and highly trained surgical teams.

Courtesy of Swedish Medical Center

If it is health-care information that patients or family members need, they can turn to Swedish's health-education centers located at the Swedish/ First Hill and Swedish/Ballard campuses. While nothing can replace a physician's expertise as a source of health information, the centers allow people to take a more active role in their own health care by putting them in touch with additional information or the appropriate resources. The centers' services include complimentary computer searches by an experienced staff; thousands of free brochures; a large selection of books, tapes, and videos; complete community resource listings; health journals, magazines, and newsletters; and equipment resources for new parents.

A VISION REALIZED

Almost a century after Swedish Medical Center's founder, Dr. Nils Johanson, opened the hospital's doors, his vision of providing the best possible health care to the people of the Northwest and beyond is thriving. Of course, meeting this commitment requires the ongoing pursuit of the latest technology and most up-to-date equipment together with a concerted effort to recruit and retain top health care professionals in all fields and specialties. Following Dr. Johanson's tradition, Swedish will forever pursue the best and most advanced health care services available, because it is an organization that understands what a privilege it is to touch thousands of lives each year.

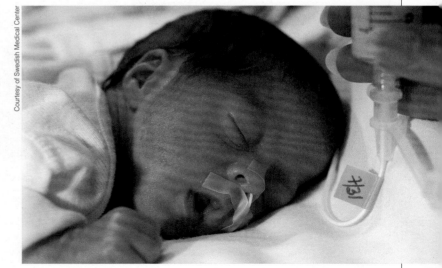

Courtesy of Swedish Medical Center

The Swedish Neonatal Intensive Care Unit offers the highest level of care for the most premature or sick newborns.

UW MEDICINE

UW Medical Center with the new state-of-the-art Surgery Pavilion.

Courtesy of UW Medicine

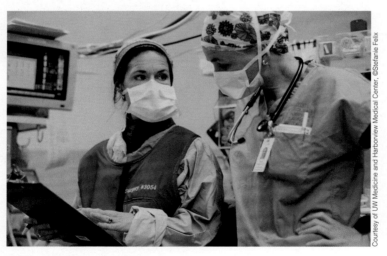

Courtesy of UW Medicine and Harborview Medical Center, ©Stefanie Felix

Harborview's team specializes in complex surgical, burn, orthopaedic, and neurosurgical treatments.

UW MEDICINE—
THE FUTURE OF HEALTH CARE
As a nationally recognized health-care system, UW Medicine provides the most complete patient care, scientific research, and physician training in the Pacific Northwest. The system includes Harborview Medical Center, University of Washington Medical Center, UW Physicians, UW Medicine Neighborhood Clinics, and the UW School of Medicine. Many clinical programs rated among the best in their fields are based at UW Medicine's two world-class hospitals, UW Medical Center and Harborview Medical Center.

Research continues to thrive at UW Medicine. UW faculty received well over $700 million in grant awards in fiscal year 2003, an increase of 14 percent over the previous year. Those numbers are but one reflection of the many significant accomplishments of faculty, fellows, students, and staff engaged in research every day. The 2003 Dean's Report highlights nearly 20 recent major advances in biomedical research, among the many more that have occurred at UW Medicine, including promising treatments for cervical cancer and muscular dystrophy, scientific advances in computational biology and medical informatics, and advances in understanding

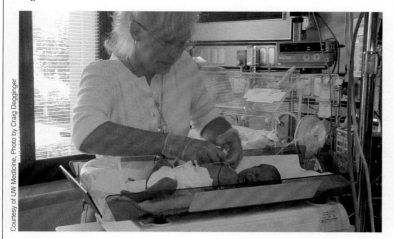

UW Medical Center nurse Kristi Diercks of the Neonatal Intensive Care Unit works with Emily Mae Hulford, the largest of the quadruplets born in August 2002.

Courtesy of UW Medicine, Photo by Craig Degginger

diseases such as tuberculosis and hepatitis C. Additionally, several faculty played a role in drafting the "NIH Vision for the Future of Genomics Research." UW Medicine's research programs continue to grow in breadth, depth, and world importance. The planned expansion of its research facilities at Portage Bay, South Lake Union, and Harborview Medical Center creates a strong foundation for continued growth and achievement in biomedical research.

UW Medicine's clinical programs have never been busier. Although the economics of medicine are challenging, the level of activity speaks to the critical role that UW Medicine's physicians, hospitals, and clinics play in meeting the needs of the sickest and most underserved citizens. Its institutions provide over 40 percent of the state's trauma care and 60 percent of the hospital-based care for the uninsured and underinsured in

King County. UW Medicine's physicians performed 100 liver transplants in 2003 for individuals who, in all likelihood, would not have lived long without a transplant. These statistics have vital meaning in the lives of many people every day.

Programs like the UW Medicine Regional Heart Center, Seattle Cancer Care Alliance, Multidisciplinary Stroke Center, and the Center for Advanced Reconstruction and Rehabilitation reflect the diverse ways the faculty and medical centers collaborate to provide the excellent patient care that is uniquely available at UW Medicine.

The future of UW Medicine is bright. The tradition of innovation and leadership in medical education and research is expected to continue. UW Medicine looks forward to an ongoing focus on the provision of high-quality patient care.

HARBORVIEW MEDICAL CENTER
Seattle's Harborview Medical Center has served the region since 1877, when it was established as the county hospital to care for the poor. Today, Harborview is a world-class trauma and patient-care center, as well as a teaching and research facility—and the hospital continues to provide care for all members of the community.

For years, King County voters have shown their steadfast support for Harborview's essential services. Most recently in 2000, residents gave Harborview another vote of confidence by passing a bond issue that, together with other funding,

Courtesy of UW Medicine, Photo by Bill Stickney

UW Medical Center is certified as a "Magnet Hospital" by the American Nurses Credentialing Center for its excellence in nursing care.

provides money for earthquake stabilization, the addition of 50 more beds over the next 10 years, and numerous other infrastructure improvements.

With the passing of a bond measure, King County voters have committed to making sure that Harborview can continue its mission to provide care for all members of the community.

Satisfying a Mission

King County retains ownership of Harborview and appoints a Board of Trustees to ensure that the medical center meets its mission in the community. Since 1967, when the University of Washington began managing it, Harborview has emerged as a critical health-care resource for King County and beyond. As the only Level I adult and pediatric trauma center in a

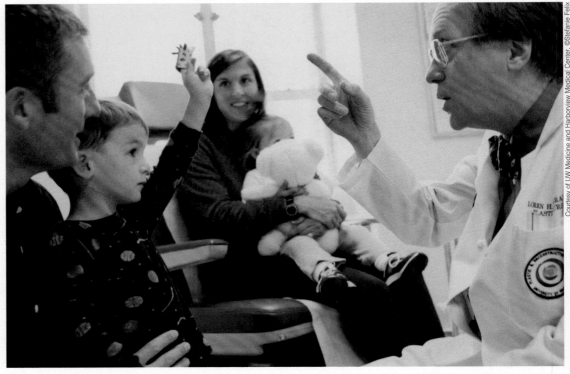

four-state area, Harborview cares for the most seriously injured residents of this region. The medical center's team specializes in complex surgical, burn, orthopaedic, and neurosurgical

treatments. The medical center's rehabilitation medicine program provides state-of-the-art services to help patients regain their ability to live independently. In addition to trauma care, Harborview houses the only Burn Center in a four-state region and provides care for complex neurological disorders of the brain and central nervous system; treatment and consultation for HIV/AIDS and sexually transmitted diseases; and services to rebuild patients' lives through the Center for Advanced Reconstruction and Rehabilitation.

The 368-bed hospital has long served as a "safety-net provider" for the underserved and disenfranchised, and Harborview continues today to address the needs of patients

Harborview Medical Center houses the only Burn Center in a four-state region and provides services to rebuild patients' lives through the Center for Advanced Reconstruction and Rehabilitation.

Harborview Medical Center.

who have nowhere else to turn to for their medical care. Additionally, the hospital offers dozens of renowned programs, including the International Medicine Clinic, Harborview Injury Prevention and Research Center, Center for Sexual Assault and Traumatic Stress, and Children's Response Center.

All of the physicians practicing at Harborview are on the faculty of UW School of Medicine, one of the country's top-rated schools. Harborview's orthopaedics department has consistently been ranked as one of the top 10 programs in the country by *U.S. News & World Report*, providing leading-edge care and treatment for an array

of orthopaedic problems including complex spine and foot-and-ankle disorders. By receiving care at Harborview, patients also have access to numerous specialty services offered at UW Medical Center, as well as primary care at convenient community-based UW clinics.

Contributing to the Community
With a strong mission to serve the community, Harborview is a leader in providing charity care. In 2002, Harborview provided $36 million in charity care to the community—by far the largest amount of any hospital in Washington state.

In addition, the medical center provides outreach services to

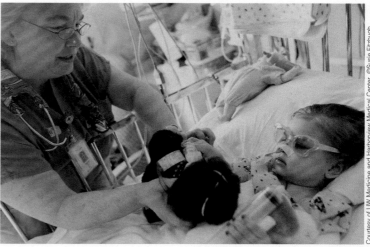

The only Level I adult and pediatric trauma center in a four-state area, Harborview cares for the most seriously injured residents.

the community. This outreach includes developing housing for the mentally ill, providing literacy programs for children and infants, and securing housing for out-of-town families of critically injured patients. Harborview also participates in

community events, providing health-care screenings and other non-reimbursable services to help enhance the community's access to health care.

Teaching and Research
To round out Harborview's comprehensive approach to health care, teaching and research are given high priority. Numerous prominent physicians provide invaluable learning experiences for the hospital's many aspiring young professionals, including medical and nursing students as well as those studying in various allied health care professions. Harborview-based staff and faculty attract more than $42 million in research funds annually to support clinical, basic sciences, and public health research. The research conducted on the Harborview campus directly impacts the services for which Harborview is best known: trauma, burns, orthopaedics, neurosciences, HIV/STD, and injury prevention.

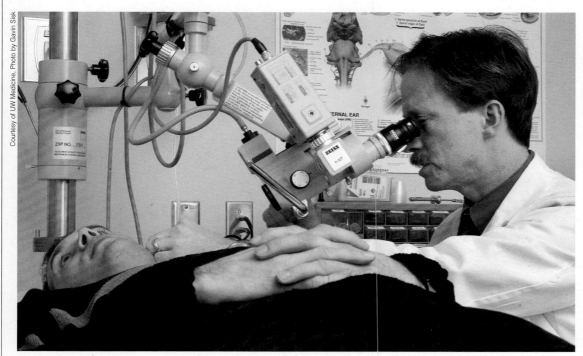

Dr. Cliff Hume is a neuro-otologist with UW Medical Center's Otolaryngology—Head & Neck Surgery Center. Dr. Hume is using an operating microscope to perform clinical otoscopy, which is an examination of the ear canal and eardrum. This type of examination is the first step in a thorough evaluation of the ear.

With advanced technology, Dr. Robert Rho, from the UW Medicine Regional Heart Center, creates a 3-D map of a heart to study a patient's atrial fibrillation.

Courtesy of UW Medicine, Photo by Bill Stickney

UNIVERSITY OF WASHINGTON MEDICAL CENTER

Established in 1959, UW Medical Center is located at the south side of the main UW campus in Seattle. Faculty physicians from the UW School of Medicine provide comprehensive primary and specialty care for area residents, and the medical center also serves as a referral and treatment center for the Pacific Northwest and Alaska.

Nationally Recognized Hospital

Regularly ranked in the top 15 of more than 1,000 major medical centers by *U.S. News & World Report*, UW Medical Center was the first hospital

in the country to achieve Magnet Hospital certification, the highest honor awarded by the American Nurses Credentialing Center.

At the forefront of medical research and leading-edge care, UW Medical Center's physicians are known for developing the world's first long-term kidney dialysis, the world's first multi-disciplinary pain center, the nation's first National Institutes of Health clinical research center, and for performing the Pacific Northwest's first heart transplant and total knee transplant.

Pioneers in Medical High-Tech

UW Medical Center has also been a pioneer in medical high-tech, using Doppler ultrasound for diagnosing heart and blood-vessel disease as well as using specialized imaging and new radiation treatments for cancer.

In 2003, the medical center opened a state-of-the-art Surgery Pavilion. Designed for operational efficiency, the latest in modern medical technology and robotics used in this facility make it an ideal environment

for patients receiving care as well as for the faculty, staff, and students who work there.

Contributing to the Community

In 2002, UW Medical Center provided over $6 million in charity care, in addition to providing leadership in health education partnerships with the Susan G. Komen Breast Cancer Foundation, the American Heart Association, and the

March of Dimes. UW Medical Center offers health career and outreach programs to area high-school students as well as health and sports fitness education to the community.

For the convenience of its Eastside neighbors, UW Medical Center has extended its specialty-care arm to the UW Medicine Eastside Specialty Center, conveniently located in Bellevue. Specialty care services

Courtesy of UW Medicine and Harborview Medical Center, ©Stefanie Felix

Harborview has long served as a "safety-net provider" for the underserved and disenfranchised, and continues today to serve patients who have no alternatives.

provided in this clinic include cardiology, gastroenterology, orthopaedics and sports medicine, rehabilitation medicine, and reproductive endocrinology and infertility, as well as general, plastic, and vascular surgery.

The combination of medical research and leading-edge technology means UW Medical Center patients receive the best care possible in the region, whether for a simple wellness visit or for a life-saving medical procedure.

UW PHYSICIANS

UW Physicians is UW Medicine's practice group of over 1,500 doctors who provide exceptional patient care, leading medical research, and advanced medical training for the next generation of doctors and researchers through the UW School of Medicine. UW Physicians practice at Harborview Medical Center, UW Medical Center, Children's Hospital and Regional Medical Center, Veterans Affairs Puget Sound Health Care System, the Seattle Cancer Care Alliance, and the UW Medicine Neighborhood Clinics.

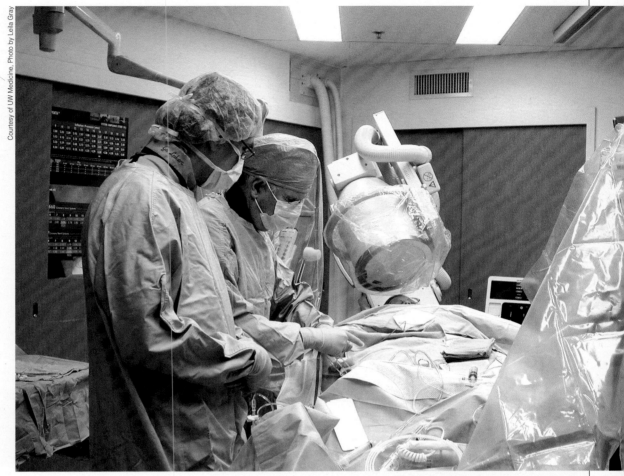

Courtesy of UW Medicine, Photo by Leila Gray

UW MEDICINE NEIGHBORHOOD CLINICS

UW Medicine Neighborhood Clinics provide primary care in eight communities in the Seattle area. Within these clinics, UW Physicians practice family medicine with obstetrics, internal medicine, pediatrics, and geriatrics, bringing world-class UW Medicine experience and skill to these sites. The system of clinics provides neighborhood access to compassionate healing with the boundless potential of medical science.

UW SCHOOL OF MEDICINE

Advanced medicine would not be possible without the UW School of Medicine. The school's biomedical research programs receive more National Institutes of Health funding than any other public school. Three of the scientists who sequenced the human genome are members of the faculty, as are four Nobel Laureates. Cumulatively, the School of Medicine's programs are helping revolutionize the treatment and prevention of disease.

The first drug-releasing stent was approved by the Food and Drug Administration on April 24, 2003. UW Medicine Regional Heart Center cardiologists implanted the stent in their first patient on April 25.

SHORELINE COMMUNITY COLLEGE

Students enjoy the natural setting of Shoreline Community College. Events are held outside under the canopy of trees during many times of the year.

For more than 40 years Shoreline Community College (SCC) has been a vital part of King County and the City of Shoreline. Since this comprehensive community college opened its doors in 1964, its mission has been to provide higher education that moves students on to a four-year university or into the workforce.

SCC is located on 83 beautifully landscaped acres just 10 miles north of downtown Seattle. Considered one of the most beautiful college campuses in the state, it is nestled among native evergreens and flowering plants that offer a landscape of colors throughout the seasons. Benches placed throughout the campus in garden areas invite students to sit outside and study or visit with friends. It is hard to find a more beautiful setting for learning in urban King County.

In addition to the main campus, SCC operates a small off-campus site at the Lake Forest Park Towne Centre in the City of Lake Forest Park. At SCC@LFP, students are surrounded by state-of-the-art technology where many high-tech vendor certification programs, including Microsoft Network Engineers, as well as programs in Oracle, Certified Software Testing, Network+, Cisco Networking and more, are taught.

Over the years, Shoreline Community College has been accredited by the Northwest Commission on Colleges and Universities and has earned stellar marks during the accreditation process. Students can earn an Associate in Arts and Sciences (AAS) degree, an Associate in Applied Arts and Sciences (AAAS) degree, or an Associate in Applied Sciences

Small classes at Shoreline Community College allow for good interaction between students and faculty. Professor Troy Wolff teaches English, a basic core requirement for all students.

More than 450 international students from over 40 countries attend Shoreline Community College to begin their university degree.

Transfer (AAS-T) degree, depending on their interests. Professional-technical students can earn degrees and certificates in over 75 programs such as automotive, visual arts, health-care, biotechnology, computer information, and business. Distance education is also becoming more popular for those students who appreciate the flexibility in scheduling and yet desire to pursue their goals for higher education.

Students can also earn college credit while still attending high school through a number of different programs. Running Start is one such program designed for those students who are high achievers and are ready for the rigor of college courses. Their credits earned at SCC are transferable to a four-year university, giving them a "running start" on their college degree.

Each year the College serves approximately 15,000 students coming from many diverse cultures and backgrounds— students just out of high school, adults who are re-entering the workforce, people who have decided to change careers, and international students from over 40 different countries. These students come to SCC to study English and to earn their associates degree.

Where Every Student Counts

Students learn as much outside of the classroom as they do in the classroom. The Ray W. Howard Library, recently reno-vated, is one of the centerpieces of the College. This library maintains numerous books and periodicals and houses a 100-seat computer lab where students can work on class assignments or browse the Internet for their personal interests.

The Pagoda Union Building (PUB) serves as the student center and central location for the Student Programs office. Many student clubs that serve the varied interests of students outside of the class are organized in the Student Programs office. Whether it is an interest in marketing or scuba diving, there are over 40 student clubs that bring people together.

Students can compete on intercollegiate sports teams or choose to participate in intra-mural sports. The intramural program features leagues, tour-naments and clubs. Basketball, soccer, racquetball, table tennis, and badminton are some of the more popular activities.

Over 50 programs in careers, such as music technology, nursing, dental hygiene, and automotive, are offered at Shoreline Community College.

The lily pond serves as a sanctuary for microorganisms and a lab for students. The College places a strong emphasis on life sciences.

Shoreline Community College is known for its natural beauty of trees, shrubs, and flowering plants.

Courtesy of Shoreline Community College

Courtesy of Shoreline Community College

Non-competitive sports clubs are also available, such as the Ski Club, Backpacking Club, and Fencing Club. A variety of non-sports clubs are also available at SCC—African Studies, American Sign Language, Art, Dance, Dead Poets Society, and Global Conversation clubs to name a few.

The Multicultural/Diversity Education Center is also a place for quiet conversation and study groups. This Center serves students of color and provides services that ensure their success at the College. The College's Women's Center provides similar services and serves as an advocacy group for women's issues.

Shoreline Community College is well known for its Artist and Lecture Series that brings to campus such speakers as former U.S. President Jimmy Carter, National Security Advisor Condoleezza Rice, Oscar-winning director Michael Moore, historian Howard Zinn, and actors B.D. Wong and Danny Glover. Each year, three

to four speakers of national prominence are invited by the Arts & Entertainment Board, a student-run committee, to give their thoughts on the world economy, political activities and other topics of interest. These lectures are free and open to the general public as well as to students.

The SCC Bookstore stocks textbooks (which can be purchased online) and class-required supplies and materials as well as software, office supplies, snacks, gifts, and casual clothing with the College logo. The Parent-Child Center offers a solution to childcare needs and the Campus Salon and the Dental Hygiene Clinic provide services at reasonable prices for community members as well as students and employees. Students feel comfortable moving across campus thanks to the College's Safety and Security Office, which provides service around the clock.

Students interested in gaining experience in leadership positions find a number of opportunities at SCC. Student Government officers, who are voted in by the student body, work side-by-side with faculty, staff, and administrators on College committees, providing a student perspective on important initiatives. As student representatives, they have the opportunity to address the College's Board of Trustees and governance committees on issues they deem important. Students can also participate on the Student Senate in volunteer positions and can participate on the Student Executive Board in paid positions.

WHY DO STUDENTS CHOOSE SCC?

Shoreline Community College has a long-standing reputation for being a place to earn an excellent education—a well-respected academic transfer program, a wide variety of professional-technical degree and certificate programs, worker retraining, and continuing education classes—SCC offers endless opportunities for successful futures.

The beauty of the campus is one of Shoreline Community College's greatest assets. Students study and relax among the trees and assorted greenery.

Many students and graduates say that the College's excellent faculty and small classroom size were the reason they came to SCC. Also on the top of the list is the fact that SCC is a place where students can meet with their instructors for one-on-one help or direction; a place where they can participate on committees and learn leadership skills; and a place to make new friends.

Regardless of the reasons for coming to the College, students find that Shoreline Community College offers students more than education. SCC provides learning for life.

Award-winning faculty are very engaged with students at Shoreline Community College. Dr. Ernest Johnson travels with students to Africa to teach them about new cultures, economic development, and international relations.

CITY UNIVERSITY

Courtesy of City University

City University's International Headquarters in Bellevue, Washington.

THE CITY UNIVERSITY STORY
With more than 11,000 current students, over 37,000 alumni worldwide, and classes offered at more than a dozen sites throughout Washington, Canada, and Europe, it is easy to forget that City University emerged from humble beginnings.

In 1973, City University (then City College) offered courses in rented classrooms at the YMCA and King County Courthouse. What was the enrollment that first year? It was a total of 86 students.

The university has experienced significant growth over the past three decades. With the unique mission to provide an opportunity to learn to anyone with the desire to achieve, "the little university that could" grew up and became the largest private, not-for-profit institution of higher education in the Pacific Northwest.

City University is focused on providing affordable, accessible, and relevant degree programs. The key reasons many students come to the university remain the same. Flexibility is a key consideration when students choose City University. Since its very beginning more than 30 years ago, City University has held classes during evenings and on weekends, a rare practice in higher education at the time.

At one point, classes were even taught on a ferry boat during the morning run from Bremerton to Seattle because it was convenient for commuting students.

Another reason people choose City University is the faculty. City University's instructors come with real-world experience—practicing professionals who work in their fields of instruction, ensuring that information is up to date and relevant.

Nothing sums up City University's success better, though, than a recent student survey that found "90 percent of City University students would recommend the university to a friend or colleague." That is a success story City University is justifiably proud of.

REACHING ACROSS THE WORLD
City University's mission knows no borders and the school remains focused on providing educational opportunities to students who would otherwise not have the chance to pursue an education. In 1991, the university established a degree program in the Slovak Republic —reaching an underserved

population for which gaining an American business degree was previously not an available option.

Since then, the university's reach has expanded to offer undergraduate and graduate degree-level business programs throughout central and eastern Europe, including the Czech Republic, Greece, Romania and Bulgaria. These programs, taught in English, fulfill a vital need for a Western-style business education. They attract and serve students eager to help develop and advance their countries. Graduates gain the skills they need to secure professional positions in both the private and public sectors and compete in an international business environment.

The addition of a partnership in Bulgaria has been among the most exciting accomplishments for City University in the last decade. The achievement was made possible with the enthusiastic support and backing of Valentin Zlatev, general manager of Lukoil and president of Lukoil Bulgaria, the country's largest company. Zlatev personally invested significant financial support to renovate and build a first-class campus for City University. In recognition of his commitment, Zlatev was awarded an honorary doctorate by City University in 2003.

For more than twenty years, City University has had a strong presence in Canada, offering degree programs in business, education, and human services in the provinces of British Columbia and Alberta. One of the many successes in Canada is the partnership with the Nisha Family and Children's Services Society, where City University jointly operates the Community Counselling Clinic in the Broadway Youth Resource Centre for at-risk youth and their families in Vancouver, B.C. The program has been used as a template by the Ministry for Children and Families in British Columbia.

Vi Tasler, president of City University's Board of Governors and Valentin Zlatev at the launch in Bulgaria.

City University also partners with the Canadian Institute of Business and Technology, along with Beijing University of Technology (formerly Beijing Polytechnic University), to provide a Master of Business Administration (MBA) program to students in China. In its first seven years, more than 1,000 students throughout China graduated from this program. These individuals, along with the students currently enrolled in the MBA program, will be among the leaders who will help shape the future of China.

These are just a few examples of how City University is reaching out across the world to bring education to those who seek it.

CITY UNIVERSITY AND THE COMMUNITY

Providing education is more than offering classes. It is about becoming a positive force in the community, and City University sees that role as part of its ongoing commitment. Whether participating in the local chambers of commerce, providing volunteers to charitable organizations, sitting on local boards of directors, or hosting public speaking events, the university is a vital, strong presence in the community.

City University plays an integral role in communities worldwide, as well, providing students with the skills, competence and confidence to work and contribute in their communities after graduation. University instructors also work for companies and organizations within these communities, bringing relevant, real-world expertise into the classroom.

One of the university's priorities in the coming years is to continue to reach into underserved areas around the world and bring higher education to those who have not had access to it before. In the last several years, City University has pursued partnerships in locations ranging from rural Canada to eastern Europe to southern China, helping these communities to transform themselves.

In recent years, City University has entered into innovative partnerships with civic organizations within the communities it serves, including the Puget Sound Business Journal, City Club Seattle and Junior Achievement. The university has also partnered with community and technical colleges throughout the region.

In the classroom.

Courtesy of City University

CITY UNIVERSITY AND
A NEW CENTURY

From the beginning, City University has been dedicated to the goal of "providing education for people anytime and anywhere." Today, with online distance learning, that goal has never been more real or achievable.

City University's distance learning program actually began in 1985, when students were first able to access quality education off-site. Back then, just 134 students were enrolled in a very small number of traditional, mail-based correspondence courses. Today, the university's correspondence program offers more than 300 courses and exceeds 10,000 enrollments.

Beginning in 1999, the nationwide educational market demand shifted from the traditional correspondence courses in favor of courses delivered online via the Internet. In response to that market shift, City University embarked on an aggressive program to convert its traditional correspondence courses to an online delivery system.

For its online courses, City University selected the Blackboard Learning Management Software System©.

People choose City University for its affordable, accessible, and relevant degree programs.

Course development began in late 2000, and the first online classes were offered in the fall quarter of the 2001-2002 year. Two years later, in fall 2003, student enrollment in these online courses exceeded 700.

At present, City University offers 400 courses through the Blackboard Learning system. Some are designed solely to enhance onsite courses, others are "hybrid courses" that combine both in-class and online instruction, and a third option provides complete online delivery to students.

CHILDREN'S HOSPITAL AND REGIONAL MEDICAL CENTER

Children's Hospital and Regional Medical Center is the pediatric referral center in the Pacific Northwest. Located in Seattle's Laurelhurst neighborhood, Children's provides premier diagnosis and care for short-term illnesses, chronic conditions and life-threatening diseases of infants, children, adolescents, and young adults from birth to 21 years of age.

Founded in 1907, Children's was the first hospital in the Northwest to provide medical care specifically for children. The spirit of innovation and commitment to improving their health continues today. The medical center is consistently ranked among the nation's top ten by *Child* magazine. In 2003, its pediatric oncology program—which boasts higher survival rates than the national average—was ranked third in the nation by *Child*.

Each year, there are 12,000 admissions to the hospital, 28,000 visits to the emergency room and 160,000 appointments in Children's outpatient clinics. Providers specialize in high-tech, high-touch care that combines the latest advances in pediatric medicine with highly compassionate care. Pediatric specialists respect the special physical, emotional and developmental needs of young patients, welcoming parents and family members as part of each patient's health care team. Parents and providers work together to develop and evaluate treatment plans as well as hospital initiatives and programs.

Children's physicians (who also are University of Washington Medicine faculty), nurses, and other providers engage in nearly 250 research projects seeking to improve patient care, prevent illness, eliminate diseases, and minimize the impact illnesses have on children and their families. Findings from Children's

Children's new patient care buildings designed to meet the medical and emotional needs of patients and families while allowing medical staff to provide care smoothly and efficiently.

Children's philosophy of care recognizes the essential role families play in the comfort and healing of patients.

Researchers at Children's are working toward a vaccine that would prevent Group B Streptococci infection of newborns.

research programs have earned international renown for researchers and clinicians in infectious disease, genetics and cancer.

Children's partners with the University of Washington to provide one of the most highly regarded pediatric residency programs in the country—currently ranked sixth by *U.S. News & World Report.* Training new graduates, providing continuing medical education to providers throughout the region, and working to improve the way physicians practice medicine has motivated Children's to create affiliations with world-class partners.

For example, the hospital is home to the University of Washington's Department of Pediatrics. Each physician is both a caring, skilled clinician and an expert educator and investigator. The hospital also

teams with Fred Hutchinson Cancer Research Center and UW Medicine to form the Seattle Cancer Care Alliance, which offers patients the most current cancer treatments while conducting research to improve these methods and discover cures.

In addition, Children's physicians partner with local providers in areas throughout Washington, Alaska, Montana and Idaho to provide specialty outpatient care. Children's also has clinics throughout the Puget Sound region so patients can access specialty care closer to home.

As its 100th anniversary approaches in 2007, Children's is preparing to meet the future by adding facilities that improve its ability to provide direct patient care and engage in research that will change the practice of medicine.

The new Janet Sinegal Patient Care Building, which opened January 2004 on the Laurelhurst campus, offers patients a home-like atmosphere and a healing connection to the outdoors while providing the space and flexibility needed to accommodate technological and treatment advances. Children's researchers now occupy two floors (47,000 square feet) on Westlake Avenue in the South Lake Union neighborhood, nearly tripling the amount of space dedicated to basic research. The facility currently hosts 15 principal investigators, with the goal of doubling this number within five years. More facility improvements are on the way.

Throughout its history, Children's has taken an active role in improving the health and well-being of children within the community, state and region. Its advocacy efforts reflect the unmet needs seen most often among the children and families it serves: access to health care, resources for children with chronic medical conditions, child safety and healthy child development. With the generous support of the community—individuals, corporations, foundations, and fund-raising guilds—Children's has remained true to the core of its mission established by founder Anna Clise nearly 100 years ago: providing the best care possible to any child who needs it, regardless of a family's ability to pay.

Compassionate care combined with the most advanced treatment options makes Children's one of the 10 best children's hospitals in the United States.

EVERGREEN HEALTHCARE

Evergreen Hospital Medical Center is located on a 35-acre campus five miles north of downtown Kirkland. The campus is also home to the freestanding Evergreen Hospice Center, Evergreen Professional Center, and the Evergreen Surgery and Physicians Center.

With today's traffic congestion, it is hard to imagine that just 40 years ago most business was done in either Bellevue or downtown Seattle, and shopping meant a trip into the city. By late 1965, however, it was obvious the growing northeast King County area needed its own hospital. A committee of concerned residents decided to form a public hospital district and raise the money to build a hospital with tax-supported bonds. The voters approved the formation of King County Public Hospital District No. 2 and on March 9, 1972, Evergreen General Hospital opened its doors.

Today, Evergreen Healthcare is a community-based health care organization serving more than 400,000 people throughout north King and south Snohomish counties.

The cornerstone of Evergreen's services is Evergreen Hospital Medical Center, a 244-bed acute care hospital located five miles north of downtown Kirkland. The 35-acre campus is also home to the freestanding Evergreen Hospice Center, as well as the Evergreen Professional Center and Evergreen Surgery and Physicians Center, which house programs and physician offices. And the Evergreen Medical Group operates primary care sites in eight locations around the community.

Evergreen's breadth of services and programs now are among the most comprehensive in the region, offering clinical excellence in all major specialties, including cardiac, oncology, maternity, and surgical care.

More than 700 physicians representing over 50 specialties are part of the Evergreen medical staff.

In April 2000, a radiation oncology center was opened. With its stunning architectural design, the center houses leading-edge equipment, including a state-of-the-art Varian linear accelerator, a CT scanner dedicated to treatment planning, sophisticated treatment planning hardware and software, a new clinical research division, and support services.

Evergreen's Level III Intensive Care Nursery was added in 2002 and was developed in collaboration with Children's Hospital and Regional Medical Center and UW Medicine. These experts participate in providing training and expertise

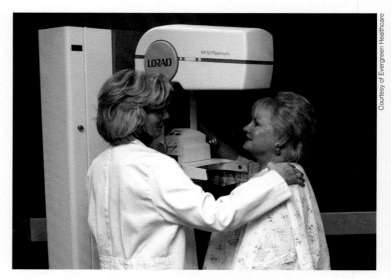

The Breast Center at Evergreen Hospital Medical Center provides leading-edge technology in a warm and supportive environment.

Evergreen's Intensive Care Nursery features private suites with space dedicated for families to stay in the same room as their newborn.

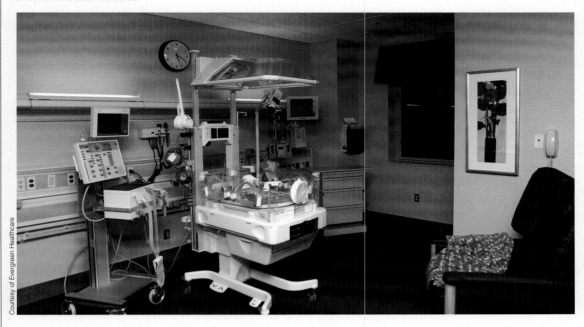

Courtesy of Evergreen Healthcare

to Evergreen staff. Also located on the Women's and Children's Services floor, is a Level II Special Care Nursery, ante partum services for women with pre-term labor or complex conditions, and a pediatrics unit. What sets Evergreen's Intensive Care Nursery apart are its private suites with space for families to stay overnight. The suites are also equipped for twins or triplets!

With the completion of expansion in 2002, Evergreen's Breast Center—ranked among the top in the nation for patient satisfaction—doubled in size. It is now one of the largest comprehensive breast centers in the Puget Sound area with eight mammography suites.

Evergreen's was one of the first breast centers in the state to use the R2 Image Checker, a computer-aided "double-check" which can find abnormalities in mammograms that may not yet be visible to the naked eye.

Evergreen is also home to the Booth Gardner Parkinson's Care Center, a regional resource for patients with Parkinson's disease and other movement disorders. Led by a national expert in Parkinson's and related movement disorders, the center serves patients throughout the Northwest, including Montana and Alaska.

Evergreen's Community-Funded Health Services offer support for the diverse health needs of individuals who reside in the communities served by the hospital. Evergreen's ongoing commitment to providing

services outside the walls of the hospital is unique on the Eastside. Serving more than 100,000 people annually, these programs contribute significantly to the health of the community.

Several Evergreen programs are national models of excellence. In 1996, the Family Maternity Center became the first U.S. hospital to be designated a Baby-Friendly hospital by UNICEF and the World Health Organization. That same year, *SELF* magazine named Evergreen one of the nation's "Top Ten Places to Have Your Baby."

As the community continues to grow and age, Evergreen keeps pace with the need for new and expanded services. A number of projects approved in 2002, including a second Cardiac Catheterization Lab and expanded Emergency care, Surgical Services, and Maternal-Fetal Medicine programs, will ensure that Evergreen continues to meet the community's need for leading-edge medical care.

Still, providing the community with quality health care goes beyond offering outstanding programs and services. This is why Evergreen combines a philosophy of patient- and family-centered care and a commitment to advancing medical solutions to provide unsurpassed care to every life it touches.

Courtesy of Evergreen Healthcare

The radiation oncology facility at Evergreen features a stunning architectural design and leading-edge equipment, including a state-of-the-art Varian linear accelerator.

AETNA

Aetna offers a wide range of health benefits choices with a variety of health plans, and pharmacy, behavioral health, and dental benefits as well as long-term care policies, disability coverage, and group life insurance.

Americans spent more than $1.4 trillion on health care in 2001 and enjoy arguably the best health care system in the world; yet, costs are rising at double-digit levels, more than 41 million Americans are uninsured, and recent reports from the Institute of Medicine have questioned the quality and safety of health care in America. Aetna is leading the development of innovative consumer-directed products that provide consumers with incentives to be more conscious of their health care spending as they are aided in making more informed decisions. This approach should lead to a more efficient system with better outcomes for patients.

ACHIEVEMENTS

In 2003, Aetna proudly celebrated its 150th anniversary, a milestone that few companies reach. Throughout its history, Aetna has remained a leader by helping people protect against the risks and uncertainties of life, promising to be there when they need it most. Aetna's long-term leadership has required constant change, while holding true to enduring values.

Today, Aetna helps employers, individuals, and families meet their comprehensive health-related benefit needs. Aetna also takes the larger view of responsible corporate citizen. The company considers part of its mission to be a leader, cooperating with doctors and hospitals, employers, patients, pubic officials, and others to build a stronger, more effective health care system.

Aetna is taking significant actions to improve the system, including:

Working to eliminate disparities in health care status that exist for racial and ethnic minority and economically disadvantaged populations with programs to increase access to quality care for members of these populations.

Proposing health insurance industry guidelines for coverage of genetic testing to promote disease prevention and management, while respecting members' privacy. Aetna believes that a small investment in testing today can prevent or mitigate human suffering, while saving on future health care costs.

Urging government action to improve access to health coverage for the uninsured, including government support programs, tax credits, and some coverage mandates. In addition, Aetna offers streamlined, cost-efficient plans that make it easier for small businesses to provide coverage for their employees.

Further, Aetna has created a culture of caring, supporting initiatives that improve the quality of life where Aetna's employees and customers work and live. Since 1980, the Aetna Foundation has contributed more than $250 million in grants, scholarships, and social investments.

Courtesy of Aetna

Aetna also has an outstanding record on diversity issues and is considered a leading employer, frequently appearing on lists of the top places to work for minorities and women.

THE PRODUCT

Aetna offers a wide range of health benefits choices with a variety of health plans, and pharmacy, behavioral health, and dental benefits as well as long-term care policies, disability coverage, and group life insurance.

Aetna members enjoy access to expansive nationwide networks of physicians, hospitals, pharmacies, and other health professionals—more than 633,000 healthcare professionals and 3,866 hospitals as of June 30, 2004. A broad national presence enables Aetna to serve large, multi-sited corporations as well as small employers.

The ability to meet employers' needs is important, because Aetna's products reach individuals at the workplace as employment benefits. Employers generally subsidize these programs, and in many cases, the employer must make difficult decisions, balancing complex options that result in different plan designs and costs.

Increasingly, many employers are interested in integrated solutions that employ health, pharmacy, and disability data that Aetna is uniquely able to provide. With access to transaction data from millions of members, Aetna analyzes information to help employers design programs that respond to the specific health and financial needs of their employees.

While working closely with employers, Aetna also is becoming more focused on the needs of individual members and their families.

RECENT DEVELOPMENTS

In September 2001, the company introduced Aetna HealthFund®, the first consumer-directed health benefit plan offered by a national health-benefits company. Aetna HealthFund is now evolving into a family of products designed to better serve the unique and varied needs of individuals and their families.

Aetna HealthFund gives individuals more control over their health-care dollars, while allowing them to become more involved in coverage and care decisions. Members get helpful tools and customized information, delivered in language they can understand, so they can make informed choices, along with their physicians.

For consumer-directed care to be most effective, the core financial incentives should be coupled with approaches that increase the likelihood that members will access cost-effective, high-quality physicians and hospitals and use patient-care management programs when needed. Patient-care management strategies include disease management programs, lifestyle interventions, information therapy, and hospital-care management programs that support effective clinical decision-making.

The success of these programs depends upon good information sharing between the health plan, the physician, and the consumer. Aetna is committed to respect and work effectively with doctors and hospitals by establishing efficient processes and providing prompt claims payments and useful information that helps them provide safe, affordable, quality health care.

Aerial view of Aetna's corporate offices in Hartford. Aetna proudly celebrated its 150th anniversary of service in 2003.

VALLEY MEDICAL CENTER

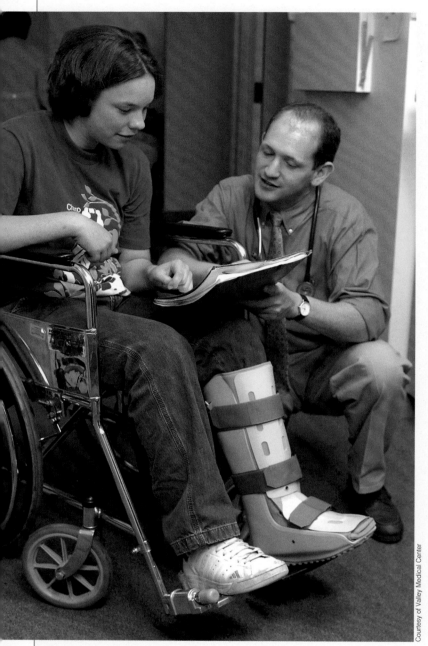

Valley Medical Center has a network of primary and specialty care clinics that stretch from Auburn to Newcastle. Through Advanced Access, patients can be seen the same day if needed.

Representing the first and largest public hospital district in Washington state, Valley Medical Center opened its doors in 1947 as Renton Hospital, a 100-bed facility. In 1969 the hospital was moved to its current location and renamed Valley General Hospital. The name changed again in 1984, becoming Valley Medical Center to better reflect the hospital's comprehensive medical services.

Today, Public Hospital District No. 1 of King County, also known as Valley Medical Center, is a 303-bed, acute-care hospital serving the cities of Renton, Kent, Covington, and most of Newcastle and Tukwila. Governed by a board of publicly elected commissioners, Valley Medical provides quality health care services in a compassionate setting through its clinic network as well as the Center for Joint Replacement, Valley Breast Center, Valley Family Center, the Sleep Center, and the Swedish Heart Institute at Valley Medical Center.

Valley Medical celebrated several major milestones in the past three years. In 2001, Valley Breast Center opened, offering a calm and reassuring environ-ment along with the most advanced diagnostic imaging technology, such as the R2 Image Checker, which helps verify mammogram results. In 2002, the Center for Joint Replacement marked its second anniversary and grew 30 percent while consistently achieving high patient satisfaction scores. Also in 2002, Valley Medical's Emergency Department served nearly 70,000 patients, making it one of the busiest EDs in the state.

Valley Medical reached another milestone in 2003, with the opening of the Newcastle Medical Pavilion. Newcastle provides primary and specialty care services, including family and adult medicine, ophthal-mology, children's health, gyne-cology, and obstetrics. Other specialty care services available through Valley Medical Center's clinic network include pediatric medicine, nephrology, behavioral health, neurology, and occupational health.

Renton Hospital, 1891.

In 2004, Valley Medical Center's Family Center, which brings more than 3,000 new babies into the world each year, opened a state-of-the-art Level III Intensive Care Nursery, enabling the hospital to care for the most fragile newborns. Valley Medical Center also welcomed the services of maternal-fetal medicine, which provides advanced consultative care for high-risk pregnancies.

Valley Medical's surgical services include general surgery, neurosurgery, and vascular surgery. Bariatric surgical services are provided on Valley Medical's campus through the Weight Intervention and Surgical Healthcare (WISH) Center. Valley Medical is a teaching facility, as well, and offers a family medicine residency program and nurse residency programs.

Valley Medical Center is committed to a healing environment, as evidenced by its lush green campus, signature soothing water fountains and the recent addition of a Healing Garden.

BASTYR UNIVERSITY

Bastyr University.

Since its founding in 1978 as a naturopathic medical college, Bastyr University has evolved into the nation's foremost academic center for advancing knowledge in natural medicine.

More than 1,100 students are enrolled each year in the university's broad natural health sciences and applied behavioral science curriculum. Bastyr Center for Natural Health is the largest natural medicine clinic in Washington state, reporting 36,000 patient visits annually and providing a venue for student clinical training. The university is proud of its international reputation for research into the effectiveness of natural therapies. Bastyr has received major funding from the NIH Center for Complementary and Alternative Medicine and is currently involved in collaborative research with the University of Washington and other local medical centers.

Bastyr's commitment to rigorous, science-based natural medicine is the foundation for all its academic programs. At the graduate level, the curriculum includes naturopathic medicine, nutrition, acupuncture and Oriental medicine, and applied behavior science (in affiliation with Leadership Institute of Seattle). Curricula for undergraduates include health psychology, herbal sciences, exercise science and nutrition.

Each year, with help from the university's Venture Grant funding, Bastyr students travel abroad to study traditional healing methods in indigenous settings. Third-year acupuncture and Oriental medicine students receive advanced training through internships at Chengdu and Shanghai Universities of Traditional Chinese Medicine in China.

To serve the community's need for natural health information, Bastyr offers a wide range of continuing and community education classes for practitioners and the public. Each May the campus welcomes the local community to an herb fair, featuring speakers, herbal products, and tours through Bastyr's medicinal herb garden, where more than 250 species of herbs and nutritional plants flourish under student care.

Bastyr faculty and alumni are continually in demand to provide expert information on natural medicine to government agencies and legislative bodies, the media and the public. The university's mission is to educate future leaders in the natural health sciences that integrate mind, body, spirit and nature, and to improve the health and well-being of the community through natural health education, research and clinical services.

Bastyr University has received international recognition for its research into the effectiveness of natural therapies.

WASHINGTON HEALTH FOUNDATION

Each year, the Washington Health Foundation helps more than 20,000 people, including children, in need of a doctor, dentist, or actual health coverage.

WE ARE ALL PART OF THE HEALTH SYSTEM

Problems in the health system are well known: high and rapidly rising costs, uninsured families, the aging baby-boom generation, preventable chronic disease, over-stressed health care budgets . . .

Too often, these problems are seen as something that "someone else" needs to fix. At the Washington Health Foundation (WHF), the belief is that "we're all someone else."

WHF has long recognized the importance of cooperation and inclusiveness in seeking solutions for health problems. Since 1992, WHF has been filling health gaps for people in need, health service providers, and community leaders. From the company's early years, it has done this through practical programs such as access services

that get health care to at-risk populations, or creative grants that assure rural providers are in place to serve those living in rural Washington.

More recently, WHF has broadened efforts to reach individuals and groups who have not been engaged in past efforts to improve health. The Foundation is providing safe venues for leaders at all levels to explore new approaches for addressing health issues. WHF has also turned its attention to the significant public policy gaps affecting our health. Without any vested interest in the outcome, WHF has been asking the people of Washington what they believe, and encouraging leaders to use this knowledge to act toward bigger, bolder and longer-term solutions.

Everyone is part of the health system. Each person has his or her problems with it. And, most have to admit to being a part of the problems even as everyone tries to solve these problems together.

The Washington Health Foundation brings people together to create better health through leader engagement, innovative programs, policy leadership and grantmaking. WHF's greatest assets are strong personal relationships, a reputation for excellence, and the belief that people can create better health by working together. The Washington Health Foundation intends to leverage these assets fully as it pursues its vision— to make Washington state and its communities the healthiest in the nation.

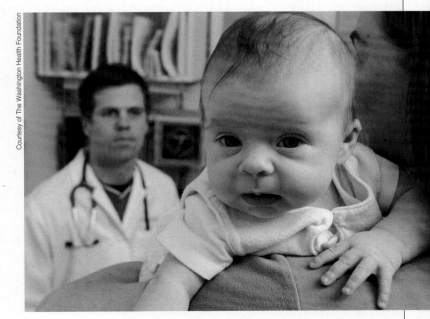

The efforts made today to improve the health care system for all will pay large dividends in the health and well being of everyone tomorrow.

Part Two

<hr>

MARKETPLACE

Bon-Macy's

When a native Northwest resident thinks about downtown Seattle, one of the first things that comes to mind is Bon-Macy's. It is of little wonder, when one considers that this premier department store has been in Seattle since 1890 and at the same location since 1929. Bon-Macy's was known as The Bon Marché until 2003, when it changed its name to include the nationally recognized "Macy's."

The history of Bon-Macy's (or "The Bon," as locals still like to call it) is rooted in the growth of the Pacific Northwest. The well-known department store was founded in downtown Seattle by an industrious couple,

Courtesy of Bon-Macy's

Edward and Josephine Nordhoff, who served the needs of local Native Americans and pioneers in the late 1800s. Bon-Macy's maintains its commitment to the Northwest with a down-to-earth attitude and local management that understands and appreciates the relaxed regional lifestyle. Macy's, on the other hand, has a long tradition as "America's Department Store," with a flair for the big, the bold, and the dramatic. Now, with the addition of the Macy's name and the retail heritage that comes with it, there is a revived emphasis on the fun of shopping, as well as on state-of-the-art conveniences that today's busy customer demands. This new brand identity—combining two strong retail names within the Federated Department Store family—is an exciting blend of Northwest know-how and national pride.

The flagship store in downtown Seattle on 4th Avenue and Pine Street remains the cornerstone for the entire Bon-Macy's operation. An extensive renovation, completed in 2000, stayed true to The Bon's roots as a retail leader in the Northwest. The building itself is high on the list of Seattle's most impressive historical landmarks, praised for its architecture that retains a handsome dignity among the modern skyscrapers that surround the site.

Courtesy of Bon-Macy's

Within each of Bon-Macy's 48 stores, customers see evidence of The Bon's commitment to serve the diverse needs of the Pacific Northwest population. A variety of fashion, home furnishings, and gifts for every taste is made even more enticing with special promotions and great values year-round.

A significant factor in The Bon's history as an outstanding retail establishment is its genuine commitment to support and serve its diverse communities. Building on the store's strong historical ties to the region, the management and staff of Bon-Macy's have earned a well-deserved reputation for giving back to the communities that helped build the company. Bon-Macy's takes its community service mission seriously. For every cause the company supports monetarily, its associates contribute time, energy, and expertise to a number of additional worthy organizations through the company's employee volunteer program, Partners in Time, now celebrating its tenth anniversary. Few Northwest charities have not felt the benefits of community service from Bon-Macy's or its employees. The company's annual report estimates that a total of 6,000 Bon-Macy's employees provided over 15,000 hours of community service.

One of the more innovative programs established by the management of Bon-Macy's has been its Follow-a-Leader contest for youngsters. Created in the mid-1990s, the program encourages local students to submit essays explaining why they would like to "follow a leader" for a day. For their essays, students may choose from a number of prominent executives and community leaders in a variety of fields. The students with the winning essays are given an opportunity to observe the business process in "the real world" and spend a full day shadowing their chosen executives. Winners also earn a $1,000 savings bond for themselves, and the top essayist wins a $5,000 gift for his or her school. Each year, 25 students are selected and Bon-Macy's, together with primary co-sponsors KING5-TV and *The Seattle Times,* provides the financial support, which to date totals well over $165,000.

One key theme in many of the community outreach programs sponsored by Bon-Macy's is cultural diversity. In the late 1980s, The Bon was the founding sponsor of a major exhibit entitled "Black Pioneers in Northwest History." This impressive exhibit still frequently travels for display in schools and organizations throughout the region. Bon-Macy's has also been a key contributor to programs highlighting cultural, social, and economic contributions from the local Chinese, Japanese, and Native American communities.

Courtesy of Bon-Macy's

Courtesy of Bon-Macy's

Courtesy of Bon-Macy's

Courtesy of Bon-Macy's

Another important aspect of Bon-Macy's community involvement is the company's several partnerships with public education programs. Employees volunteer their time and expertise to tutor students from local elementary schools. Others initiate "pen pal" relationships with students, offering encouragement and support for their academic efforts and future aspirations. All of these activities reflect the commitment of Bon-Macy's management and its employees to take an active role in the communities where they work and live.

With more than a century of service to its customers, Bon-Macy's continues to adapt to the changing realities of the retail marketplace in the new millennium. Management and staff pride themselves on knowing how people live, what they want, and the flexibility they need in their shopping. Bon-Macy's credit card customers, for example, may use their card at any of the 450 stores nationwide that share the Macy's name. In recent years, Bon-Macy's has championed a new culture for

employees and customers called "BONlife." Simply put, it is a day-in and day-out effort to make Bon-Macy's the best place to work and the best place to shop. For employees, that includes creating a better balance of their professional and personal lives through options such as telecommuting, flexible work arrangements, casual dress days, and summer hours. The company also finds numerous ways to celebrate its employees' successes and diverse contributions.

For customers, BONlife means enjoying a shopping experience that meets or exceeds their expectations. Using information from customer feedback groups, Bon-Macy's looks for ways to create a more exciting store environment that delivers a faster, simpler, and more relaxing way to shop. That includes better merchandise selections, more knowledgeable sales

Courtesy of Bon-Macy's

definitely breeds loyalty, bringing customers back again and again, for many years.

Loyalty is held in high regard at The Bon—not only customer loyalty—but also loyalty the company owes to the communities it serves, too. In the entrance to the renovated flagship store in downtown Seattle, a particularly compelling work of art greets customers. It is a series of historic-reproduction panels that pay tribute to the major indus-

tries that formed the foundation of the Pacific Northwest economy. Displayed in the center of a striking two-story opening, the five-foot square panels represent such industries as aviation, mining, logging, and others. This art is a graphic reminder of Bon-Macy's historical ties to the region, as well as a statement of The Bon's determination to maintain its own positive influence in the economy of the area for years to come.

Courtesy of Bon-Macy's

associates, helpful directional signs, and more spacious and comfortable fitting rooms.

Ultimately, BONlife is about the good life. One promise to customers motivates every BON employee: "We understand you have a style that's all your own. You can trust Bon-Macy's for the quality, style, selection, and service that you deserve . . . for yourself and your home . . . to look good and feel right."

Evidence of Bon-Macy's extraordinary corporate culture can be seen in the career longevity of many of its associates. Numerous employees boast 10, 15, and 25 years of service to the company, and some have reached the amazing milestone of 35 years or more with The Bon. That kind of commitment

THE FAIRMONT OLYMPIC HOTEL

The tattered pages of a copy of *The Seattle Daily Times* from 1924 tell the beginnings of a story still true 80 years later:

In words of highest praise—praise for the indomitable spirit of the men who conceived and carried it through to completion, praise for the civic pride that made it possible, praise for the hands and minds that accomplished the artistry with which it is wrought —The Olympic was dedicated to the Queen City in a series of programs following the opening banquet last night.

It was obviously a celebration of the highest caliber when The Olympic opened. Now The Fairmont Olympic Hotel, the beautiful building in the center of Seattle's downtown still reflects the same degree of elegance and civic pride seen through the eyes of that newspaper reporter in 1924. A current publication describes The Fairmont Olympic as the "center of social life in the Seattle/King County area." Indeed, thousands of current and past residents of the Seattle area can recite stories of senior proms, debutante balls, engagement parties, wedding receptions, anniversary celebrations, and civic galas from recent years or distant memory. All were made that much more beautiful because they took place at The Olympic.

Built on what was originally the site of the first campus of the University of Washington, The Fairmont Olympic has evolved from "the grandest inn

The Georgian is one of Seattle's most exquisite fine dining restaurants, featuring French-inspired and regional cuisine.

west of Chicago" in 1924 to Washington's only AAA Five Diamond hotel (earning its twentieth consecutive Five Diamond designation in 2004). Fully restored in the mid 1980s, this 450-guest-room hotel, which includes 216 suites, has been lauded for retaining and, indeed celebrating, the "old world charm," of its Italian renaissance architectural design. Listed on the National Register of Historic Places and a member of Historic Hotels of America, the hotel continues to receive national and international recognition.

From plush furnishings to complimentary high-speed Internet access, the hotel ensures a stay that is both comfortable and productive.

The lobby of The Fairmont Olympic Hotel, with its original chandeliers and hand-carved woodwork, remains true to the hotel's original 1924 Italian Renaissance construction.

Even with all these honors, today's management and staff continually look for ways to make each visitor's stay memorable. Weekend guests are treated to warm cookies and milk at the time of their Sunday departure. Children find a bag of toys or complimentary snack awaiting them at check-in. Teens receive popcorn, soda, and popular video games on their arrival. For the business traveler, there are all the high-tech amenities one would expect in Seattle, including complimentary high-speed Internet access in all guest rooms. Frequent guests can enroll in Fairmont President's Club, a program that honors repeat guests with exclusive privileges.

Whether the visitor to The Fairmont Olympic is in town for an extended stay, an overnight business trip, or is a local resident dropping by for some fine dining, the elegance of the superbly appointed hotel leaves a lasting impression. A walk through the lobby, a visit to the arcade shops, or award-winning cocktails in The Terrace bar all engender a feeling of luxury and pampering. The hotel's chefs are recruited from among the world's finest, and the dining experience in The Georgian or Shuckers will attest to their experience.

The Fairmont Olympic's commitment to service extends beyond the needs of hotel guests and into the local community. Numerous charity functions and special hotel-sponsored events carry out that commitment. The Teddy Bear Suite and the Festival of Trees are recognized throughout the Northwest as exciting holiday traditions that raise thousands of dollars each year for Children's Hospital. A seasonal chestnut roasting in front of the hotel features local "celebrity roasters" and reflects the "old-world-charm" people expect from The Olympic, while raising even more money for a local charity. The sponsorship of an annual run an "Happy Hour" auction, which benefit Fred Hutchinson Cancer Research Center, further speak to the hotel's corporate citizenship. The full list of events supporting local charities is too long to recite and keeps growing.

Indeed, the 1924 "founding fathers" would be proud to visit The Fairmont Olympic today. They would be following in the

footsteps of six sitting United States Presidents, numerous foreign heads of state, royalty, and countless celebrities who have found the hotel's allure and luxury irresistible. At the 1924 opening gala, the President of the United Hotel Corporation, the original owners and builders of the hotel, said, "I want the Olympic to be an influence for good, to be a helpful factor in the development of those higher things in life not measured by material success."

By delivering luxury, timeless style, and unparalleled service in unrivalled surroundings, The Fairmont Olympic Hotel aims to live up to that reputation and gain a place in the heart of each guest who passes through its doors.

Earning the AAA Five Diamond award for 20 consecutive years in 2004, The Fairmont Olympic delivers impeccable service from the moment visitors arrive at the hotel's Grand Motor Entrance.

PACIFIC NORTHWEST BALLET

Kaori Nakamura and Christophe Maraval in The Merry Widow.

"Pacific Northwest Ballet would stand out in the richest of seasons."—*The New York Times.*

The Northwest's premiere ballet company, Pacific Northwest Ballet (PNB), presents full-length and mixed repertory ballets September through June at Marion Oliver McCaw Hall. Founded in 1972 and under the artistic guidance of Kent Stowell and Francia Russell since 1977, PNB is one of the most highly regarded ballet companies in the United States. PNB's 47 dancers dazzle thousands each year, offering the finest in dance. Known for versatility, PNB shines in presenting the full-length classics such as *Swan Lake, A Midsummer Night's Dream, The Sleeping Beauty,* and *Cinderella.* Equally popular are PNB's mixed-repertory ballets featuring new works by today's leading choreographers, gems from the Balanchine repertory, and favorites from around the globe. Each holiday season, delighted fans flock in droves to McCaw Hall for PNB's *Nutcracker,* with sets and costumes by Maurice Sendak and choreography by Kent Stowell.

Pacific Northwest Ballet has toured throughout the United States, Canada, Australia, Europe, and Asia. The Company made its debut at the John F. Kennedy Center in Washington, D.C. in 1987 and has since returned three times.

Kaori Nakamura and Jeffrey Stanton in Rush.

Noelani Pantastico in
Divertimento No. 15.

Courtesy of Pacific Northwest Ballet; Photo by Angela Sterling

In October 1995, PNB opened the Melbourne International Festival of the Arts to great acclaim. PNB's Manhattan debut, in October 1996 at City Center, was celebrated by both audiences and press. PNB made its European debut and critically acclaimed appearance in August 1998 at the Edinburgh Festival, and became the first American company to perform at London's newly renovated Sadler's Wells Theatre in February 1999 and was invited back to perform in July 2002.

Pacific Northwest Ballet resides in The Phelps Center, one of North American's most innovative dance facilities, on the grounds of Seattle Center. The Phelps Center houses Pacific Northwest Ballet dancers, administrative staff, PNB School, and a costume and wardrobe shop.

PACIFIC NORTHWEST BALLET SCHOOL

Under the direction of Francia Russell, Pacific Northwest Ballet School (PNBS) has become one of the nation's most respected ballet training facilities. PNBS serves over 800 students in two locations: The Phelps Center in Seattle and The Francia Russell Center in Bellevue. The Francia Russell Center opened in November 2002, to suit the needs of the growing Eastside community, to great acclaim.

PNBS trains professional ballet dancers as well as youngsters who love to dance. It is a central philosophy of the School to demand of each student, whether or not a dance career is planned, the very best efforts of which he or she is capable,

and to give in return the care and attention the student deserves. PNBS students have the opportunity to perform with PNB, with over 200 appearing in *Nutcracker* each year!

In 1994, PNB launched DanceChance, PNB's innovative Outreach program, which reaches into the community to discover talented Seattle-area elementary school students. Children who show they have the physical ability to become professional dancers are provided with classical training, allowing them the opportunity they might not otherwise have to pursue a dance career.

Students attend classes twice a week on full tuition scholarship with dance attire, transportation, and complimentary tickets to company performances provided.

PNBConditioning is PNB's Pilates program, created to work with people from all walks of life to strengthen and sculpt their bodies. PNBConditioning develops core strength and stability, promotes long, lean muscles, increases flexibility, and works with any fitness level. Fifty-minute private- and small-group apparatus classes are offered Monday through Saturday at both PNBS locations.

Maria Chapman in The Merry Widow.

Courtesy of Pacific Northwest Ballet; Photo by Angela Sterling

COSTCO WHOLESALE

From its cavernous warehouses to its immense buying power, Costco is a giant among retailers. With its first retail unit opening in 1983, this King County behemoth pioneered the warehouse club concept right in Seattle. Today, the company maintains its status as the recognized leader in its field and is the most respected retailer in the country for pricing authority.

Costco's mission? It is to continually provide its members with quality goods and services at the lowest possible prices. Costco runs a tight operation with the lowest overhead in retailing and leverages its buying power to buy low and then pass the savings along to its members.

More than 43 million members all over the world are happy to pay for the privilege of shopping at Costco. The Issaquah-based retailer is known for its innovative merchandising and treasure-hunt atmosphere. Its own private-label goods, under the Kirkland Signature name, set the standard for excellence while representing a significant savings over national brands.

Number 44 in the Fortune 500, Costco has been named one of the state's best companies

Courtesy of Costco Wholesale, Photo by France Freeman

Costco, the nation's largest wine seller, sells more Dom Perignon than any other retailer in the U.S.

Courtesy of Costco Wholesale

Costco Wholesale, the originator of the warehouse club concept, now has 43 million members and over 400 locations worldwide.

Courtesy of Costco Wholesale

Costco members are accustomed to being dazzled by great deals on products ranging from cream cheese to crystal.

to work for in *Washington CEO* magazine. Over 100,000 employees call Costco home, and more than 4,000 of them live and work in King County. They are respected for their high integrity, excellent customer service, and charitable involvement. Costco employees regularly volunteer in their local communities through company-sponsored events dedicated primarily to the health and education of children.

Costco currently operates 416 warehouse stores in seven countries, including 36 U.S. states and Puerto Rico, Canada, the United Kingdom, South Korea, Taiwan, Japan, and Mexico. Costco warehouses are legendary for their unique mix of quality, name-brand products at prices often half of what other stores are charging. America's number three grocer, the company is the nation's top seller of toilet paper and also leads the country in wine sales. Aficionados often buy fine wines by the case at Costco, finding it hard to pass up the great everyday low pricing, which includes $90 bottles of Dom Perignon champagne.

In fact, the juxtaposition of basic products alongside luxury items is a big part of the Costco mystique, and a big reason why the big spenders enjoy the shopping experience.

While new radial tires are being installed on their SUVs, shoppers can peruse the aisles for large-screen plasma TVs, computers, best-selling books, clothing, and fine collectibles like Lalique crystal. Costco is also the largest diamond dealer in the United States, offering outstanding values in fine jewelry. From its fresh-foods products to its value-based optical and pharmacies, Costco carries a great mix of products and services, and company leadership foresees continued success for the $40 billion-plus retailer.

Courtesy of Costco Wholesale, Photo by France Freeman

For more casual refreshment, there is the famous Costco hot dog and soda for only $1.50.

SEATTLE SYMPHONY

Courtesy of Seattle Symphony; Photo by Ben VanHouten

Maestro Gerard Schwarz celebrates his 20th year as Music Director of the Seattle Symphony.

Since its first performance on December 29, 1903, the Seattle Symphony has held a unique place in the world of symphonic music. During its formative years, Sir Thomas Beecham developed the orchestra's skill and reputation. In 1954, Milton Katims began his 22-year tenure as Music Director, greatly expanding the Symphony's education program. Rainer Miedél, Music Director from 1976 until his death in 1983, led the Orchestra on its first European tour in 1981.

Since Gerard Schwarz's appointment as Music Advisor in 1983, the Seattle Symphony has experienced an era of unprecedented artistic growth, with a reputation for innovative and adventurous programming and recording. Schwarz has been Music Director of the Seattle Symphony since 1985. The Orchestra has given 46 premieres in the past 20 years, including commissions by six

major American composers during the Symphony's 2003-2004 Centennial Season.

The Symphony has presented several festivals of music by composers from the countries of the Pacific Rim nations, including the varied musical traditions of Latin America. These special celebrations and new music presentations support the creative efforts of contemporary composers and serve to bring vital new audiences to the concert hall. With an ever-growing subscriber base of nearly 40,000 patrons, the Symphony performs or presents 220 performances annually to an audience of more than 330,000 people.

In 1998, the Seattle Symphony inaugurated its new home, Benaroya Hall, noted for its architectural and acoustical splendor. Three years later, the Orchestra opened the doors to *Soundbridge* Seattle Symphony Music Discovery Center, where people of all ages are welcomed

to explore the world of symphonic music. Other education initiatives bring over 10,000 fifth graders each year to Benaroya Hall to hear the Orchestra.

In 2003, the Symphony implemented the ACCESS project—Artistic and Cultural Community Engagement with Seattle Symphony. Evolving from an initiative of the Orchestra's Community Engagement Council, the ACCESS project is made up of Seattle Symphony Board Members and prominent members of the Asian, Latino, and African-American communities in the Puget Sound region. The ACCESS project is a multi-tiered project intended to generate opportunities for diverse population groups to begin and develop a life-long relationship with symphonic music through the Seattle Symphony and to make arts experiences available to all people in the community.

Courtesy of Seattle Symphony; Photo by Yuen Lui Studio

The 92-member Seattle Symphony on stage in Benaroya Hall, a far cry from the 24-member ensemble that gave its first performance on December 29, 1903.

BURKE MUSEUM OF NATURAL HISTORY AND CULTURE

Home to Washington's only real dinosaur fossils and a world-renowned collection of Northwest Coast Native art, the Burke Museum of Natural History and Culture has thrilled and educated visitors for more than 100 years.

Founded in 1885 and designated the Washington State Museum in 1899, the museum holds nationally ranked collections totaling over five million specimens. A vital education program reaches 120,000 children a year. Through exhibits, public programs, and research, the museum promotes a better understanding of the natural world and the cultural heritage of the region. Located just minutes from downtown Seattle on the northwest corner of the University of Washington campus, the Burke is accredited by the American Association of Museums.

The collections of the Burke are the heart of the museum. They are the foundation of its public and research programs. They preserve an irreplaceable record of the natural and cultural heritage of Washington State and beyond and are world-renowned in many areas. The Burke's collections are housed within three primary research divisions: anthropology, geology, and biology.

ANTHROPOLOGY

The Burke's anthropology collections are focused on Pacific Rim and Pacific Island peoples and cultures. The archaeology collections number more than one million specimens and include significant prehistoric materials from sites throughout Washington State and the Northwest. The ethnology collections include major collections of Melanesian, Micronesian, Southeast Asian, and Asian materials as well as American Arctic, Northwest Coast, and Plateau Native American materials.

GEOLOGY

The Geology Division maintains the museum's paleontology and mineral collections, including over 2.75 million fossil invertebrates, fossil vertebrates, fossil plants, and modern mollusks. The mineral collection is one of the finest in the Pacific Northwest, and contains rock and mineral specimens of every major chemical group.

BIOLOGY

The Burke's biology collections include both botany and zoological specimens. The zoology collection includes birds, mammals, fish, amphibians, and reptiles in addition to an excellent collection of spiders and 40,000 butterflies. The bird collection alone is one of the largest and most diverse in the North Pacific Rim.

The museum's botanical holdings are housed at the University of Washington Herbarium, the largest herbarium in the Pacific Northwest, and contain more than 560,000 specimens.

From Dinosaur Day to Native American Arts celebrations, a Thursday night lecture, or a summer camp for kids—the Burke Museum offers programs of interest to people of all ages.

Native American mask (detail). Masks are an important part of the Burke Museum's ethnology collections.

The front exterior of the Burke Museum at night.

Part Two

GOVERNMENT AND COMMUNITY
ORGANIZATIONS

KING COUNTY EXECUTIVE OFFICE

View of Seattle from Lake Union.

Founded in 1852 by act of the Oregon Territorial Legislature, King County is located on Puget Sound in Washington state and today covers more than 2,200 square miles. It is nearly twice as large as the average county in the United States. With more than 1.7 million people, it ranks as the 13th most populous county in the nation.

In 1969, King County was the first county in the state of Washington to adopt a home charter rule establishing two branches of government, executive and council. This basic restructuring of county government has allowed King County to manage the increasingly complex range of services demanded by its residents.

Since the creation of the King County Executive Office, six individuals have held this position: John Spellman, Ron Dunlap, Randy Revelle, Tim Hill, Gary Locke, and the current executive Ron Sims.

There are many facets to the job of the King County Executive. As a political leader of the second largest government in Washington state, the County Executive oversees the delivery of such services as criminal justice, governance, transportation, environmental protection, wastewater treatment, public health, and human services.

Like other metropolitan regions, King County faces challenges while it prospers. This includes threats to the environment, increasing traffic congestion due to explosive growth, and rising home prices. The role of the County Executive must also include improving the quality of life for residents.

Sailing on Lake Washington.

Providing essential, core services to the people of King County through sound financial planning and regional leadership is the way to maintain that quality of life for the area's children and for all generations that will follow. Through the leadership of the County Executive, King County works to ensure the safety and well being of its residents and provides opportunities for them as well. Fulfilling opportunities means helping to make things happen for those who need the assistance.

Snoqualmie Falls.

Sunset over Lake Washington.

Throughout its 152-year history, King County government has intertwined with local cities, the Puget Sound region, and the state. Since its earliest days, King County, along with other Washington Territory counties, took the initiative in establishing numerous ordinances that managed their county according to local preference. There has never been a status quo for King County government. That is because its people have consistently demanded change for the better. From property taxes to sewage treatment, King County residents have never hesitated to speak up and call for change.

As King County government and its leaders continue to build on its century-and-a-half of history and progress, they must ask, "What will our legacy be? Are we prepared to do right by our children? How do we fully realize the great potential among the residents of King County?" The King County Executive Office must continue to work

Snoqualmie River.

with its regional partners including schools, businesses, cities, and rural communities to ensure long-term economic growth and an exceptional quality of life.

Looking at where King County has been can help government leaders and residents shape the future for this govern-ment and its people. With effec-tive and sound leadership, King County can take the path toward greater progress and prosperity. Working together, it can create a sustainable future so people can continue to earn a living wage, afford a home, and develop a sense of community.

Pioneer Square in downtown Seattle.

Courtesy of Wyndham Images

KING COUNTY COUNCIL

The 2004 Metropolitan King County Council consisted of: (back row from left) David Irons, Rob McKenna, Kathy Lambert, Steve Hammond, and Jane Hague; (middle row) Julia Patterson, Dow Constantine, Dwight Pelz, Carolyn Edmonds, and Bob Ferguson; (front row) Larry Gossett, Council Chair Larry Phillips, and Council Vice Chair Pete von Reichbauer.

Courtesy of King County Council

King County is as unique a mix of urban, suburban, and rural lifestyles as can be found in the U.S. It is bisected by two major interstate freeways, home to two major airports, and is the gateway to the Pacific Rim. The goal of King County Government is to sustain the economic, social, and environmental infrastructure needed to support the 1.8 million people who live and work within the 2,200 square miles of the thirteenth most populous county in America.

King County government is headed by an elected Executive and a 13-member Council elected by the residents within their districts. Independently elected officials include the sheriff, prosecutor, assessor, and various district and superior court judges.

The Metropolitan King County Council, the legislative branch of King County government, sets policies, enacts laws, and adopts the annual county budget—the second largest budget in the state of Washington. The Council is also responsible for the oversight of services ranging from Metro Transit bus service to records, elections, and

licensing to King County International Airport (Boeing Field). The Council also oversees the Harborview Medical Center, the level one trauma center for not only the state of Washington, but also for Idaho, Montana, and Alaska as well.

While there are 39 incorporated cities within King County, 350,000 residents live within unincorporated communities. For those citizens, the Council is their local government, responsible for providing services ranging from law enforcement to criminal justice to road construction.

Protection of the natural environment is an ongoing goal for the Council, which has preserved thousands of acres of open space for the enjoyment of future generations and for the protection of salmon and wildlife habitat. To encourage innovative preservation of open space, the Council has enacted legislation such as the

Conservation Futures Trust that dedicates a portion of county property taxes to the acquisition of open space.

As King County enters the twenty-first century, its regional government, led by the County Council, is also entering a new era. The economic challenges that have buffeted the country left their mark on county government. The Council has been instrumental in helping create a more regional approach to governance, but it has not been without costs. King County has divested itself of a number of county parks, working out

King County's Harborview Medical Center is the Level 1 trauma center for the entire Northwest Region. It is also one the few public hospitals in the nation that operates in the black.

Metro Transit bus service is one of the best transit systems in the nation. The Council strives to keep fares low while providing excellent service throughout the county.

agreements that transferred the facilities to the incorporated cities where they reside. Out of that has come a regional-based park system that focuses on rural parks and trails as well as regional and nationally known facilities such as the Weyerhaeuser King County Aquatic Center and Marymoor Park, home of the Marymoor Velodrome.

The Council has also taken the lead on trimming the single largest item of the County's general fund budget—the operating budget of county government. Nearly three-quarters of the general fund budget is devoted to criminal justice agencies: the sheriff, courts, adult and juvenile detention, prosecution, and the public defender. In order to manage the crisis of increasing costs with dwindling revenues, while still meeting government's basic responsibility to enforce the law and keep the public safe, the Council required the criminal justice system to find efficiencies and develop appropriate alternatives to incarceration— thus reducing costs without compromising public safety.

Those efforts, dubbed the Adult Justice Operational Master Plan (AJOMP), have reduced the average daily population within the King County Jail by more than 400 inmates a day while saving $6 million a year in the operation of the King County Jail.

King County remains home to large agricultural concerns as well as the base for industrial giants Boeing and Weyerhaeuser and high-tech icon Microsoft. But it also remains an area of small communities that are working with King County Council members to maintain a high quality of life for all residents.

The public is welcome to visit the King County Council, located in the historic King County Courthouse in downtown Seattle.

Protection of the natural environment is an ongoing goal for the Council, which has preserved thousands of acres of open space for the enjoyment of future generations and for the protection of salmon and wildlife habitat.

ECONOMIC DEVELOPMENT COUNCIL

The Seattle region scintillates with natural beauty, in heart-stopping vistas of mountains, lakes, and forests. The natural environment is what people treasure most and it goes to the very core of the Northwest lifestyle. The region's education and research institutions have produced three Nobel Laureates. The spirit of entrepreneurship has encouraged some of the wealthiest individuals in the world to make the Northwest their home.

All this has drawn a rich, diverse population to the region and it has grown tremendously.

This represents some challenges for residents, but one thing is clear, Northwesterners never compromise their assets or their investment in them. Whether its the infrastructure, the salmon-filled streams, the architecture, or the coastline,

the people of the Northwest maintain the same high standards and this is not up for debate, because without them there is no future.

Washington is the envy of many states. *Forbes* magazine said it all: " What do you call a town that is home to America's richest entrepreneur; its biggest exporter amongst many other flourishing enterprises; home to one of the country's biggest ports and state universities; home to some of its most breathtaking scenery including sea, lakes, mountains and forest. You'd call it the best city for global business in the U.S.—Seattle."

Poised on the Pacific Rim, Seattle is located midway between Asia and Europe. The state is one of the most livable states in the nation. The region excels in livability with a full range of arts, cultural, and sporting events, and easy access to outdoor recreational events. It rains, but never pours, from October through April, so many trees and flowers bloom year round. Annual Seattle rainfall is

36 inches—that is less than New York, less than Atlanta, less than Boston.

King County's world-renowned research centers, large biotechnology and software industry clusters, access to capital, and highly educated workforce give the region a competitive edge. The county is a leading center for advanced technology in aerospace, computer software, bioinformatics, genomics, telemedicine, electronics, medical equipment, and environmental engineering.

King County's most important economic resource is people. The region is consistently ranked among the top five in the nation

in terms of education, productivity and experience. Almost 40 percent of Seattle-area residents have a college degree, one of the highest rates in the nation—higher than San Francisco, New York, Philadelphia, Chicago, and Boston.

A premium location offering unparalleled intellectual capital is the reason why so many international companies are headquartered in the area: Microsoft, Starbucks, REI, Amazon.com, Costco, Nintendo, Nordstrom, Washington Mutual, Weyerhaeuser, Alaska Airlines.

But, if all the other variables are pushed aside, there is no question that quality of life is an underpinning of the Northwest's economic miracle

When people talk about Seattle, they are usually not speaking about the exact same towns and neighborhoods, but

they generally are talking about some part of the region that lies within the borders of the Puget Sound and the Cascade range. King County has an interesting and diverse topography. Beaches, pasture, and forest lands, and ski trails are all accessible within an hour's drive, with the elevation ranging from sea level to 6,270 feet at Snoqualmie Mountain. The region offers a wide range of lifestyles, from the sophisticated urban environment of Seattle and Bellevue to the picturesque,

small-town life offered by King County's many rural communities like Snoqualmie, Enumclaw, and Carnation. Other cities like Renton, Federal Way, Kirkland, and Auburn provide the ideal locations to work, play, and live.

Seattle is a unique and exciting visitor destination. With a number of world-class attractions including The Space Needle, Major League Baseball's Seattle Mariners, and Pike Place Market, there is no shortage of interesting sightseeing opportunities.

Pioneer Square is in the southern part of the downtown area. The neighborhood of Pioneer Square consists of about 30 blocks, the houses mostly date from after the Great Fire of 1889. The buildings in the area were mostly designed by one architect, so the appearance is particularly harmonious and well planned. Today the area is full of boutiques, galleries and coffeehouses and it has a charming relaxed atmosphere.

The Pike Place Market is one of the great marketplaces of the

Courtesy of Wyndham Images

world. The market was originally opened in 1907, and has served as a city focal point ever since. Situated above the waterfront, the market's myriad displays of fish and seafood are very photogenic. Street entertainers perform and add a carnival atmosphere. The market has numerous arts-and-craft stalls, boutiques, some great restaurants, and coffeeshops.

The main site for the 1962 Seattle World's Fair was The Seattle Center where the vestiges of the fair still remain. The view from the top of the 520-foot Space Needed is awesome, especially considering Seattle's dramatic scenic setting. Visitors can walk outside on an observation deck, or eat in the revolving restaurant. Seattle Center has become somewhat of a center for the arts. It is home to the city opera, symphony orchestra and ballet companies. The Pacific Science Center is a very innovative and wide-encompassing museum particularly suitable for children.

The Museum of Flight is located at the Boeing Field at Renton about 10 miles south of downtown. Much of the museum is housed in the original 1909 Red Barn that was the first Boeing plant. The museum covers the history of flight from

Courtesy of Wyndham Images

Icarus and Leonardo da Vinci to the current NASA programs. Many actual aircraft are on display, some spectacularly hanging from the ceiling of the museum to appear as if in flight, including the venerable DC-3 airliner manufactured by Boeing's former rival, which it now owns - McDonnell Douglas. Also suspended from the roof is a replica of the Mercury capsule that took John Glen on his space journey in 1962. The museum also restores aircraft, and new items are always being added to the museum's collection.

MASTER BUILDERS ASSOCIATION OF KING AND SNOHOMISH COUNTIES

In 1909, a group of Seattle builders came together to promote the American dream of home ownership. Since its founding, the Master Builders Association of King and Snohomish Counties (MBA) has grown to nearly 3,500 members, representing all facets of the residential construction industry in the Puget Sound region. In addition to builders and remodelers, the association's membership includes developers, architects, suppliers, bankers, and other professionals associated with the industry.

Several issues surrounding the housing industry have changed since MBA's founding, but its focus has remained the same: to ensure the economic viability of the industry and the livability of the region. For more than 20 years, the most critical issue facing the building

industry has been how to provide affordable housing for the majority of the region's residents. To achieve this, MBA staff and members work with elected officials and local governments to create an environment that allows builders to meet the area's housing needs.

To raise professionalism and industry expertise, MBA offers courses on a wide range of topics that include safety, best practices, and other subjects that help them run their companies more efficiently. The association's dedication to community involvement is longstanding. In 1939, the MBA sponsored the first Seattle Home Show. Today, the show's tradition continues each February and October. Through two non-profit organizations, the association gives back to the community in many ways. The Master Builders Care

MBA relocated to its current Bellevue location in spring 2003.

Foundation undertakes a variety of service projects each year including Rampathon, in which volunteers build handicapped access ramps for low-income residents. The Master Builders Education Foundation sponsors programs with Seattle-area schools, colleges and universities that encourage students to enter the building profession. Another program of the MBA is Built Green™, which promotes environmentally friendly building practices for remodeling and new home construction.

After almost 100 years of serving its members and residents of the Puget Sound region, the MBA continues to provide its members with quality services, programs and legislative representation and remains the leader in providing consumers information about building or remodeling a home.

Community service has always been at the heart of many association activities, including Rampathon, which provides free wheelchair access ramps to low-income residents.

NATIONAL OCEANIC AND ATMOSPHERIC ADMINISTRATION

The National Oceanic and Atmospheric Administration's (NOAA) mission is to provide environmental assessments, predictions and stewardship, which will ensure quality of life and healthy commerce for generations to come. NOAA was formed in 1970 as the umbrella organization for several dispersed federal scientific agencies, and its roots date to the earliest years of the nation. In the interest of national security and commerce, President Thomas Jefferson signed an act in 1807 to conduct surveys of coastal waters. In 1814, the Surgeon General ordered surgeons to keep weather diaries, which marked the first government collection of weather data. The nation's first Federal conservation agency was initiated in 1871 to protect, study, manage

and restore fish. Today, the work NOAA conducts touches the lives of every American on a daily basis.

The NOAA community in Seattle represents the agency's largest contingent outside of Washington, D.C. All major line elements, NOAA Weather Service, NOAA Fisheries, NOAA Ocean Service, NOAA Research and NOAA Satellites and Information are represented in Seattle. NOAA Marine and Aviation Operations Marine Operations Center supports four Seattle-based ships and additional vessels based in San Diego, Honolulu, and soon, Ketchikan and Kodiak. The NOAA Diving Program, also under the Marine and Aviation Operations office, is located in Seattle. The Western Administrative Support Center

NOAA Ship Rainier *conducts hydrographic surveys used in the production of nautical charts.*

provides administrative services in the western region to NOAA and the Department of Commerce, NOAA's parent organization.

Three major facilities house the majority of NOAA personnel in Seattle. The Western Regional Center located at Sand Point along the western shoreline of Lake Washington is the largest. The two other major components are the Marine Operations Center on the eastern shore of Lake Union and the Montlake facility on Portage Bay near the University of Washington. The facilities include offices, laboratories, auditoriums, equipment assembly and maintenance areas, warehousing, ship piers and staging areas, a cafeteria and health services building and a day care center.

NOAA's WP-3D Orion turboprop and Gulfstream-IV jet aircraft participate in Pacific Ocean Jet Stream and winter storm research to improve Pacific Northwest forecast warning times and accuracy.

WASHINGTON COUNCIL ON INTERNATIONAL TRADE

The Washington Council on International Trade (WCIT) is a private, non-profit, non-partisan association comprised of businesses, government agencies, non-profit organizations, academia, consular groups, and individuals. Founded in 1973, the Council works to support public policies favorable to expanded opportunities in the global marketplace. Because Washington is the most trade-dependent state in the union, international trade is crucial to the state's continuing prosperity and growth. WCIT is the only organization in Washington State whose only mission is to educate, inform, and advocate for international trade.

The Council advocates for pro-trade policies at federal and state levels by focusing on key trade-related issues that impact the health of our businesses and our communities. Washington is home to many of the nation's leading companies in aerospace, software, forest products, financial services, communications, legal services, agriculture, and food products. International trade is a growing part of their customer base. Smaller, entrepreneurial companies also depend on international trade to grow and expand.

Every year the Council publishes Trade Picture, a colorful, graphic compilation of annual trade statistics for Washington State and its trading partners. Trade Picture is available by calling the WCIT offices.

WCIT has a web-information base. This web site includes articles on current trade issues and trade-related issues such as poverty, corporate responsibility, sustainability, globalization vs. localization, labor rights, etc. The site also has a separate section for educators that features information about WCIT's trade curriculum for middle and high schools.

Courtesy of Wyndham Images

PUGET SOUND REGIONAL COUNCIL

View of Downtown Seattle from Magnolia Bluff.

The central Puget Sound region rises from the tideflats of the Sound to the crest of the Cascade Mountains and extends through the glacially sculpted lowlands of the Olympic Peninsula. High mountains, forests, and abundant water surround the region, shape the land, and set a snowcapped and shimmering stage for its people, who enjoy life's opportunities within one of the world's most distinctively successful places.

King County is the geographic, cultural and economic heart of this lush and temperate region. Its economy, environment, and people are interconnected and interdependent with the rest of the region, which combines to form the largest and most richly diverse metropolitan area in the Pacific Northwest.

The Puget Sound Regional Council is where the elected leadership of King County, as well as diverse community interests, assemble with counterparts from Snohomish, Pierce, and Kitsap counties, to assess the region's long-range challenges and chart the region's growth, economic and transportation future.

Central to the Regional Council's mission is sustaining the region's outstanding natural environment, its robust recreational and cultural resources, its gateway location on the Pacific Rim, and its amazing cultural diversity as the region continues to grow and prosper.

The region's landmark VISION 2020 growth, economic, and transportation strategy, produced through the assembly provided by the Council, lays the foundation for the region's future. It is a nationally acclaimed road map that balances the region's economic needs with a coordinated land-use strategy which focuses growth within already urbanized areas—connected by diverse and efficient transportation choices, including roads, transit systems, and ferries.

The region's work is never done. The people of the Puget Sound region can count on the Regional Council to always be asking: What's Next? It is where the people of the region chart a common vision for the future and create the pathways to get there.

Carkeek Park, Seattle.

CITY OF SEATTLE

Aerial view of Seattle's waterfront.

WELCOME TO SEATTLE! This wonderful city is one of the most picturesque places in the country. Seattle encompasses a great deal of natural beauty, from the panoramic views of the snow-capped Cascades to the scenic Puget Sound. Whether one is boating on Lake Washington, taking in the views from the top of the Space Needle, or strolling through Pike Place Market, Seattle is truly a great city to visit or call home.

Seattle is home to more than half a million residents in many distinct and vibrant neighborhoods. Its communities are rich and lively, whether one prefers the cosmopolitan bustle of the downtown area or the small-town feel of West Seattle. From the historic Pioneer Square to the hip and trendy Capitol Hill, each Seattle neighborhood has a unique identity.

The city enjoys a richly diverse culture and strong multi-national community. Seattle citizens are appreciative of the social, artistic, and economic contributions that stem from a variety of different ethnic traditions.

Seattle residents are proud of their city's inventive and groundbreaking economic community. The city is the home of some the world's greatest entrepreneurs, from Bill Boeing to Bill Gates. Today Seattle is a recognized leader in aerospace, information technology, education, and retail. Microsoft, Amazon.com, Nordstrom, Starbucks, and the University of Washington are all proud to call Seattle home. In addition, Seattle is on its way to becoming a national center for biomedical research. The city has a unique opportunity to lead a global industry—find cures for cancer, malaria, HIV, and other diseases that shorten life and bring misery to families worldwide—and to do great things for the future.

Mayor Greg Nickels.

Seattle City Council 2004, clockwise from upper left: Councilmembers Jim Compton, Richard Conlin, David Della, Richard McIver, Peter Steinbrueck, and Jean Godden, Council President Jan Drago, Councilmembers Tom Rasmussen and Nick Licata.

the City. The public is always urged to participate in public meetings or hearings.

Every Monday at 2 PM, the Council considers proposed legislation put forward by City departments, the council members, or sometimes by citizens. Adoption of the city budget, proposed by the Mayor, is one of the most important tasks of the Council. Although Seattle adopts a biennial budget, the budget is reviewed every year.

Council members are non-partisan and elected at large citywide to serve four-year terms. They work with the Legislative Department's Central Staff and their own individual office staffs, researching and developing ideas and issues under consideration. Council members' offices also provide constituent services to citizens who are having difficulty getting responses from a City department to problems.

SEATTLE CITY COUNCIL

The City of Seattle is situated in a beautiful setting in the Pacific Northwest between Lake Washington and Elliott Bay, a part of Puget Sound, and looking out to the Olympic Mountains to the west and the Cascade Mountains to the east, with majestic Mount Rainier looming large to the south. The mountain forests and the water have played an important role in Seattle's economic history, from the Native American tribes here when the first settlers arrived, to the logging and fishing industries that have survived and thrived since the late nineteenth century. Seattle was named for Chief Sealth, whose tribes—the Duwamish and Suquamish—welcomed the first settlers and helped them survive their first winters.

The nine-member Seattle City Council is the City's full-time legislative body and considers listening to the citizens of Seattle its primary responsibility. Public hearings and briefings from policy experts and City staff are held in Council Chambers downtown at Seattle City Hall. Hearings are also often held in community centers throughout

Cedar Falls, Cedar River Watershed.

CITY OF BELLEVUE

Bellevue's skyline glows with the calm waters of Lake Washington in the foreground and the frosted peaks of the Cascade Mountain Range in the background.

BELLEVUE DELIVERS ON PROMISE OF QUALITY SERVICE
The Bellevue City Council is committed to Bellevue's future as an urban center, working to help businesses grow and prosper, while maintaining the high quality of life that has attracted people to the community for more than 50 years.

Bellevue is recognized throughout the region as an exceptionally well-managed city known for delivering a high-quality environment for both business and living. The city is bolstering a long tradition of excellent public service with innovative new approaches to customer service, supplemented by the use of technology—such as on-line building permits and reservations for parks programs, plus a web site that allows businesses to make detailed, up-to-date searches for commercial property in the city, complete with city demographic and zoning information.

The city also manages with a long-term perspective, both financially and in terms of land use and infrastructure. Taxes are moderate and predictable. Bellevue's financial fitness is strong enough to consistently earn it the highest credit rating for bond issues because the city maintains strong reserve funds to replace equipment and fundamental infrastructure such as water and sewer systems. At the same time, Bellevue takes advantage of modern technology and techniques to manage the size and cost of government while maintaining high standards for the services delivered to citizens.

Bellevue makes continuous, substantial investments in streets, sidewalks, and other transportation projects that maintain the customer and employee lifeline to businesses while supporting and updating the city's high-quality neighborhoods. More than 25 years of intensive planning and development have made Bellevue exceptional among suburban cities. Bellevue successfully created a strong, well-defined downtown urban business, residential, and shopping district while it protected and enhanced quiet, safe, highly livable neighborhoods. Bellevue truly has the best of both worlds, and the Bellevue City Council is committed to building on that quality that makes the city unique in the Puget Sound area.

2004 Bellevue City Council, left to right: John Chelminiak, Conrad Lee, Deputy Mayor Phil Noble, Mayor Connie Marshall, Grant Degginger, Don Davidson, Claudia Balducci.

Bellevue Square is festive during the holiday season.

Courtesy of City of Bellevue

SAFE, SMART, ATTRACTIVE: BELLEVUE MAKES A GREAT HOME BASE

Most people in the Puget Sound region know at least two things about Bellevue: it has lots of nice, green suburban neighborhoods and Bellevue Square is the best shopping mall in the Northwest.

Those perceptions are true, but there is more.

Bellevue's quality neighborhoods have been attracting people since the 1950s, and a variety of quality, single-family homes can be found. Increasingly popular in Bellevue, however, are condominiums and apartments. Downtown Bellevue in particular is becoming the city's newest neighborhood as new units are added at a substantial pace. The number of housing units downtown is expected to increase fivefold by 2020, to more than 10,000 dwellings.

Three important features that draw people to Bellevue are its great parks system, top-quality public schools, and safe environment. In annual scientific surveys, the majority of Bellevue residents say they feel safe walking in their neighborhoods before and after dark—and in fact, an already low rate of property and violent crime has declined 7.6 percent in the past ten years. There are plenty of great places to walk in the city's 1,900 acres of parkland and open space and more than 50 miles of walking and bicycle trails. Bellevue public schools consistently rank among the best in the state, and three Bellevue School District high schools were rated in 2003 by *Newsweek* magazine as among the best in the nation.

An increasingly diverse population also now calls Bellevue home. Nearly one-quarter of Bellevue's residents were born outside of the U.S., according to the 2000 Census, adding an expanding mix of cultures to what has become the leading city among the Seattle-area's Eastside communities and center for culture and commerce.

QUICK FACTS ABOUT BELLEVUE

- Percentage of Bellevue residents age 25 and older with a Bachelor's degree or higher (2000 Census): 54 percent
- Population (2004): 116,400
- Workforce (2004): 125,000
- Percentage of Bellevue residents with Internet service at home (2003): 77.4 percent
- Projected employment growth citywide by 2020: 25-30 percent
- Projected employment growth downtown by 2020: 80 percent

Courtesy of City of Bellevue

There are plenty of great places to walk in the Bellevue's 1,900 acres of parkland and open space and more than 50 miles of walking and bicycle trails.

CITY OF ISSAQUAH

Issaquah has established itself as a prime Northwest business location and attracts regional, national, and international businesses to its scenic and friendly community. At least 40 percent of the state's population is located within a 40-mile radius of Issaquah, providing businesses with an expansive market for commerce. In recent years, corporations with continental and global interests have found a home in Issaquah, developing custom offices in close proximity to Seattle's port, with access to the Pacific Rim. Issaquah is a new hub of commercial and corporate development on the Eastside. Microsoft and Siemens are two of Issaquah's major employers, as is Costco with international headquarters in Issaquah.

Along Front Street, historic downtown Issaquah remains the heart of the city, where quaint shops and restaurants mingle with the early 1900s train depot, now a museum. The Issaquah Historical Society works with Main Street Issaquah, the Issaquah Chamber, and the City of Issaquah to maintain the charm and vitality of this town's humble beginnings in logging, dairying, and coal mining.

The fresh paint on historic buildings, the variety of regionally known restaurants, the generations of local merchants, and seasonal plantings and decor reflect the close-knit community spirit of Issaquah. Issaquah's recent business growth has expanded its pool of talent, expertise, resources, and services as many business people and professionals participate in local government, community service, and public events through the Issaquah Chamber. Such involvement enhances the quality of life for all and ensures the economic vitality of Issaquah's future.

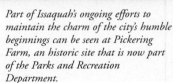

Part of Issaquah's ongoing efforts to maintain the charm of the city's humble beginnings can be seen at Pickering Farm, an historic site that is now part of the Parks and Recreation Department.

The Washington State Salmon Hatchery is in the center of historic downtown Issaquah. As the state's only hatchery in an urban setting, the Issaquah facility offers up-close observation of Chinook, Coho, and Sockeye salmon returning from the Pacific Ocean and spawning in the gravel of the creek bed.

The Issaquah City Council, clockwise from upper left: Councilmembers Bill Conley, Hank Thomas, Joe Forkner, Russell Joe, Nancy Davidson, David Kappler, and Fred Butler.

Issaquah's neighborhoods—from the white picket fences of historic homes, to the tree-lined drives of new subdivisions—retain the small, hometown feeling that is one of the community's most cherished assets. Issaquah's close proximity to neighboring business districts, downtown Seattle, and recreational areas makes it an ideal place for families to live.

New residential developments continue to add to the diversity of housing options in Issaquah, from high-density urban apartments in a glade of mature conifers to luxury homes on acreage, and everything in between. Issaquah is home to two master-planned communities, which feature clustered neighborhoods that preserve a large percentage of the available land as permanently preserved parks and open space. In Issaquah, fast-paced growth does create concern about zoning,

transportation, and environmental preservation, but in-depth public scrutiny and the support of the Issaquah Chamber has made the community an integral part of the planning and developing process. This balance will ensure Issaquah remains a great place to live.

Excellent education is a hallmark of the rapidly growing Issaquah School District, which ranks among the highest in test scores in the state. Issaquah residents have easy access to several main and branch campuses of area colleges and universities.

Issaquah is surrounded by 200 miles of gentle and rugged hiking trails through conifer forests. Paragliders have discovered the perfect launch spot at Poo Poo Point, a cliff at the 1,800-foot level on the west side of Tiger Mountain. Swimmers, water skiers, boaters, anglers, and picnic enthusiasts enjoy nearby Lake Sammamish State

Park, the most-used state park in Washington. Snow skiers, snowboarders, and sledders flock to Snoqualmie Pass ski areas—just 30 minutes east. World-famous Snoqualmie Falls, with its spectacular vistas and easy walking trails, is just a brief drive from Issaquah.

Each fall, the Washington State Salmon Hatchery in the center of historic downtown overflows with visitors awed by the spectacular return of the salmon to Issaquah Creek. Issaquah celebrates this remarkable odyssey with the annual Issaquah Salmon Days Festival, the city's most treasured event. Presented the first weekend of October for more than 30 years, more than 150,000 visitors flock to town during the two-day event, which serves as the Chamber's primary fund-raising activity.

Like a walk back in time, the annual Down Home Fourth of July Kids, Pets 'n Pride Parade leads hundreds of families down historic Front Street and into a patriotic day full of old-fashioned fun. Summer evenings are dedicated to weekly Concerts on the Green, a perfect time and place for picnicking with baskets or with Kiwanis barbecued burgers and hot dogs. In August, two of Issaquah's favorite tastes complement each other perfectly at the Chamber's annual Chocolate, Wine and All that Jazz event, presenting an evening of music, merriment, and fine dining. Three Art Walk events take place on Main Street: Late Spring, Late Summer, and the Holiday Extravaganza, featuring regional artists, horse & buggy rides, music and entertainment located in the Historic District of Issaquah.

Mayor Ava Frisinger.

CITY OF KENT

The Kent City Council, clockwise from lower left: Coucilmembers Debbie Raplee, Ron Harmon, Tim Clark, Les Thomas, Bruce White, Deborah Ranniger, and Julie Peterson.

"On behalf of the City of Kent, I'm proud to share with you this information about South King County's largest city."

—Mayor Jim White

POPULATION AND DEMOGRAPHICS

Kent's breathtaking setting features a view of Mt. Rainier rising majestically over the landscape, and the Cascade and Olympic Mountains on the horizon. Kent is centrally located on the Interstate 5 corridor between Seattle, 18 miles to the north, and Tacoma, 18 miles to the south. In addition, Kent is just seven miles from Seattle Tacoma International Airport. Other major routes include the Valley Freeway (SR-167), which

traverses Kent north/south, and I-405 and SR-516, which run east/west through South King County. Both the Union Pacific and Burlington Northern Railroads provide services to many business and industrial properties, and Kent is now a stop for the regional commuter rail system, which provides service between downtown Tacoma and Seattle. When doing business in Kent, business is connected.

Kent is centrally located in the Puget Sound Region of Washington state, an area of over two million people. The largest city in South King County and the seventh largest in the state, Kent's population of 84,210 live within a geographic area of 29 square miles.

Population	84,210
Number of Employees	67,019
Number of Businesses	3,895
Number of Households	30,693
Average Household Income	81,094

(Source for population: State Office of Financial Management, 2003; source for other data: *Claritas, 2002*.)

LOCAL ECONOMY

One of the largest warehouse and distribution centers in North America, Kent has more than 45 million square feet of industrial space and is a major manufacturing center. Companies making their home in Kent include Flow International, Hexcel Corporation, Mikron Industries,

Kent's Riverbend Golf Course is the most frequently played public golf course in Washington state.

Kent was named "Sportstown Washington" by Sports Illustrated *for its tremendous community sports programs and facilities.*

Starbucks Roasting Plant, Oberto Sausage Company, REI, and Boeing. There is still vacant land available for office and industrial development.

PARKS AND RECREATION

The Kent Parks Department has been recognized nationally for Excellence in Parks and Recreation Management, and was recently named by *Sports Illustrated* as Sportstown Washington. The City of Kent operates 68 parks, 1,349 acres of parkland, 26 miles of trails, 31 ball fields, and 15 tennis courts. In addition, the City owns the Kent Meridian Pool, which is operated under a sublease by the Aquatic Management Group.

In 2000, 2001, and 2002, the Park Maintenance division received the National Softball Association Outstanding Park Award for Russell Road Park, which features five softball fields. Wilson Playfields, a Youth Sports Complex consisting of three ball fields, with special turf allowing year-round play, was completed and dedicated in 2002.

Golfers can enjoy 27 holes of first-class golf between the 6,666-yard, 18-hole course (the busiest in the state) and the 1,174-yard, Par 3 course of the City's Riverbend Golf Complex. The driving range features 32 covered hitting stations with lights, multiple target greens, and a learning center.

The Kent Senior Activity Center is a 21,000-square-foot facility offering a variety of programs and social activities for those 55 and older.

HOUSING

There is a wide variety of housing available, including single-family, condominiums, and apartments. The average price for a home sold in Kent is $229,652, with an average market time of 52 days. The average sales price for a condominium is $143,310, with an average market time of 47 days (source: *Northwest Multiple Listing Service, 2003*). The average rents for apartments are $533 for a studio, $637 for a one-bedroom, $713 for a two-bedroom/one-bath, $824 for a two-bedroom/two-bath, $998 for a three-bedroom/two-bath (source: *Dupre & Scott Apartment Advisors, Inc. 2003*).

DOWNTOWN KENT

Downtown Kent is the vibrant traditional center of the Kent Valley. Kent's historic downtown district offers great restaurants, specialty retail, office space, and plenty of free parking. Almost 12,000 employees work within one mile of downtown. Downtown Kent is also the financial hub of the City, with numerous banks and deposits of over $300 million.

Coming in 2005 is Kent Station, a town-center project with a 12-screen multiplex theater, a branch campus of Green River Community College, and additional retail and restaurants. This project, to be located adjacent to the Sounder commuter rail station, will create a community focal point and gathering place, making downtown Kent an economic and community cornerstone for years to come.

Downtown is also home to the City's civic center, including City Hall, the Kent Downtown Library, the Kent Downtown Post Office, and the King County Regional Justice Center. Each day, 150 jurors arrive at the Regional Justice Center with time to shop and sample restaurants.

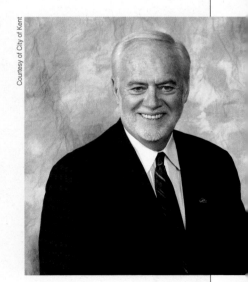

Mayor Jim White.

CITY OF SEATAC

SeaTac City Hall.

Incorporated in February 1990, the City of SeaTac is located midway between Seattle and Tacoma and is the home of the Seattle-Tacoma International Airport. The city is vibrant, economically strong, environmentally sensitive, and people-oriented. The airport brings in approximately 14,000 visitors daily, and many stay, dine, and shop in the City of SeaTac. Both Horizon and Alaska Airlines are headquartered in SeaTac. The Boeing Spares Distribution Center distributes parts worldwide from SeaTac.

SeaTac has certainly evolved through the years and has established itself as an important part of the region. Recently, SeaTac took ownership of its own City Hall facility and opened a police precinct at City Hall in 2003 to better serve the community.

Over the years, the City has made substantial improvements to its parks, including a skate park, outdoor basketball courts, lakeside performing arts stage, children's play equipment, picnic shelters, and much more. The annual International Festival and Parade, Shakespeare in the Park, and the Music in the Park Series have become summer traditions. The Highline Botanical Garden is a beautiful, relaxing place to get away from it all. It is located in close proximity to the community center at the 240-acre North SeaTac Park.

Transportation and pedestrian improvements have been a high priority. Phase III of the International Boulevard Improvements were completed in late 2003 and Phase IV will begin by mid-2004. Improvements to International Boulevard and other city streets have added to the safety and aesthetics for its citizens and visitors.

SeaTac is a thriving, culturally diverse community projected to grow by 60 percent over the next 25 years. About one-fourth of the people who live in the city are employed in manufacturing in the region. Most of the remaining are employed in the retail trade, professional services, and transportation sectors. More people work in SeaTac than live there. The labor force is attracted primarily by jobs in the airline industry and related services. Diversification of job opportunities will occur over the next 25 years as a natural result of population growth and of attracting more manufacturing and distribution businesses to the area.

The Music in the Park Series every summer at Angle Lake Park is a popular way to picnic in the park.

Arbor at Angle Lake Park.

The leaders of SeaTac have succeeded in fulfilling their vision of the future by transforming the city into the key transportation and business hub for the region while creating a first-rate living and working environment.

The City of SeaTac has a seven-member City Council elected by the citizens. The Council chooses from among themselves who will serve as Mayor and Deputy Mayor for a two-year term. The Mayor is recognized as the head of the City for ceremonial purposes and is the chair for the Council meetings.

The Mayor appoints the chairperson and membership for each of the Standing Council Committees. The standing committees include Transportation and Public Works, Administration and Finance, Land Use and Parks, and Public Safety and Justice.

The Mayor or a majority of the City Council may also establish Ad-Hoc Committees to consider special matters that do not readily fit the standing committee structure. The Mayor also appoints Council representatives to various intergovernmental councils, boards, and committees.

The City Councilmembers are the leaders and policymakers elected to represent the community and to concentrate on policy issues that are responsive to the citizens' needs and wishes. The SeaTac Council makes

policy, land use, and budget decisions for the City. The Council's mission is to keep SeaTac economically strong, environmentally sensitive, visually pleasing, and people-oriented with a socially diverse but cohesive population and employment mix. These attributes create a positive identity and image for the community.

The City Council appoints a full-time City Manager to oversee the daily operations of the City and to advise, implement, and administer the policies adopted by the City Council.

A sign welcomes visitors to the City of SeaTac at the south exit of Sea-Tac International Airport.

KEY PLAYERS

AETNA
413 Pine Street, Suite 200
Seattle, Washington 98101
Telephone: 206.701.1035
Facsimile: 206.701.1150
Page 170

AMERICAN LIFE
3223 Third Avenue South,
Suite 200
Seattle, Washington 98134
Telephone: 206.381.1690
Facsimile: 206.381.3927
Page 143

BASTYR UNIVERSITY
14500 Juanita Drive NE
Kenmore, Washington 98028
Telephone: 425.823.1300
Facsimile: 425.823.6222
Web Site: www.bastyr.edu
Page 174

BON-MACY'S
Third & Pine Streets
Seattle, Washington 98181
Telephone: 206.506.7000
Facsimile: 206.506.7722
Web Site: www.bonmacys.com
Page 178

BURKE MUSEUM OF NATURAL
HISTORY AND CULTURE
University of Washington,
Box 353010
Seattle, Washington 98195
Telephone: 206.616.3962
Facsimile: 206.616.1274
Web Site: www.washington.edu/
burkemuseum
Page 189

CHILDREN'S HOSPITAL AND
REGIONAL MEDICAL CENTER
4800 Sand Point Way NE
Seattle, Washington 98105-0371
Telephone: 206.987.2000
Facsimile: 206.987.5215
Web Site:
www.seattlechildrens.org
Page 166

CITY OF BELLEVUE
P. O. Box 90012
Bellevue, Washington
98009-9012
Telephone: 425.452.6800
Web Site:
www.ci.bellevue.wa.us/
Page 210

CITY OF ISSAQUAH
P. O. Box 1307
Issaquah, Washington 98027
Telephone: 425.837.3000
Facsimile: 425.837.3009
Web Site:
www.ci.issaquah.wa.us/
Page 212

CITY OF KENT
220 Fourth Avenue South
Kent, Washington 98032
Telephone: 253.856.5200
Web Site: www.ci.kent.wa.us/
Page 214

CITY OF SEATAC
4800 South 188th Street
SeaTac, Washington
98188-8605
Telephone: 206.973.4800
Web Site: www.seatac.wa.gov/
Page 216

CITY OF SEATTLE,
CITY COUNCIL
P. O. Box 34025
Seattle, Washington 98124-4025
Telephone: 206.684.8888
Facsimile: 206.684.8587
Web Site:
www.seattle.gov/council/
Page 208

CITY OF SEATTLE,
OFFICE OF THE MAYOR
P. O. Box 94749
Seattle, Washington 98124-4749
Telephone: 206.684.4000
Facsimile: 206.684.5360
Web Site:
www.seattle.gov/mayor/
Page 208

CITY UNIVERSITY
11900 Northeast 1st Street
Bellevue, Washington 98005
Telephone: 1888.42CITYU
Web Site: www.cityu.edu
Page 162

COSTCO WHOLESALE
999 Lake Drive
Issaquah, Washington 98027
Telephone: 425.313.8163
Facsimile: 425.313.8103
Web Site: www.costco.com
Page 186

ECONOMIC DEVELOPMENT
COUNCIL OF SEATTLE &
KING COUNTY
1301 Fifth Avenue, #2500
Seattle, Washington 98101
Telephone: 206.389.8650
Facsimile: 206.389.8651
Web Site: www.edc-sea.org
Page 200

EVERGREEN HEALTHCARE
12040 NE 128th Street
Kirkland, Washington 98034
Telephone: 425.899.1000
Web Site:
www.evergreenhealthcare.org
Page 168

THE FAIRMONT OLYMPIC
HOTEL, SEATTLE
411 University Street
Seattle, Washington 98101
Telephone: 206.621.1700
Facsimile: 206.623.2270
Web Site:
www.fairmont.com/seattle
Page 182

KING COUNTY COUNCIL
516 Third Avenue, Room 1200
Seattle, Washington 98104-3272
Telephone: 206.296.1000
Facsimile: 206.296.0198
Web Site:
www.metrokc.gov/council/
Page 196

KING COUNTY DEPARTMENT OF
TRANSPORTATION
201 South Jackson Street,
KSC-TR-0815
Seattle, Washington 98104-3856
Telephone: 206.684.1481
Facsimile: 206.684.1224
Web Site:
www.metrokc.gov/kcdot
Page 130

KING COUNTY
EXECUTIVE OFFICE
516 3rd Avenue, Room 400
Seattle, Washington 98104
Telephone: 206.296.4040
206.296.0190
Web Site:
www.metrokc.gov/exec
Page 192

KING COUNTY
INTERNATIONAL AIRPORT
P. O. Box 80245
Seattle, Washington 98108
Telephone: 206.296.7380
Facsimile: 206.296.0190
Web Site:
www.metrokc.gov/airport
Page 124

MASTER BUILDERS ASSOCIATION
FOR KING AND SNOHOMISH
COUNTIES
335 116th Avenue SE
Bellevue, Washington 98004
Telephone: 425.451.7920
Facsimile: 425.646.5985
Web Site:
www.masterbuildersinfo.com
Page 204

NOAA MARINE AND
AVIATION OPERATIONS
Marine Operations
Center-Pacific
1801 Fairview Avenue East
Seattle, Washington 98102-3767
Telephone: 206.553.7656
Facsimile: 206.553.1109
Web Site:
http://www.moc.noaa.gov
Page 205

PACCAR INC
777 106th Avenue NE
Bellevue, Washington 98004
Telephone: 425.468.7400
Facsimile: 425.468.8216
Web Site: www.paccar.com
Page 138

PACIFIC NORTHWEST BALLET
301 Mercer Street
Seattle, Washington 98109
Telephone: 206.441.9411
Facsimile: 206.441.2440
Web Site: www.pnb.org
Page 184

PUGET SOUND
REGIONAL COUNCIL
1011 Western Avenue, Suite 500
Seattle, Washington 98104
Telephone: 206.464.7090
Facsimile: 206.587.4825
Web Site: www.psrc.org
Page 207

SEATTLE CITY LIGHT
700 5th Avenue, Suite 3300
Seattle, Washington 98104-5031
Telephone: 206.684.3508
Fax: 206.684.3326
Web Site:
http://cityofseattle.gove/light/
Page 135

SEATTLE PUBLIC UTILITIES
Key Tower, 700 Fifth Avenue,
49th Floor
Seattle, Washington 98104
Telephone: 206.684.8180
Facsimile: 206.684.4631
Page 134

SEATTLE SYMPHONY
P. O. Box 21906
Seattle, Washington 98111-3906
Telephone: 206.215.4700
Facsimile: 206.215.4701
Web Site:
www.seattlesymphony.org
Page 188

SHORELINE COMMUNITY
COLLEGE
16101 Greenwood
Avenue North
Shoreline, Washington 98133
Telephone: 206.546.4101
Facsimile: 206.546.4630
Web Site: www.shoreline.ctc.edu
Page 158

SKILLS, INC.
715 30th Street NE
Auburn, Washington 98002
Telephone: 206.782.6000
Facsimile: 253.939.2126
Web Site: www.skillsinc.com
Page 142

SWEDISH MEDICAL CENTER
747 Broadway
Seattle, Washington 98122-4307
Telephone: 206.386.6000
Web Site: www.swedish.org
Page 146

UW MEDICINE
University of Washington,
Box 356350
Seattle, Washington 98195-6350
Telephone: 206.543.7718
Facsimile: 206.685.8767
Web Site: www.uwmedicine.org
Page 152

VALLEY MEDICAL CENTER
P. O. Box 50010
Renton, Washington
98058-5010
Telephone: 425.228.3450
Web Site: www.valleymed.org
Page 172

WASHINGTON COUNCIL ON
INTERNATIONAL TRADE
2200 Alaskan Way, Suite 430
Seattle, Washington 98121
Telephone: 206.443.3826
Facsimile: 206.443.3828
Web Site: www.wcit.org
Page 206

WASHINGTON HEALTH
FOUNDATION
300 Elliott Avenue West,
Suite 300
Seattle, Washington 98119-4118
Telephone: 206.285.6355
Facsimile: 206.283.6122
Web Site: www.whf.org
Page 175

WASHINGTON MUTUAL
1201 Third Avenue
Seattle, Washington 98101
Web Site: www.wamu.com
Page 140

THE WOODINVILLE WEEKLY
P. O. Box 587
Woodinville, Washington 98072
Telephone: 425.483.0606
Facsimile: 425.486.7593
Web Site: www.nwnews.com
Page 133

BIBLIOGRAPHY

Chapter 1
Works Cited
Hanford, Hon. C. H., Ed. *Seattle and Environs: 1852-1924.* Chicago and Seattle: Pioneer Historical Publishing Co. 1924.

Kaplan, Jim. *Historic America: The Northwest.* San Diego: Thunder Bay Press. 2002.

Kirk, Ruth. *Tradition & Change on the Northwest Coast: The Makah, Nuu-chah-nulth, Southern Kwakiutl and Nuxalk.* Seattle: University of Washington Press. 1986.

"Native American Tribes of the Northwest: Contemporary Reservations, Reserves, and Communities." Bauu Institute. 2000. http://www.bauuinstitute.com/Native/Nalistnw.html. Downloaded 4 Sept. 2003.

Ruby, Robert H., and John A. Brown. *A Guide to the Indian Tribes of the Pacific Northwest.* Norman and London: University of Oklahoma Press. 1986.

Schwantes, Carlos A. *The Pacific Northwest: An Interpretive History.* Lincoln and London: University of Nebraska Press. 1989.

Seattle City Light. "A Brief History." Published 19 July 2001. http://www.cityofseattle.net/light/aboutus/history/ab5_brhs.htm. 1 Sept. 2003.

Snowden, Clinton A. *History of Washington: The Rise and Progress of an American State.* Volume 2. New York: The Century History Company. 1909.

"State and County QuickFacts: King County, Washington." U.S. Census Bureau. 15 Jul. 2003. http://quickfacts.census.gov/qfd/states/53000.html. 6 Dec. 2003.

"State and County QuickFacts: Washington." U.S. Census Bureau. 2000. 15 Jul. 2003. http://quickfacts.census.gov/qfd/states/53000.html. 6 Dec. 2003.

White, Sid, and S.E. Solberg. *Peoples of Washington: Perspectives on Cultural Diversity.* Pullman: Washington State University Press. 1989.

Chapter 2
Works Cited
"2002 Washington Biotechnology & Medical Technology Annual Report." Washington Biotechnology & Medical Technology Online. http://www.wabio.com/industry/annrpt/annrpt_intro.htm. 2 Sept. 2003.

"King County Profile." Washington State Employment Security. Labor Market and Economic Analysis Branch. March 2001: 1.

"Office of Trade & Economic Development 'International Trade.'" http://www.oted.wa.gov/trade/statsmiser/2001countriesmiser.htm. 28 Aug. 2003.

Puget Sound Maritime Historical Society. *Images of America: Maritime Seattle.* Chicago: Arcadia Publishing. 2002.

Strong, Kathy. *The Seattle Guidebook.* 12th Edition. Guilford: The Globe Pequot Press. 1975 - 2001.

"Washington State Fact Sheet." Economic Research Service, U.S. Department of Agriculture. Updated 15 July 2003. http://www.ers.usda.gov/StateFacts/WA.htm. Downloaded 28 Aug. 2003.

Chapter 3
Works Cited
Dunphy, Stephen H. "Times Watch: Trading Up." *The Seattle Times.* 19 Oct. 2003.

Puget Sound Maritime Historical Society. *Images of America: Maritime Seattle.* Chicago: Arcadia Publishing. 2002.

"Seattle Datasheet: Transportation." City of Seattle. Revised 29 Jan. 2002. http://www.cityofseattle.net/oir/dataasheet/transportation.htm. Downloaded 9 Aug. 2003.

Spector, Robert. *The Space Needle: Symbol of Seattle.* Seattle: Documentary Media LLC. 2002.

Chapter 4
Works Cited
"Key Facts About Higher Education in Washington." Washington Higher Education Coordinating Board (HECB). http://www.hecb.wa.gov/Docs/Factbook.pdf. Published Aug. 2002. Downloaded 6 Sept. 2003.

"Preparing Washington Students for the 21st Century: Five-Year Strategic Plan for the Office of Superintendent of Public Instruction 2002-2007." April 2003.

Chapter 5
Works Cited
"King County City Profiles." Economic Development Council of Seattle & King County. http://www.edc-sea.org/Research_Data/CityProfiles.cfm. 1 Sept. 2003.

Chapter 6
Works Cited
Dolan, Maria and Kathryn True. Nature in the City Seattle: Walks, Hikes, Wildlife, Natural Wonders. Seattle: The Mountaineers Books. 2003.

Kaplan, Jim. Historic America: The Northwest. San Diego: Thunder Bay Press. 2002.

Schwantes, Carlos A. The Pacific Northwest: An Interpretive History. Lincoln and London: University of Nebraska Press. 1989: 6.

Chapter 7
Works Cited
Donnelly, Peter F. "Direct Link Between Vitality of Arts Community and Region's Economic Prosperity." The Seattle Times. 7 Sept. 2003.

Chapter 8
Works Cited
Cook, John. "Seattle is Quickly Becoming the Boardwalk of Popular Board Games." *The Seattle Post-Intelligencer.* 31 Oct. 2003. D1-D6.

Droker, Howard. *Seattle's Unsinkable Houseboats.* Seattle: Watermark Press, 1977: 7.

Kaplan, Jim. *Historic America: The Northwest.* San Diego: Thunder Bay Press. 2002.

Means, Beth and Bill Keasler. "A Short History of Houseboats In Seattle." 1986. Seattle Floating Homes Association. http://www.seattlefloatinghomes.org/shortHist.htm. Downloaded 8 Sept. 2003.

Rex-Johnson, Braiden. *Inside the Pike Place Market: Exploring America's Favorite Farmers' Market.* Seattle: Sasquatch Books, 1999.

INDEX

PHOTO CREDITS

Page 1
Courtesy of Wyndham Images

Page 2-3
Autumn in Japanese Garden, Washington Park Arboretum.
© Wolfgang Kaehler/CORBIS

Page 4-5
All images courtesy of Wyndham Images

Page 6-7
Left: Dr. Paul Ramsey rows down the Montlake Cut, just under the Montlake Bridge, near the University of Washington.
Courtesy of University of Washington, Photo by Dan Lamont
Inset Photo: Courtesy of University of Washington

Page 8-9
Left: A hiker looks out at Mt. Rainier and the moon during sunset from Mt. Si.
© Chase Jarvis/CORBIS
Inset Photo: Courtesy of Senator Patty Murray

Page 20-21
Bell Harbor International Conference Center at Seattle's waterfront.
© Richard Cummins/CORBIS
Inset Photo: Courtesy of Metropolitan King County Council

Page 38-39
A golden sunset glows over Puget Sound. Downtown Seattle just emerges from the luminous haze of the horizon.
© Neil Rabinowitz/CORBIS
Inset Photo: Courtesy of National Oceanic and Atmospheric Administration

Page 54-55
Fruits from a Chinese lantern plant.
© Darrell Gulin/CORBIS
Inset Photo: Courtesy of Swedish Medical Center

Page 66-67
Mount Si.
© Darrell Gulin/CORBIS
Inset Photo: Courtesy of The Woodinville Weekly

Page 84-85
A skier takes flight.
© Chase Jarvis/CORBIS
Inset Photo: Courtesy of Liberty High School

Page 96-97
Hammering Man *stands outside Seattle Art Museum.*
© Philip James Corwin/CORBIS
Inset Photo: Courtesy of Seattle Art Museum

Page 110-111
Hiking in the Cascade Mountains.
© Charles Mauzy/CORBIS
Inset Photo: Courtesy of Puget Sound Regional Council

Page 122-123
Olympic Iliad *and the Space Needle.*
© Richard Cummins/CORBIS

Page 136-137
Pergola in Pioneer Square.
Courtesy of Wyndham Images

Page 144-145
Pike Place Market display.
Courtesy of Wyndham Images

Page 176-177
Neon signs at Pike Place Market.
© Randy Faris/CORBIS

Page 190-191
Mt. Rainier from Lake Washington.
Courtesy of Wyndham Images

SEATTLE & KING COUNTY

GATEWAY TO THE PACIFIC NORTHWEST–VOLUME II

LIMITED FIRST EDITION

Front Cover Illustration: Created by Craig Overbey, Shoreline Community College, Winner of the 2004 Wyndham Publications Art Cover Contest for the *Seattle & King County: Gateway to the Pacific Northwest, Vol. II* Project.